Anonymous

Cook and Wylie's Stirling Directory

Anonymous

Cook and Wylie's Stirling Directory

ISBN/EAN: 9783337102579

Printed in Europe, USA, Canada, Australia, Japan

Cover: Foto ©Andreas Hilbeck / pixelio.de

More available books at **www.hansebooks.com**

COOK & WYLIE'S
STIRLING
DIRECTORY

CONTAINING

STREET AND GENERAL DIRECTORIES
(Including Causewayhead, Cambuskenneth,
and St. Ninians),

BUSINESS AND PROFESSIONAL DIRECTORY,

LISTS OF PUBLIC OFFICIALS.

OFFICE-BEARERS OF LOCAL SOCIETIES, CLUBS,
AND INSTITUTIONS:

also

COUNTY INFORMATION, JUSTICES OF THE
PEACE. &c., &c.

STIRLING:
COOK & WYLIE, 9 BARNTON STREET

1906.

Established a Quarter
of a Century.

Silver Medal,
Highest Award, 1895.

The only Gold Medal
Awarded, 1896.

STIRLING
STEAM LAUNDRY

And Carpet Beating Works.

WYLLIE, SANDEMAN & CO.

Highest Class LAUNDRY WORK.

FAMILY WORK in all its Branches.

Orders for Vans to call may be sent by Post Card, or left with Misses E. & J. REID, 32 Murray Place.

FRENCH CLEANING.

DRESSES.   SUITS.   CURTAINS.   DRAPERIES.

CARPET BEATING by Patent Machinery.

DYEING in First=Class Style.

Prompt and Careful Attention bestowed.

STREET DIRECTORY.

ABBEY ROAD.

1 David Henderson, ironmonger
  Thomas Logan, brushmaker
  William Haslar, clerk
3 Samuel Howie, carter
  John Wallace, engine driver
  A. Thomson Gardiner, clerk
  Miss Sarah Dunlop
5 David Pearson, reporter
  Miss Janet M'Gibbon
  John M'Fadyen, lorryman
  John Drummond, lorryman
7 John Murdoch, traveller
  George Crombie, plasterer
  Dugald Campbell, butcher
  Alex. Lindsay, mechanic
9 Peter Stewart, grocer
  Robert Ritchie, tailor
  Jas. M'Farlane, foreman printer
  John L. Galloway, draper
11 Arthur Goldsmith, postman
  James M'Kenzie, weaver
  Alex. Glenday, compositor
  A. M. Swan, clothier
13 Wm. Baird, retired farmer
  Charles Duncan, pensioner
  David Gilchrist, mason
  Peter Balfour, draper
17 James Maitland, guard
  James M'Laren, guard
  James Donaldson, joiner
  James Jerrat, cooper
  Robert Millar, miner
  Mrs Agnes Currie
  Fred Walker, lorryman
19 David Bean, tailor
  Alexander Taylor, guard
  Thomas Whitehead, guard
  Robert Keddie surfaceman
  Alex. Miller, cooper

6 Robert Young, saltworker
8 Mrs Jane Francis
10 Parlane M'Farlan, drysalter
12 Mrs Mary Johnstone
16-18 Dunn Bros., wood merchants
20 John Syme, smith
26 David Craig, engine cleaner
28-30 Jas. Johnston, wood mer.
32 John Gourlay
  Haldane & Co., Forth Cooperage
34 Wm. Hutchison, sawyer
  Robert Thornton, brakesman
  Mrs Renfrew
  Thos. Kennedy Kellie, cooper
  Herbt. Stevens, rubberworker
36 Robert M'Robbie, cooper
  William Pye, tailor
  Wm. Sutherland, fireman
  William Gordon, saddler
  William Monteith, lorryman
38 Francis Cooper, guard
  Alex. Innes, goods porter
  Joseph Kennedy
40 John Hall, grocer
44 George Craig, foreman porter
  Duncan Duff, brassfinisher
  James Wilkie, sawyer
48 M'Ewen & Co , Perambulator
  Works
52 Wyllie, Sandeman & Co., Stir-
  ling Steam Laundry
54 Alex. Nish, grain porter
  John C. M'Donald, mason
56 David Ferguson, fireman
  Isaac M'Gowan, miner
Ferry—Thomas Dow, ferryman

ABBEY ROAD—Continued.

19 William Kay, blacksmith
   David Ramsay, weaver
21 John M'Lay, stair railer
   James Rouney, miner
   Patrick Marshall, settmaker
   Chas. Gillespie, cabinetmaker
23 Mrs Elizabeth Townsend
   Robert Meiklejohn, engineer
   James Galloway, brakesman

23 John Jackson, traveller
25 Robert Buchan, clerk
   Peter M'Ewan, brassfinisher
   William Brown, weaver
   Mrs Janet M'Cormack
27 Mrs Annie Thomson, laundress
   Mrs Helen Bolton
   Dugald Harrower, fireman

ABBEY ROAD PLACE.

1 Thomas Gordon, storeman
3 David Goldie, coachtrimmer
5 Henry Binnie, cooper
7 Mrs Elizabeth Ritchie
9 Mrs Christina Murray
11 John Henry Oliver, foreman,
   Ordnance Store
   Bannockburn Hosiery Co.

2 James Spowart, engineer
4 Henry Hunter, contractor
6 Wm. Cunning, clerk
8 John Lambert, joiner
10 John Cree, sawyer
12 Andw. Thomson, carter
Abbey Road Dairy — Miss Jessie
   Fraser

ABERCROMBY PLACE.

1 Thomas Menzies, draper
3 Henry Robb, writer
5 John Millar
7 James Jackson, traveller
9 E. Gentleman, writer
11 Rev. D. P. M'Lees, minister
13 Andw. Simpson, auctioneer
15 Mrs Jessie Duncanson
17 Andw. Buchanan, grocer
19 Alex. Crowe
21 Miss Low

2 William Morrison, joiner
4 Charles E. Panton
6 Sam. F. Millar, baker
8 Miss Mitchell
   Mrs M'Lauchlan
10 Misses Graham, teachers
   Mrs Margaret Graham
12 T. M. Morton, ironmonger
14 Eben. Simpson, architect
16 Thomas Lupton, writer
18 Miss Mary Campbell

ALBANY CRESCENT.

6 Wm. C. Clarke
7 Arth. Chapman, Sergt. A.O.C.
9 Wm. Goodwillie, hawker

11 Miss Helen Norwell
12 John Anderson, blacksmith
13 Wm. Rogers, gardener

ALBERT PLACE.

Wellwood—Alex. Galbraith, grocer
    John Steel, plumber
1 John S. Ralston, restaurateur
2 Robert Macewen, grocer
3 Rev. Matthew Mair, minister
4 Mrs Margaret Harvey
5 Hugh Ferguson, bootmaker
6 John Dempster, tobacconist
7 Robert Waugh, law clerk
8 Wm. Shirra, bookseller
9 Wm. H. Dobson, organist
10 Miss Annie Buchanan
11 Miss Mary Cunnintor.
12 Miss Esther Symon
    Miss Margaret Symon

13 Wm. Boswell, bootmaker
14 Mrs Nicol
15 Miss A. M'Ewen
16 John T. Drummond, jeweller
17 Miss Gentleman
    Miss Alice Gentleman
18 William Cullens, flesher
19 Thomas Henderson
21 Mrs Watson
22 Leonard Baker, drawing teacher
23 Peter L. Jeffrey, traveller
24 Patrick M'Dougall
25 Miss Goldie
26 Wm. Bell, Lieut.-Colonel
27 Patrick Drummond, seedsman

ALEXANDRA PLACE.

Albert E. Shakespeare, cycle agent

ALLAN PARK.

1 Geo. Plenderleith, blacksmith
3 John Brown, draper
5 Mrs Gardner
    Alex. Gardner. Sheriff-Clerk-Depute (Falkirk)
7 Wm. Carstairs Shaw
9 Wm. M'Farlane, traveller
11 James Kinross, coachbuilder
13 Eben. Morrison, writer
15 J. Venters, In Revenue officer
17 Mrs Ireland
19 James M'Rae, writer
21 Robert MacEwan, merchant
23 P. D. Nairn, Allan Park Studio
25 Miss Feahrenbach
    Thomas Moore, chemist
    James Gavin, draper
    Joseph Cook, traveller
    William Nairn, traveller
    P. D. Nairn, photographer
    J. W. S. Chivers, traveller

2 Y.M.C.A. Institute—
    John Blyth, caretaker
4 Thomas Lamb, joiner
6 George Charleston, plumber
    Miss M. A. Baldie, dressmaker
8 Jas. M'Ewen, iron merchant
10 Robert M'Culloch, draper
12 Ronald Walker, architect
14 Alexander Walls, plasterer
16 Donald M'Kerchar, traveller
20 Miss Caroline Graham
    Miss Mary Blackburn
22 Rev. Mr M'Kay, ret. minister
24 Rev. Wm. Agnew, editor, Tract Depot
38 Andrew M'Ewan, stockbroker
Allan Park House—
    Mrs Haldane
    Dr Graham Skinner
    Thos. Houston, vet. surgeon
    Whaley H. Young, accountant

ARCADE.

1-3 Stirlingshire Rubber Co.—
    David Paton, manager
5-7 A. T. Paul, general draper
9-11 Misses Thomson, milliners
15-21 Craig's stationery, hardware,
    and toy warehouse
23 Chas. P. Stevenson, musicseller
25 Wm. Low & Co., grocers
27 Arcade Hall—Wm. Crawford's
    Trustees
    Wm. Ogilvie, caretaker
29 T. Adamson & Co., grocers
31 Mrs S. Galashan, bootmaker
33 Miss K. M'Farlane, baby linen
35 M. Dewar, art dealer
37 A. T. Paul, draper
39 John T. Drummond, jeweller
41 Peter Stevens, Crown Hotel
43 Peter Comrie, baker
    J. Galashan, hairdresser

2 William Brown, outfitter
2½-4 Mrs Morgan, Douglas Hotel
6-8 Mrs E. Brown, fruiterer
10 Bankrupt Stock Realisation Co.
12 Miss A Danskin, draper
14 Thomas Marshall, confectioner
16 South U.F. Church Hall
18-20 Ladies' Lavatory and Cloak-
    Room
22 Miss L. Whyte, baby linen
24 Michael Hannan, bootmaker
26 Miss Stevenson, confectioner
28 Miss C. M'Bain, tobacconist
30-34 A. Johnstone, painter
36 Miss Isabella Jollie, milliner
38 "Flower of Stirling" I.O.G.T.
    Lodge-room
40 Miss B. Hamilton, confectioner
42-44 Miss A. Oswald, tea rooms
46 Miss Rutherford, milliner

50 Donald M'Killop, hotelkeeper
    Miss Agnes Aird

BAKER STREET.

1 M'Culloch & Young, drapers
3 W. & J. Aitken, bakers
5 David Sinclair, barman
    John Cunningham, cabman
    Peter Doig, police constable
    James Gibson, saltworker
    John Fraser, blacksmith
7 William M'Kenzie, jeweller
9 Andrew Buchanan, grocer
11 George Thomson, billposter
    Peter Eadie, joiner
    Mrs Jane M'Naughton
    William Reid, hatter
13 Thomas Stevenson, stationer
    and ironmonger
15 James Neil, baker
17-25 Lawsons, Ltd., furnishers
23 George Aimer, hairdresser
    L. M'Donald, gamekeeper
    James Robb, plumber

2 James Page, Star Bar
4 Ferguson & Struthers, drapers
6 John Campbell, coachman
    Robert Robertson, cellarman
    John Gray, labourer
    James Seardison, labourer
    William Ferguson, cabman
8 E. & B. Kyle, fancy warehouse
10-12 W. & J. Cullens, butchers
14 Wm. Drummond, mason
    Thomas Younger, tailor
    John Brunton, lather
    J. Mitchell, spirit merchant
    Andrew Buchanan, painter
    Peter Cuthill, carter
    James Dow, carter
    Andrew Dow, labourer
    Martin Ging, labourer
    Archibald Cowan, gardener
    Patrick Donnachie, miner

BAKER STREET—Continued.

23 Andrew Crichton, permanent way inspector
Mrs M. Aitken
William Forrester, plumber
David Todd, miner
W. S. Williamson, town officer
John Dawson, engine driver
27-29 Alexander Roberts, publican
31 Raff. Giuliani, ice-cream shop
33 James Ormiston, tailor
Miss Elizth. Glass, dressmaker
Robert Finlayson, wheelwright
35 Miss Margaret Donaldson, tobacconist and fancy goods
37-39 John Brown, draper
41 James White, labourer
John Fleming, fireman
Arthur Prowe, miner
William Galloway, broker
Alexander Thomson, tanner
John Kerr, fireman
Thomas Davidson, blacksmith
Mrs T. L. Glass
Mrs Helen Johnston
43 Oliver P. Derrick, auctioneer
45 Roberto Corieiri, ice-cream shop
47 Thomas Munro, labourer
Wm. Smith, 'phone linesman
James Gundry, traveller
49 W. Galloway, broker
51 Don. M'Killop, restaurateur
53 James Rintoul, spinner
53 and 57 David Hunter, grocer
55 And. Murdoch, spirit merchant
59 Miss C. Nealus, broker
61 John M'Dougall, hairdresser
63 John Duncanson, plumber
James Buchanan, lathsplitter
William Jamieson, waiter
John Littlejohn, miner
65 Alex. Watters, spirit merchant
67 Leathley Bros., fish merchants
69 William Morrison, tailor
Michael Kenny, waterman
Thomas Bain, mason
Mrs Susan Miller
71 Dugald M'Donald, grocer

14 Henry Scully, cabman
16 John Mitchell, Derby Inn
18 Wm. Boswell, bootmaker
20 Dugald Campbell, butcher
22 H. P. Watt, auctioneer
24 James Rollo, gardener
Mrs Lilias Reid
Bernard Youlle, moulder
Alex. M'Intosh, blacksmith
Thomas Aitken, vanman
Mrs Jessie Campbell
Peter Harkins, storekeeper
Misses Finlayson, dressmakers
James Mackin, mason
D. Lumsden, station policeman
Wm. Burmie, scavenger
25 George Aimer, hairdresser
28 Andrew Cumming, grocer
30 John Blyth, confectioner
32 H. P. Watt, cabinetmaker
John Murray, blindmaker
James Fullarton, dairyman
English Church Home
J. Youl, manager (Lawsons, Ld.)
34 Lawsons, Limited, drapers
36 William Goudie, baker
Mrs Mary Boreland
Alexander Robertson, labourer
38 James Dickson, bootmaker
40 A. Giannandrea, ice-cream shop
42 Miss M'Culloch, refresh. rooms
44 John Johnstone, hawker
Jas. Carmichael, shoemaker
Mrs Jane Ferguson
Mrs Robertson
Matthew M'Farlane, labourer
Mrs Jane M'Cormack
Mrs Thomas Rankine
John Mackie, bricklayer
James M'Guire, miner
Alex. M'Farlane, cabinetmaker
Richard M'Que, miner
Patrick Darcy, labourer
Charles Soddin, baker
John Queen, miner
Hugh Harley, labourer
Thomas Barrat, miner

BAKER STREET—Continued.

73 Hugh Kaney, labourer
   Mrs Mary Smith
75 Thomas Cannon, labourer
   Henry M'Culloch, miner
   Adam Murray, carter
77 Thos. Mowat & Sons, butchers
79-81-83 J. Brown, furniture dealer
81 Alex. Ferguson, joiner
   Miss A. Heatley
   James Hutton engine driver
85 Alan Lorimer, slater
   Mrs M. Brown, french polisher
87 Mrs Wm. Brown, confectioner
89 Charles Holmes, carter
   Hugh Munro, boiler washer
91 C. Mowat, butcher
93 A. Giannandrea, ice-cream shop
95 James W. Dalgetty, tailor
   Mrs Janet Judd
   Mrs Bridget Fitzpatrick
   John Finlayson, shoemaker
95-97 Henry Dalgetty, shoemaker
101-103 Patrick M'Kay, broker
103 Mrs J. Duff, lodging-house kpr.
   Donald M'Kay, hawker
105-107 Mrs C. Bremner, restaur.
109 Mrs Holland, broker
111 George Farmer, miner
   Mrs Mary Joyce
113 William Bremner
   John Paterson, slater
   John Geegan, labourer
   Archibald Paterson
   Wm. Bremner, restaurateur

44 Hugh Clark, labourer
   Mrs C. Gwynne
   Robert Farmer, sawyer
   A. Giannandrea, confectioner
   Wm. M'Kutcheon, miner
   B. Giannandrea, confectioner
46 Eastmans, Limited, butchers
46½-48 Clark Donaldson, restaur.
48 John Bryce, shoemaker
   Mrs Michael Monachan
   Jonathan Roberts, labourer
   William M'Lean, lorryman
   John Kelly, labourer
   Andrew Barclay, miner
   James M'Coll, miner
50 Peter Mackintosh, tobacconist
52 William Aitken, baker
   Mrs Crabtree
54 W. & J. Aitken, confectioners
56 Thomas Young, fruiterer
58 John Livingstone, chemist
60 J. Cuthbert, tailor
   Mrs Peter M'Ewan
   James Johnstone, labourer
   Robt. Lickrish, coachtrimmer
   Robt. Pender, coachtrimmer
   William Taylor, labourer
   Anthony Cassidy, shunter
   John Stevenson, cabman
   James Haggart, banksman
   John Cameron, guide
   Miss Agnes Macpherson
   James White, baker
   Wm. Cunningham, tailor
   Peter Sinclair, lorryman
   Thomas Young, gardener
   James Johnston, fitter
   Alex. Thomson, blacksmith
   Janet M'Lean, millworker
   George Rankine, miner
   Hector Henderson, slater
   John Fraser, miner
   Mrs Margaret M'Nab
   Walter Rutherford, fireman
62 Ferguson Bros., grocers
64-66 M. Hogan, furniture w'house
66 Mrs Jane Laurie, spirit merc.

BAKER STREET – Continued.

66 Thomas M'Gregor, lorryman
And. Stewart, rubber worker
Andrew Hardie, machineman
William Davie, moulder
Mrs Elizabeth Fraser
Hugh M'Dougal, bricklayer
68 Mrs Laurie, spirit dealer
70 Wm. Mailer, cabinetmaker
72 John Carmichael, woodman
Wm. S. Mailer, cabinetmaker
Henry M'Lauchlan, baler
Patrick Cavanagh, mason
John Parker, carpet dresser
James Parker, patternmaker
74 Eben. Millar, fancy goods shop
76 Michael Welsh, labourer
Mrs James M'Guire
Thomas Scotland, painter
Working Men's Reading Room
80 Jas. Duguid, refresh. room
82 Mrs M. Boreland, pastrycook
84 John Lickrish, shoemaker
Thomas Bain, residenter
84 Baker Street Mission Hall
Pietro Togneri, confectioner
Robert Denovan, gardener
Donald Corbett, labourer
James M'Farlane, baker
John M'Farlane, polisher
Mrs M'Gonville, broker
86 Wm. Brown, furniture dealer

88 D. Giovanelle, ice-cream shop
92-94 Mrs M. Lees, spirit merchant
92 John M'Dougall, hairdresser
96-98 George Bulloch, broker
98 George Sutherland, labourer
John Livingstone, wood turner
Robert Oliver, carter
George Watson, labourer
Alex. Wotherspoon, labourer
Francis Preston, labourer
John M'Donald, carter
104 William Easson, grocer
106 Alex. Adam, shoemaker
108 Mrs Anne Bennett
Thos. Gillon, setmaker
108 Donald M'Kay, broker
110 Henderson & Bennett, grocers
112-114 John Brown, broker
114 Mrs Elizabeth M'Guire
Golan Hislop, painter
Mrs William Dick
John Johnston, painter
116 P. Togneri, ice-cream shop
118 William Marshall, labourer
John Healy, surfaceman
John Murray, wood carter
Mrs Susan Wells
James Walker, miner
Thomas Carruthers, gardener
120 W. Gordon, newsagent, &c.,
sub-Post Office

BALLENGEICH ROAD.

1 Thomas White, pensioner
2 Charles Smith
Mrs Langford
3 Mrs Catherine Catchel

4 W. Watchman, retired mining
surveyor
5 Thos. Marshall, electrician
6 John Hamilton, retired baker

BALMORAL PLACE.

1 Asa Clay, accountant
2 John M'Aree, draper
3 Wm. Reid, electrician

4 Miss Margaret M'Gregor
5 Miss Margaret Bain

BANK STREET.

1 Sam. Goudie, janitor
Mrs Lawrie
Jas. Lyle, cooper
3 Edward Kettrick, labourer
5-7 John Howie

4 Mrs Leathley, fish merchant
Matthew Lyle, weaver
Francis Reynolds, mason
David M'Donald, rubber worker
J. Campbell, tailor
6 Mrs Jane Drummond
Richard Copley, gardener
6-8 A. J. Mullan, pawnbroker

BANNOCKBURN ROAD, St. Ninians.

1 John Crawford, nailer
Mrs Mary Cooper
3-5 William Mitchell, baker
7 James M'Gregor, baker
Andrew M'Naughton, nailer
9 Jas. M'Farlane, quarryman
Peter Gardener, confectioner
Robert Armstrong, blacksmith
Thomas Mailley, tanner
11 Thomas Walls, smith
13 George Ewing, plumber
15 Mrs Janet M'Gregor
17 Alex. Sinclair, mason
19 William M'Farlane, mason
21 Alexander Harvey, tailor
23-25 James D. Kemp, dairyman
25 St Ninians Mission Hall
27 Miss Kennedy, confectioner
29 Mrs Helen Lennox
Mrs Mary Gillespie
31 William Kerr, blacksmith
33 James Paton, nailer
35 Mrs Jane Henny
37 Mrs Dobbie
James Wingate, roadman
39 Henry Forgie, miner
Bernard Hughes, miner
Mrs Paterson
40 Patrick Rafferty, miner
40½ Mrs J. M'Lachlan
41 David Cairney, miner
43 Alex. Stevenson, miner
45 Daniel M'Intyre, cartwright
47 James M'Farlane
49 Peter Nimmo, labourer

2-4 John Brimber, spirit merchant
6 Henry Liddell, insurance agent
8 George Paton, miner
10 Mrs Agnes Paton
James Robertson, labourer
12 Wm. M'Naughton, millworker
14 Alex. Taylor, carter
16 Thomas Taylor, contractor
Thomas Cook, labourer
18 Jas. Cook, railway surfaceman
20 Mrs Margaret M'Donald
John Gibb, carter
Archibald Young, quarryman
24 Alex. Lamond, saddler
26 William Cook, miner
David Meiklejohn, labourer
David Taylor, contractor
28 William M'Farlane, labourer
30 John Gardner, joiner

Aitken's Buildings—

James Irving, vanman
James Clark, butcher
Hugh Ewing, nailer
John Denovan, shoemaker
Robert Blennie, lorryman
Henry Knox, engine keeper
Archibald M'Ewan, painter
Thomas Walls, blacksmith
John Adams, coal merchant
John Paton, blacksmith
Peter Connal, engineman

BANNOCKBURN ROAD—Continued.

51 John Taylor, hawker
53 William Lawrie, labourer
55 John Struthers, nailer
37-59 James M'Arthur, contractor
61 Mrs M'Arthur
63 David Ireland, labourer
65 James Thomson
   Mrs Mary Hunter
   Misses Fotheringham, laundry
69 William Bennett, labourer
71 James Kelly, miner
73 Thomas Thomson, lathsplitter

BARN ROAD.

1 Wm. Johnston, publican
3 Patrick Reilly, poulterer
5 Thos. M'Gribben, miner
7 Wm. Harkins, labourer
   Cornelius Leary, labourer
2 Mrs Jane M'Leod
   James M'Cue, labourer
4 Patrick Dunagan, labourer
   John Simpson, moulder
   Mrs Ann Salton
   Mrs C. Bardsley
6 Thomas Smith, cabinetmaker
8 James M'Ewan, miner
10 Mrs Margaret Sussams
   John Watt, baker
12 Peter Mills, confectioner

Crofthead—

1 James Dowell, clothier
2 And. Fowler, greenkeeper
3 Wm. Monachan, miner
4 Wm. M'Lay, warehouseman
5 Thos. D. Peebles, water bailiff
6 John Gunn, miner
6 Wm. Glasgow, lorryman
   James Paterson, fireman
   John Skinner, miner
7 Neil M'Caffer, dairyman
   Neil Lamont, insurance agent

BARNSDALE PLACE, St. Ninians.

Alexander Martin, nailmaker
William Gall, contractor
Miss Mary Stewart

BARNTON STREET.

1-5 Stirling Co-operative Society
7 Miss J. Roxburgh, confectioner
9 Cook & Wylie, printers and
   publishers. Tel. No. 0169.
11 R. Smith, joiner
13 And. Buchanan, fish merchant
15 Wm. Watson, shoemaker
17 Mrs C. Robertson, china merc.
33 P. M. Forfar, draper
2 Wm. Somerville, newsagent
4 H. G. Mathie, hatter
6 Joseph Mackieson, hairdresser
8-10 H. C. Nisbet, dairyman
10 Brown & Murray, solicitors
   Misses Liston
   Mrs Jane Flockhart
   Mr Graham, traveller
   Mr Pattison, electrician

BARNTON STREET—Continued.

35-37 J. Creagh, house furnisher
37 Mrs Taylor
   John Dun, traveller
39 Harvey & Harris, tailors
41 W. S. Palmer, umbrella maker
43 Mrs Borrowman, milliner
45 W. & J. Aitken, bakers
47 Lipton, Ltd., merchants
49 A. Fisher, draper
51 John Hunter, spirit merchant
53 R. W. Salmond, hatter
55 Miss Allan, tobacconist
57 D. Gilmour, bootmaker
59 Richard Copley, fruiterer
61 Miss Agnes Elliott
   Miss M. Elliott, nurse
   J. P. Welsh, postman
   John Edgar, baker
   Miss Gowans, tobacconist
63 Miss Gardner, milliner
65 Alex. Bennie, flesher
67 W. Strang & Co., drapers
69 Miss M. George, tea rooms
71 Mrs George
   J. M'Kenzie, trav. sec., Y.M.C.A.
   Mrs Jane Oswald
   J. Findlay, compositor
   Alex. Young, residenter
   James Young, residenter

10 Miss Boreland, saleswoman
12 John A. Gordon, chemist
14 Geo. Arthur & Son, drapers
16-18 MacEwen Bros., grocers
20 Pearl Life Assurance Co. Office
   Stirlingshire Conservative Asso-
      ciation Committee Rooms—
   John Parnie, agent
   M. P. Constable, teacher
   William Thomson, saddler
   David Fenton, grocer
   John Young, traveller
   Miss Margaret M'Intyre
   Sutherland Bremner, fish mer.
22 Singer's Sewing Machine Co
24 Bremner & Co., fruiterers
26-28 Cameron Harley, ironmonger
30 George Kerr Hardie, clerk
   Mrs William Bain
   Mrs Mary Duncan
      Mr Downie
      Mr Kennedy
32 Shakespeare & Chalmers, cycle
      agents
34 James Stevens, hairdresser
36 Duncan M'Ewan, grocer
38 Mrs Gasser, restaurateur
40 A. Denovan, residenter
   Wm Stevenson, potato mer.
   Adam Herron
   Mrs M'Que
   John Stewart, bootmaker
   Mrs Cowie
   Misses Davidson, dressmakers
   Mrs Gentles
40 42 Mrs A. Forrester, fish merc.
44 Andrew Simpson, auctioneer
46 Morrison & Taylor, solicitors
   Stirling Public Hall Co., Ltd.
48 Henry D. M'Lellan, solicitor
   D. Cox, county road surveyor
   John Barr, county san. inspec.
50 T. Gentles & Son, saddlers
52 John Walker, peram. maker
   Miss Bain, dressmaker
   J. Y. M'Intosh, compositor
   Mrs Hume, dressmaker

BARNTON STREET—Continued.

52 George Chisholm
 J. Fyfe, chemist
 Mrs M'Gowan

54 Mrs Collins, newsagent
56 James Dowell, clothier

BAYNE STREET.

1 John Baxter, joiner
 Wm. M'Queen, vanman
 Peter Laing, engine driver
3 Wm. Aikman, joiner
5 Robert Cairns, goods guard
 John Bradley, labourer
 John Davie, coachbuilder
 John Brogan, rubber worker
7 John White, miner
 Thos. Haggerty, motor driver

4 Walter Reekie, tailor
 Thos. Sullivan, labourer
6 John Ferguson, vanman
 George M'Innes, cartwright
8 Miss H. Gregor
 Patrick Docherty, shoemaker
10 Daniel M'Gregor, labourer
 Mrs Helen Young
 Wm. Hunter, miner
 James Clark, joiner
 Thos. Myles, miner
 Joseph Bundy, grocer
 Alex. J. Aitken, signalman
 John Hunter, blacksmith
 Hugh Jackson, miner
 James Campbell, labourer
 Lance-Sergt. Bibbie, A. & S. H.
 John Rennie, engine driver
 Daniel Griffiths, tailor
 Alex. Gray, labourer
 George Horsburgh, brushmaker
 Peter Gilchrist, plasterer
12 James Hutchison, cooper
 Mrs Ann Hunter
 James Brady, mason
 Alex. Rodgers, gas collector
 Mrs Margaret Wadsley
 Wm. Porter, baker
 Hugh Stewart, clockmaker
 James Jackson, sawyer
 Andrew Hunter, lorryman
 Alex. Webster, guard
 Peter Kerr, wheel inspector
 Hugh Stewart, labourer
 James Stevenson, cabinetmaker
 James Hutchison, roadman
 Miss E. Westwater
 Mrs Mary Comrie
14 A. Oliphant, biscuit agent

BORESTONE CRESCENT, St. Ninians.

1 Jas. Burnett, spirit merchant
7 Thomas Meldrum, labourer
  Owen Hughes, engineman
  Wm. Tabor, locomotive driver
  David Clelland, miner
  Mrs M. Denovan
  Robert Crawford, gardener
  Abraham France, miner

7 James Paterson, labourer
9 James Davidson, vanman
  Richard Brown, miner
  Peter Wright, coachpainter
  A. Cowan, farmer
  William Evans, painter
  Alex. Thomson, miner
  Malcolm M'Callum, miner

BORESTONE PLACE, St. Ninians.

Holly Bank—John White
Borestone Cottage—Jas. Welsh
13 James Kay, joiner
15 Mrs Minnie L. Dowie

2 Mrs Ann Paterson
4-6 Duncan M'Alpine, grocer
8 Mrs Jane M'Cann
10 John Currie, miner
  John Watt, Borestone Guide
  Duncan Davidson, slater
14 Robert Walker, engineman
16 James Hay, joiner
18 Mrs Agnes Hutton
20 Mrs Mary Graham
22 John M'Nair, clerk

BOW STREET.

1 Thos. O'Brien, shoemaker
3 James Neil, butcher
5 Mrs M'Cormack, pawnbroker
7 Mrs Isabella Morgan
  Mrs Elizabeth Counter
11 Mrs Livingstone
13 James Cattanach, tobacconist
15 Thomas Kerr, engine driver
  Wm. Macher, bricklayer
  Thomas Ryan, broker
  Wm. Wylie, carter
  Miss K. Nealus

2 George Barr, hairdresser
4 Mrs Mary Derrick
  Thomas Conn, labourer
  Mrs Margaret Marshall
  John Balloch, hawker
  Mrs Catherine Brown
6 Thos. Ryan, broker
8 And. Simpson, undertaker
10 John Upfold, church officer
  Wm. Campbell, moulder
  Wm. Brunton, miner
  Thos. O'Brien, bootmaker
12 Dunlop & Co., grocers
14 Thomas Kaney, slater
  John M'Figgins, painter
  Wm. M'Ewan, labourer
  Robert Marshall, labourer
  Robert Smith, painter
  John Docherty, slater
  John Dempster, baker
  Mrs Jane M'Arthur
  George Young, carter
  John Machar, mason

BOW STREET—Continued.

16 Miss Ann Nicol
  John Dermidy, labourer
  Anthony Thornton, labourer
16-18 Jas. Peebles, furniture dealer
20 Thomas Hislop, surfaceman
  John Gallacher, surfaceman
  Mrs M'Kay
  John M'Vey, labourer
  Mrs Watson
  John Cameron, labourer
  George Barr, hairdresser
  Peter Turner, labourer
  Mrs Mary Fraser
  Mrs Gibson
  J. M'Kerron, labourer
  Miss Kerr
22 Robt. Menzies & Co., grocers
24 Mrs M'Nab
  William Telford, shoemaker
  J. Aitken, upholsterer

24 W. M'Donald, rubber worker
  J. Kirkwood, miner
  Daniel M'Nab, lorryman
  Mrs Janet Finlayson
  A. M'Nab, carter
  Mrs Dobbie
  Mrs Aitken
  Peter Martin, lathsplitter
26 Miss C. Finlayson, confectioner
28 Miss B. Henderson, newsagent
30 Miss J. M'Laren, dressmaker
  Mrs Isabella Robb
  Andrew Ferguson, plumber
  Thomas Coleman, warder
  Mrs Henderson
  C. Donaldson, dyer
  J. Cattanach, newsagent
  Miss M'Neil
32 Wm. Simpson, pawnbroker
34 Christie & M'Donald, grocers

BRIDGE STREET (UPPER).

1 Thomas Green, miner
3 John Currie, miner
5 James Melrose, maltman
7 Duncan Stirling, vanman
11 Rev. Jas. Angus, clergyman
15 Miss Fanny White
  Miss Kate Goodfellow
17 Children's Home—
    Miss Annie K. Croall
  Miss Nellie Harvey
23-25 David M'Aree, draper
71 George Porteous, lorryman
  Robert Cowie, miner
  Adam Wilson, miner
  William M'Neil, miner
  James Swanston, fireman
73 Mrs Mary M'Pherson
75 Wm. White, rubber worker
  Wm. Ferguson, labourer
77 Mrs Helen M'Kay, widow
  Mrs Janet Stirling
  Thomas Machar, bricklayer
  John Kinmonth, vanman
79 Robert Brown, miner

4 Jas. James, labourer
  John Bundy, carpenter
  Thomas Bremner, painter
  Jas. Anderson, cabinetmaker
6 Jos. Houston, rubber worker
  Alex. Primrose, gardener
8 John Booth, stableman
  Mrs Margaret Robertson
10 Michael Burke, engine driver
  Henry Hynd, tailor
  John Donaldson, plumber
  James Tainsh, coachpainter
  John Finlayson, engine driver
  Walter Williamson
  Thomas M'Lean, tailor
  John Charleston, labourer
  George Hendry, brushmaker
  Mrs Honeyman, laundress
  Robert Baxter, engine driver
  A. M'Intosh, police constable
  Robert Henderson, tailor
  William Smith, cabinetmaker
  George Smith, joiner
12 Henry Pearson, fruiterer

BRIDGE STREET (UPPER) – Continued.

14 Mrs Helen M'Intosh
James Forsyth, clothier
Mrs Catherine Taylor
16 R. & J. Greenhorn, fleshers
20-24 E. Boyes, maltman
26 N. M'L. Murphy, insur. mangr.
Matthew D. Murphy
28 Girls' Club
David Imrie, rubber worker
30 Miss Danskin, dressmaker
Mrs Helen M'Lauchlan
32 Robert Houston, lathsplitter
William Battison
John Martin
Thomas Stirling, corkcutter
Alex. Primrose, gardener
Miss Mary Marshall
Mrs Alice Lauder

36 Miss Christina Nicol
38 Mrs Mary Wiggan
Andrew Murphy, miner
40 Robert Walker, miner
42 T. B. Jones, asst. inspr. of poor
James Clark, engine driver
44 Thomas M'Rorie, gardener
Misses M'Rorie, laundresses
Henry England, clerk
Miss Agnes Eadie
46 Mrs Catherine Martin
J. D. Smith, painter
Thomas Drysdale
50 Mrs J. Weir
John Parnie, Organising Secy.
Conservative Association
52 Mrs Sarah Guthrie
54 Mrs Janet Wright

Bellfield—

J. G. Taylor, Sergt.-Major
Mrs Isa Cowpar
Alex. Henderson Taylor

Thomas Gentles, saddler
James Gentles, saddler
Mrs Elizabeth Kay

BRIDGE STREET (LOWER).

1 William Paul, seedsman
3 John Welsh, labourer
Mrs Rebecca Sharp
Miss E. Russell
5 John M'Farlane, shoemaker
7 Robert Goodwillie, fish hawker
9 D. B. M'Diarmid, grocer
11 James Morton, baker
Donaldson Fleming, miner
Thomas Brown, rubber worker
John Millar, miner
Mrs Mary M'Lean
John Thomson, labourer
And Davidson, telegraphist
James Somerville, scavenger
13 Mrs Janet Murray
James Fairley, traveller
Donald M'Innes, baker

2 A. Porter, spirit merchant
4 Miss C. M'Laren
James M'Nab, labourer
William Hutton, lorryman
Hugh Gray, wool sorter
6 Thomas Murray, mason
Mrs M. Farish
George Birrell, rubber worker
Henry Peddie, carter
8 David Manning, ret. teacher
Mrs Finlayson, nurse
Alex. Fraser, contractor
Eben. Robertson, labourer
10 Mrs A. M'Pherson
John Smeaton, carter
James Marshall, tailor
Charles M'Nab, miner
David Ritchie, labourer

BRIDGE STREET (LOWER) - Continued.

13 William Kirk, joiner
William Yorkston, organist
Thomas Wylie, draper
M. Killingbeck, carpet designer
Alex. Greenhill, water bailiff
15 William Wilson, miner
Robert Chester, guide
John Watson, warehouseman
John Laidlaw, compositor
Hugh Jamieson, engine driver
Thomas Fyfe, sawyer
John M'Kenzie, lorryman
William Ketchen, blacksmith
29 Peter M'Neill, draper
31 James Murphy, miner
Donald M'Laren, drover
William Darg, rubber worker
William Roy, engine driver
Wm. Finlayson, engine driver
James Kirk, plumber
Alex. Battison, porter
John Moir, engine driver
Mrs Jane M'Dermont
Robert Millar, labourer
33 Wm. M'Keen, labourer
35 Geo. Galloway, plumber
John M'Farlane, lorryman
37 James Dow, engine driver
Mrs Marion Hastie
39 Mrs Sarah Noble, grocer
39½ Bernd. M'Kinlay, goods guard
43 Robert Gilvear, dairyman
Mrs Janet Fotheringham
45 John Fotheringham, builder
John Henderson, roadman
47 George Henderson, vanman
53 Mrs Menzies
Charles Conaway, signalman
James H. Campbell, reader
John Campbell
Charles Sands, joiner
Peter M'Gregor, moulder
John Symon, blacksmith
Andrew Ferguson, joiner
55 Peter Ferguson, labourer
Andrew Roy, grocer
A. Jackson, inspt. of postmen

10 Mrs Cochrane
Mrs Janet Black
12 Chas. Haxton, engine driver
James Leitham, labourer
Joseph Farquharson, vanman
Alex. Fisher, labourer
Mrs Mary Reid
14 Mrs Margaret Harris
16 Mrs Jane Dawson
Eben. Millar, vanman
Miss Mary Coutts
Mrs Allardice
24 Mrs Janet Chalmers
Alexander M'Ewan, smith
26 Hugh M'Adam, butcher
A. M'Allister, rubber worker
44 Peter Jenkins, fisherman
Samuel Reid, labourer
Mrs Catherine Gow
46 John Pinkerton, miner
Thomas Meffen, lorryman
Mrs Bridget Fagen
William Welsh, blacksmith
48 John Lawson, shoemaker
50 Mrs Catherine Stalker
52 James Campbell, carter
Michael O'Connor, miner
54 Farq. Bethune, ret. coachman
Thomas Hughes, miner
56 James M'Donald, labourer
William Louden, miner
Don. Thomson, cabinetmaker
Edward Duffy, rubber worker
58 Robert Drummond, labourer
60 Mrs A. Mathieson, dressmaker

BRIDGE STREET (LOWER)—Continued.

55 George Moore, goods guard
John Kettrick, mason
Mrs Mary M'Donald
William M'Figgins, painter
Mrs Jane Christie
57 Herbert Cotton, rubber worker
Thos. Finlayson, engine driver
Wm. Lindsay, scripture reader
Peter Robertson, tailor
Patrick H. Kelly, storeman
Mrs Grace Buchanan
D. Cameron
Mrs Catherine Watt
61 Mrs Isabella Young
63 William Ferguson, hostler
65 Alexander Dow, fisherman
67 Peter Reynolds, bricklayer
69 John Bowie, cooper
Robt. Sinclair, rubber worker
Arthur Wentworth, store worker
Robert Littlejohn, gardener
71 James Rhind, foreman
73 Mrs John Henderson
75 James M'Ewen, coachpainter
79 Martin O'Neil, labourer
81 Jas. M'Leod, rubber worker
Mrs Jane Graham
83 Mrs Mary O'Connor
85 Adam Lindsay, mason
93 Robert M'Lean, plasterer

93 James M'Lean, tailor
95 Thomas Crawford, joiner
Mrs Janet Robertson
97 Fred Hislop, labourer
Thomas Pryde, cooper
John M'Ilreid, labourer
Mrs Christina Robertson
97½ James Spalding, plasterer
99 Richmond Wilkins, storeman
101 Mrs Ferguson
Mrs Thorley
Mrs Margaret M'Laren
103 John Philip, joiner
C. C. Spalding, engine driver
Francis Coyle, miner
William M'Kay, miner
105 Miss Marion Conley
Mrs Peyton
Mrs Elizabeth Syme
Colin Gardiner, brakesman
Miss Jane Christie
David M'Innes, baker
107 Andrew Christie, cooper
Archibald Brown, waiter
111 Mrs Mary Galloway
James M'Kay, engine driver
Alex. M'Kenzie, rubber worker
George Rankine, miner
Mrs Barbara Brooksby
Wm. Partridge, rubber worker

Bridge Lane—

1 Bothy
3 John Harris, sawyer
4 D. M'Kerracher
6 Town Stables

Bridge Haugh—

Alexander Esslemont
Geo. Johnston, insur. agent
William Hood, joiner
Alexander Lauder, guard
Thomas Noble, woodcarver
Raines, Ltd., engineers, &c.
John Louden, mason
John M'Ewen, electrician

BROAD STREET.

1 Stirling Co-Operative Society
3 Robert Walker, sawyer
John Given, postman
Arch. Henderson, compositor
Mrs M'Kinnon
Mrs Mary Grant
3-5 Arch. Speed, ironmonger
7-9 John Buchanan, grocer
9 James Buchanan, joiner
Hugh Conway, labourer
William Miller, painter
William Clarke, painter
11 F. R. France, refresh. rooms
13 John Archibald, baker
William Glasgow, miner
Mgt. Chrystal, outdoor worker
Frank Morris, miner
15 James Neil, baker
17 Mrs Mary Ann M'Arthur
Mrs Peacock
Mrs Ann Coyle
Mrs Mary M'Donald
William Smith, labourer
19 Wm. M'Callum, dairyman
21-23 Mrs Euphemia Tritton, grocer
23 Patrick Shirra, waste merchant
Charles Day, labourer
Miss H. M'Neil, outdoor worker
Mary M'Kenzie
John Smeaton, labourer
John Smeaton, gardener
Martin Harkens, labourer
Peter Greig, caretaker
Walter Morrison, mason
Alexander Jude, painter
Thomas Fulton, labourer
Mrs Margaret Anderson
William Hurley, labourer
Peter M'Farlane, labourer
Mrs Mary Johnstone
Wm. Orr, colliery fireman
Mrs Mary Freeland
Lawrence Monro, labourer
James Mitchell, labourer
John Moran, labourer
Mrs Margaret Peddar
Miss Bella Fulton

2 William M'Andrew, carter
4 Miss Janet Hunter, confect.
6 Peter Watt, grocer
8 Ann Leyden, millworker
James M'Garry
Michael Brannan, labourer
Patrick Horn, labourer
James Peebles, hawker
George Anderson, labourer
William Galloway, joiner
John Wylie, carter
Sam M'Adam, labourer
Robert Campbell, tailor
Robert Menteith, hawker
Mrs Agnes Dunagan
Peter Whiteford, hawker
James Morrison, carter
Patrick Donnachie, labourer
John M'Ewan, labourer
10 G. Gianandrea, ice-cream vendor
12 Patrick M'Glennan, miner
14 William Ritchie, labourer
Robert Ferguson, plasterer
Edward Welsh, grocer
Robert M'Kenzie, insur. agent
16 Edward Welsh, general dealer
18 David Brock, spirit merchant
20 Mrs Mary Burke
Mary Gibbons, outdoor worker
William Ross, hawker
Daniel Comrie, miner
Daniel Donnelly, labourer
Thomas Bermingham, hawker
Michael Kelly, stonebreaker
22 J. Bermingham, general dealer
24 Thomas Black, blacksmith
John Cattanach, plumber
James Gilchrist, plasterer
John M'Kellar, miner
Mrs Ann Blair
J. Livingstone, chemist
Hugh Crawford, cabinetmaker
John Duthie, coachbuilder
John Monaghan, labourer
William Yule, policeman
Donald Scott, shepherd
Lawrence Christie, merchant

2

BROAD STREET—Continued.

23-27 Mrs Cath. Darmody, general
    dealer
25 Francis Grogan, basket maker
33 John Winter, miner
    John Thomson, lorryman
35 Burgh Police Office
37 Court House and Police Office
    T. Ferguson, chief constable
    Parish Council Office—
    John Paterson, inspector
39 Butter Market
41 David Forrester, fish dealer
    William Wright, labourer
43 Patrick M'Vey, labourer
45 Wm. Stocksley, shoemaker
    Peter Allan, hairdresser
    Michael Cussack, labourer
    David Gardener, labourer
    Pat. M'Vey, labourer
    Mrs Janet Kerr
    James Scott, railwayman
    Michael Lundie, mason
    Mrs Lamb
47 William Hill, greengrocer

26 James Doyle, miner
30 James Fairley, miner
    Mrs Brown
    George Reid, miner
    William Ferguson, labourer
    Alex. M'Millan, miner
    John M'Pherson, soldier
    John Lewyllen, labourer
32 James O'Hare, miner
34 James Kilgannon, miner
36 John Turner, labourer
    Mrs Helen Hodgson
    John Dougal, coach painter
    Mrs Margaret Forbes
    Peter Brannan, stoker
    William Quinn, labourer
    John M'Alpine, saltman
    Mrs Catherine M'Connachie
    John Moran, labourer
    Duncan Sinclair, baker
    Patrick Convery, mason
    Francis O'Hare, miner
38 Robert M'Knight, miner
40 Alex. Munro, upholsterer
    Thomas Wilkinson, labourer
    Mrs Shaw
    Andrew Greig
42 And. S. Greig, spirit dealer
44 Mrs Galashan
    George Allan
    Mrs Ann Innes
    John Wallace, watchmaker
    Mrs Susan Conway
    James Claxton, labourer
    William Kerr, plumber
48 Thomas Gray, miner
    John O'Donnell, miner
    Michael Finn, labourer
    Miss Ann Ging
    Matthew Fleming, miner
    Mrs Mary Paterson
    John Robertson, labourer
    David Greenhill, policeman
    Miss Helen Maxwell
    Wm. Dempster, cabinetmaker
    David Brock, spirit dealer
    Edward M'Creadie, gardener

BROAD STREET—Continued.

52 Miss H. Turner, dressmaker
Bartholomew Kidd, tailor
James M'Nicol, clerk
Mrs Elizabeth Fallon

52 Wm. John Dormer
Mrs Hamilton
54 James Williamson, baker
58 William Cunningham

BRUCE STREET.

1 James Ramsay, engine driver
3 Duncan M'Donald, tailor
Robert M'Millan, baker
Charles Shirra, postman
Chas. Robertson, engine driver
Thomas Ross, sculptor
J. Menzies, engine driver
5 Andrew M'Innes, baker
David Cunning, postman
Louis Bayne, joiner
John Wingate, compositor
Richard Martin, carter
William Cairns, plumber
7 Miss Janet Donaldson
Mrs Marshall
James Abercromby, plumber
Peter Cameron, joiner
John Crawford, clerk
Mrs Allison Chalmers
9 Mrs Jessie Louden
Misses M'Culloch, restaurateurs
John Anderson, engine driver
John Wallace, postman
David Robertson
James Denovan, labourer
11 James F. Fenton, watchmaker
James Simpson, clerk
Mrs Helen Denovan
Alex. M'Kenzie, waiter
Wm. Duncanson, fireman
Wm. M'Laren, engine driver
13 Robert Dyball, draper
Mrs Jane Marshall
George Hall, guard
Robert Buchanan, baker
Robert Campbell, mason
Allan Brown, butcher
15 Mrs Mary Ritchie
George M'Kay, mason
John Henderson, plumber
William M'Ewan, joiner

2 Alex. Muirhead, shepherd
Thomas Campbell, plumber
John Wilson, tailor
Peter Wallace, policeman
4 David Moores, traveller
Alex. Dalgetty, joiner
Mrs Marr
J. M'Cuaig
T. Hynd, tailor
— Richardson, miner
6 Robert Hislop, waterman
Thos. B. Weir, traveller
James Jenkins, baker
Michael Stewart, engine driver
Mrs Smith
Matthew B. Forsyth, clerk
8 Charles Stewart, labourer
Andrew Turpie, plumber
Robert Strang, traveller
Thomas Brown, draper
Mrs Maxton
John Hunter, cabinetmaker
10 George Leslie, insur. agent
Hugh G. Mathie, hatter
Chas. Thomson, coachpainter
Alexander Cousin, fireman
John Bennie, draper
James C. Brown, clerk
12 Joseph Taylor, clerk
Duncan Thomson, butcher
David Millie, traveller
Wm. C. Shaw, traveller
David Graham, traveller
A. Pollock, miner
14 John Ramsay, clerk
David Thomson, ironmonger
John Blackadder, draper
George Thomson, joiner
John Coulthart, gardener
John Lindsay, clerk
16 Wm. Dobbie, draper

BRUCE STREET – Continued.

15 George M'Kechnie, tailor
  James King, guard
17 Henry D. Strachan, rubber
  worker
  Mrs Margaret Robertson
  Robert Gardner, engine driver
  Jas. Buchan, lathsplitter
  Colin Lennox, painter
  James Thomson, plumber
19 James Christie
  Mrs Margaret Gow
  Mrs Mary Stewart
  Robt. Thomson, storekeeper
  Robt. M'Innes, joiner
  William Comrie, miner
21 Archd. Oliphant, confectioner

16 Alex. M. Guild, grocer
  Andrew Robertson, postman
  A. H. Robertson, postal clerk
  Jas. Sellars, draper
  Jas. Neil, butcher
18 James Kerr, coachman
  Alfred Kenny, linotype operator
  Alex. Murray, railway inspector
  Wm. M'Kinlay, grocer
  Wm. Smith, traveller
  Jas. Dawson, ironmonger
Bowling Green—Spittalmyre Club
20 Arch. Greenhorn, tailor
  Jas. Dewar, ironmonger
  Mrs Lawson
  Wm. M'Dougall, draper
  George Stevens, draper
  Walter Francis, wheelwright
22 Mrs Bennett, residenter
  Robert Bennett, grocer
  George Isitt, grocer
  Robert Fenwick, contractor
  John Sutherland, telegraphist
  Wm. Griffiths, blacksmith
  James G. Rae, insur. agent
  Rev. A. Ashby (Baptist assist.)
24 Mrs William Gilmour
  Mrs William M'Intosh
  Thomas Henderson, joiner
  Andrew Brown
  Alex. Beaton, engine driver
  Jas. Gordon, teacher of dancing

BURGHMUIR.

1 Peter Reid, lorryman
3 Mrs Cecilia Scotland, nurse
  James Conner, weaver
13 Mrs Janet Allan
15 Mrs M'Laren
15½ James Somerville, tailor
17 Robert Gilfillan, wool merc.
19 David Crowe, fitter
21 Wm. Macpherson, Co-op. Soc.
  Secy.
23 James Kemp, platelayer
25-29 J. & J. Miller, brewers
31 John Nisbet, upholsterer

33 David Gerrard, cabinetmaker
35 Peter M'Laren, warehouseman
37 Graham & Morton, furnishers
39 Malcolm M'Farlane, porter
Burnbank—Miss M'Farlane
  P. Skinner, cutter
Elmbank—Robert Morrison, tailor
Rowanlea—W. Ferguson, traveller
The Linden—R. Foster, plasterer
Thistlecroft—R. F. Smith
Woodbank—R. Marshall, residenter
  Robert Maclaurin
  W. Towers, electrician

CAMBUSKENNETH ABBEY.

Main Street.

Thomas Dow, ferryman
Abbey Rope Works—Charles Robertson
Dunlora—Mrs Eliz. Henry
Alex. Christie, joiner
Alex. Rolland
John Welsh, carter
Alexandra Cottage—A. Dewar, slater
Rose Cottage—Mrs E. Bauchop
Tower Orchard—J. Stewart, market gardener
St. James' Orchard—A. Watson, market gardener

May Cottage—Miss E. Fisher
Ivanhoe Cottage—T. Watson, cartwright
Abbey School
Bute Cottage—James Baillies, rubber worker
Comely Bank—Mrs A. Nimmo
Mrs Janet Connell
Robt. Ferguson, ploughman
W. Henry, insurance agent
Peter Davie, cartwright
Hood Farm—John Kinross

High Street.

1 Abbey Inn—George Milne
3 Richard Marshall, saddler
Alex. Black, painter
Mrs Catherine Hunter
Mrs Pryde
5 Mrs Christina Christie
7 James M'Anany, blacksmith
9 H. E. Bruce, tailor
11 Mrs Ann Frew
13 Mrs Jane Westcott
15 Mrs Jane Nicholson
17 Alex. Dewar, ironmonger
19 Henry Knowles, insur. agent
Finlay Taylor, painter
21 John Lyall, dentist
23 John M'Queen
25 John Fyfe, waggon inspector
27 C. Mathieson, patternmaker
29 James Cameron, joiner

2 Thistle Cottage—Mrs M. Aitken
4 James Hutchieson
6 Miss Glen, confectioner
8 Mrs A. Sutherland
10 Abbey Cottage—James Smith, painter
12 Mrs Catherine Johnstone
14 Mrs Ann Taylor
16 The Rowans—J. G. Murray, artist
18 Ferry Orchard—
Alex. Baxter, market gardener
20 Mrs Graham, grocer
Ladysneuk Farm—John Lucas

CASTLE.

Major Aytoun, D.S.O.
Captain D. Darroch
Captain A. Beattie
Adjt. H. P. Moulton-Barrett
Lieutenant Sceales
Lieutenant M'Lean
Private George Finn

Qr.-Mr.-Sergt. J. Sutherland
Colour-Sergeant D. M'Lean
David Haston, soldier
Alfred G. Furr, soldier
Wm. Martin, canteen steward
Sergeant-Major Lindsay

CASTLE - Continued.

Married Quarters—

1 Pipe-Major Smith
2 Colour-Sergeant Matthews
3 Sergeant Dickson
4 Private Stewart
5 Private Gallagher
6 Sergeant Watson
7 Private John Gray
8 Private Robert Duncan
9 Sergeant Joseph Moore
10 Colour-Sergeant Newport
11 Sergeant Oliver
12 Private Robert Thomson
13 Private Samuel Reid
14 Sergeant H. Farish
15 Corporal G. T. Rodwell
16 Private Charles Girgan
17 Sergeant James Elrick
18 Sergeant John Rae
19 Private James M'Lauchlan
22 Sergeant A. Oliver
22B Private M'Culloch
23 Private Hugh Paton
24 Sergt. Ketchtall, prison staff
25 Private J. L. Buchanan
26 Private Roderick M'Lauchlan
27 Private John Connell
28 Corporal Phillips, prison staff
29 Corporal Robertson
30 Private Henry Davies

CASTLE ESPLANADE.

1 Miss Jane Buchan
2 3 Mrs Hamilton, hotelkeeper
   Fred. E. Bussell, photographer
   Peter Lees, sexton
   James Minty, clothier

Waterloo House—
   David Raphael, labourer
   John Allan, miner
   William Machan, barman
   Thos. Lees, assistant sexton

CASTLEHILL (UPPER).

17 George Milne, labourer
19 William Lenton, pensioner
37 James M'Phee, labourer
   Peter Neilson, labourer
   Michael Murphy, labourer
39 Mrs Mary Robertson
   Mrs Margaret Lawson
41 Charles Moncrieff, shoemaker
43 William Ferguson, tailor
   Michael M'Gibbon, labourer
24 James M'Avoy, porter
   Mrs M'Lachlan
   William M'Kay, labourer
   Jas. Binnington, prison warder
26 Mrs Janet Honeyman
28 James Rennie, cooper
   David Jackson, labourer
   Mrs Mary M'Donald
30 Peter Mailley, labourer
32 John Wood, miner
   Mrs Bridget Quin
   Mrs Christina M'Donald
   Robert Robertson, plasterer
34 David Muir, tobacconist
   John Vance, tailor
36 Peter Gardner, mason
38 William Cherry, smith
   Mrs Marion Scully
   R. B. Honeyman, miner
40 Mrs Mary M'Gloan

CASTLEHILL (UPPER)—Continued.

40 Andrew Burgess, labourer
   Miss Mary Dawson
   Alex. Harvey, labourer
   Robert Honeyman, sawmiller
42 Mrs Ellen Yule
   Hugh M'Gregor, miner
44 William Watson, tailor

44 Alex. M'Donald, labourer
46 Mrs Ann Stewart
   Michael Kenny, labourer
   Edward Kenny, fireman
48 John Gardner, mason
52 James Gunn, guide
   John Porter, plumber

CASTLEHILL (LOWER).

7 Allan Park Mission Hall
33 Mrs M'Luckie
   Peter M'Gregor, guide
35 Alex. Law, goods porter
37 Mrs C. M'Donald
39 Mrs Margaret Girvan

12 Donald Fisher, surfaceman
   Alex. Pirrie, carter
   William Morrison, miner
   John Welsh, labourer
14 Mrs M'Que
16 Peter M'Gregor, engine driver
   Peter Jack, carter
   Caldwell Morrison, miner
18 Edward Derrick, labourer
   John Mills, labourer
20 Mrs Cassidy
   William Stewart, pedlar
   Thomas Robertson, cooper
   John Hamilton, miner
   Mrs Margaret Robertson
   John M'Intosh, labourer
22 Mrs Marion Gilvear
24 Andrew Black, shoemaker
   Fred. Edwards, labourer
   Thomas Allan, labourer
30 Ebenezer Monteath, labourer
32 Mrs Sarah Ann Downie
36 Mrs Janet Cruickshanks
38 John M'Innes, labourer
40 Andrew Buchanan, dairyman
42 James Welsh, labourer
44 Thomas Donoghue, miner
   Thomas Jamieson, surfaceman
46 John Leathley, fish merchant
   Mannus O'Donnel, miner
48 Mrs Mary M'Kenzie
   Patrick Kaney, labourer
   John Wood Blakey
   William Allsworth, labourer
50 Michael Marrie, labourer
   Hugh Thomson, miner
52 William Meldrum, groom
54 John Moore, miner

CASTLE WYND.

9-11 Fever Hospital
Lorne Tavern—
    Andrew Hunter, spirit merc.

Mar Lodge and Palace Tea Rooms—
    Mrs Craig
Military Hospital—
    Sergeant-Major Hardie
    Colour-Sergeant M'Culloch
    Qr-Mr-Sergeant F. Meston
    Sergeant Jackson
    Colour-Sergeant Bertram
    Colour-Sergeant Gordon

CHURCH WYND.

1 Andrew Johnstone, miner
  Thomas Stevenson, newsagent
3 John Turner, labourer
5 George Henderson, mason

7 Michael Monnachan, hawker
  Charles Faulds, miner
  Alex. Hall, fish hawker

CLARENDON PLACE.

1 Mrs Calder
3 Mrs Elizabeth M'Lean
5 John Landale
7 Andrew Swan, jeweller
9 D. Arbuthnot, engineer
11 Captain Darroch
13 Mrs Sarah Muir
15 D. Crawford, china merchant
19 John G. Murray, solicitor
21 Edmund Baker, art master
23 Mrs Anne M'Donald

2 John Barr, surveyor of taxes
4 Andrew Young
6 James MacAulay
10 Rev. Percival Brown
12 Robert Kidston
14 Miss Risk
16 Miss Elizabeth Drummond
18 Mrs Woodburne
20 A. Whytt, M.D.
22 Captain Tasker
24 Wm. Dobbie, commission agent

CLIFFORD ROAD.

1 Peter Brodie, baker
2 Mich. Thomas Wing, traveller
3 John Johnston, fishmonger
4 Miss Easton
5 Mrs Elizabeth Rae
6 William Maxwell, merchant
7 Peter Murray, coal merchant

9 W. Meiklejohn, ret. draper
10 David Carson, painter
11 John Jenkins, writer
12 Rev. John M'Ewan
13 Thomas M'Kay, shipowner

COBURG AVENUE.

1 John M'Kay, factor
3 D. Stewart, jun., jeweller
5 David T. James, teacher
7 John Stevenson, potato merc.
9 F. G. Mann, surveyor
11 James G. Bailey, traveller
13 William Brown, clothier
15 John Walker, chemist
17 William T. King, traveller
19 William Hood, artist
21 D. Mackie, Inland Rev. officer

2 John Cairns, traveller
4 Miss Mary Mills
6 Mrs Catherine Smith
8 Mrs Hagemann, teacher
Forthview—John Fowler
Parkview—
    James Johnston, wood merc.

COLQUHOUN STREET.

William Place—

1 Alex. M'Laren, engine driver
  John M'Donald engine driver
  William Easson, joiner
  James Richardson, jun., clerk
3 James Crabb, weaver
  Mrs Buchanan
  John Donachie, railwayman
  Peter Jeffray, brakesman
5 George Ramsay, painter
  J. C. Robertson, watchmaker
  James Sharp, compositor
  Gavin Weir, miner
7 William Forrester, sinker
  David Naismyth, miner
  John Ogilvie, upholsterer
  Miss Jane M'Millan
  Burgh Electric Light Station

2 Henry Jamieson, mill overseer
  William Lewis, upholsterer
  J. Kerr
  Peter Easton, weaver
4 James Stevenson, weaver
  John Donaldson, bottler
  Mrs Campbell
6 Isaac Hunter, timekeeper
  James Blair, miner
  Alex. Crichton, engine driver
  Thomas Thomson, saddler
8 Arch. Beveridge, checkweigher
  Robert Naismyth, miner
  John Yeardly, engineman
  Peter Stirling, pointsman

CORN EXCHANGE ROAD.

W. M. Reyburn, banker
Stirling Public Library—
  Wm. C. Waugh, librarian
Arch. M'Kinlay, lorryman
John Walker, baker

Corn Exchange Bar—
  Public-House Trust, Ltd.

CORNTON ROAD.

Forth Bridge Mills—
  John E. Thurman & Co., wool
  and flock merchants
  Kennedy & Co., Ltd., manufacturing confectioners.

Forthvale Cottage—Walter Cotton,
  manager, rubber works
Forthvale Works—Rubber Co. of
  Scotland, Ltd.—R. B. Black,
  managing director

COWANE STREET.

3 Mrs Janet M'Donald
5 Mrs Mary Dawson
13 John Hunter, lorryman
Robert Wilson, tailor
Miss Jane Colquhoun
George Cuthill, signal fitter
Thomas Hunter, lorryman
Mrs Maggie Russell
15 Robert Wilson, sailor
John Millar, plasterer
Mrs Catherine M'Donald
Mrs Ferguson
And. M'Callum, blacksmith
James M'Millan, gardener
17 Mrs L. Wilson
Mrs Agnes M'Callum
Alex. Wright, plumber
Thomas Bowie, joiner
William Guthrie, storekeeper
Miss Agnes Melville
19 John M'Innes, sawyer
Robert M'Neil, finisher
Alex. Campbell, plumber
Alex. Bowie, clerk
Miss Mary Henderson
Mrs Janet Monteath
23 David Millar, plasterer
William M'Leod, carter
Mrs Boag
John Begbie, clerk
John Roy, lorryman
Alex. Bremner, tailor
25 William Munnoch, tailor
George More, tailor
Mrs Janet Squair
David Pattie, baker
T. B. M'Intosh, baker
William Neilson, gardener
27 Robert M'Donald, brakesman
Henry M'Connachie, traveller
Miss M. Cameron
Wm. Donaldson, sculptor
Robert Craig, machineman
29 Jas. Robertson, cabinetmaker
31 John Duff, labourer
33 Jas. Sutherland, signal fitter
35 James Ross, plasterer

2 John M'Gregor, publican
4 Alex. Henderson, butcher
Mrs Millar
John Hood, baker
Allan Hood, clerk
4½ R. Guiliani, ice-cream shop
6-10 John Henderson, dairyman
12 John Dewar, joiner
14 John M'Cormack, mason
Miss Wilkinson
Mrs Lily Kerr
16 Peter Hood, labourer
Thomas Harley, conductor
20 William Munro, gardener
Alex. Fyfe, barman
Mrs Thomson
Mrs M Moncrieff
22 Miss Agnes Christie, grocer
24 George Robertson, plasterer
John Anderson, blacksmith
Mrs Donaldson
Robert Don, lorryman
Miss Jessie Duncan
28 Robert Paterson, tailor
Andrew Paterson, warder
30 James Proudfoot, guard
Mrs Margaret Dow
Mrs Brown
John Heaps, miner
32 Allan Murdoch, cartwright
34 James Walker, joiner
William Main, vanman
John Henderson, mason
Robert Kinlay, compositor
William Summers, vanman
36-38 Co-operative Society—
Butchery and Grocery Depts.
38½ Mrs Helen Fergie
William Buchanan, miner
40 John Wright, draper
42 Archibald Stewart, plumber
44 John Lockhart, coal agent
Miss Kate Sharp
James Black, plasterer
46 John Anderson, painter
48 William Fraser, gardener
James Aitken, labourer

COWANE STREET – Continued.

35 Wm. Dougal, coachpainter
Alex. Anderson, labourer
Frances Rollo, clerk
William M'Kay, baker
Miss Gillespie
David Kirk, engine driver
Miss Janet Taylor
John M'Lauchlan, butcher
A. M'Ewan, baker
37 John Shaw, bootmaker
39-41 Robert Paterson, dairy
43 Mrs Catherine Duthie
Mrs Elizabeth Halley
Mrs Elizabeth Donaldson
James Taylor, tailor
Mrs Janet Bryce
Thomas Arthur, joiner
43½ Mrs Agnes Watson
William M'Arthur, painter
James Mathers, guard
William Robb, porter
John Horn, vanman
J. Simpson, foreman yardsman
45 Mrs Edith Gill, confectioner
47 John Gill, traveller
Alex. Armstrong, vanman
John Paterson, tailor
William Derrick, gardener
Mrs Margaret Stalker
Charles M'Kinnon, joiner
Hugh Harper, mechanic
Wm. Bayne, labourer
Wm. M'Robbie, lathsplitter
49 Jas. Speirs, grocer
49½ J. W. Shennan, bootmaker
51 Jas. M'Donald, rubber worker
Miss Jessie Swanston
John Dunsmuir, miner
51-53 Peter Meiklejohn, dairyman
53½ Michael Connoboy, plasterer
Henry Rae, signalman
Wm. Marshall, labourer
Edward M'Donald, smith
Henry M. Richards, labourer
Thomas Rawding, engineer
Henry Taylor, bootcloser
James M'Rorie, porter

48 Miss Jane Henderson
Colin M'Lean, carter
Jas. Marshall, candlemaker
Mrs Mary Elliot
50 James M'Kenzie, clothier
52 Andrew Burt
Wm. M'Callum, tailor
Miss Margaret Haggart
Miss M Pow, nurse
Peter Francis, cooper
54 Mrs Anstruther, confectioner
56 Archd. P. Smith, carter
Charles Duncanson, slater
Mrs Mary M'Cartney
Miss Janet M'Kay
58 Joseph M'Gregor, goods guard
Joseph Young, rubber worker
Mrs Lizzie M'Farlane
Tom Black, glazier
Wm. Adams, labourer
60 Hugh Eadie, labourer
62 Mrs M. Marriott, newsagent
64 George M'Intosh, labourer
Mrs Mary M'Pherson
Miss Janet White
Mrs Helen M'Intosh
Mrs Crae
James Flockhart, fireman
Mrs Jessie Donnelly
Anthony Thornton, labourer
66 John Clark, miner
Wm. Lenord, candlemaker
Mrs Mary Ritchie
Alex. Clark, miner
Jas. Anderson, tacklemaker
Mrs Margaret Harley
Mrs Jane Ritchie
James Gray, joiner
68 Michael Malley, labourer
Alex. Stewart, railwayman
And. Kemp, car. inspector
Daniel M'Lean, carter
Wm. Watson, tinsmith
Hugh Phee, miner
Patrick Dinnet, labourer
72 George Moir, mason
74 Mrs Agnes Collis

COWANE STREET—Continued.

53½ John Steele, engine driver
 55 Miss C. Thomson, bookseller
 57 Alex. Dick, plasterer
 59 James Urquhart, brakesman
    Mrs Abercrombie
    Mrs Margaret Crerar
    Mrs Margaret Gray
    Robert Anderson, plumber
    Miss M. M'Gregor, dressmaker
    Miss Helen Ogilvie
    Mrs Jane Johnston
    David Cousin, plumber
    Wm. White, draper
 61 Wm. Clink, warehouseman
    John Stirling, joiner
    Mrs Margaret Struthers
    J. F. Lorimer, cabinetmaker
    P. Battison, gilder
    John Riddle coachman
 63 Mrs Tetstall
    James Wilson, labourer
    James Tetstall, cooper
    Arch. Mitchell, cabinetmaker
    Miss Stewart
    Territorial School
    West U.F. Church—
        Rev. James Angus

 74 James Pullar, porter
    Mrs Duncan
    Miss C. Thomson, saleswoman
    Miss Christina Thomson
 76 George Monaghan
    Miss Alice Suttie
    John Pattie, engine driver
    John Barclay, warehouseman
    Elizabeth Lee
    Mrs Margaret Ritchie
    Alex. Reid, carter
    Mrs Janet Mathieson
 80 Peter Sinclair, gardener
    Andrew Black, mason
    Miss Harvie, dressmaker
    Miss M. M'Arthur
    Mrs Lorimer
    George Tait, painter
    Samuel Fishington, rubber worker
 82 Adam Aitken, labourer
 84 Mrs A. Stewart
    Mrs C. Swanston
    Miss Horn
 86 Miss Johann Strachan
 88 Mrs Jane Cormack
    George Marshall, tailor
    James Drummond, carter
    David Powrie, sawyer
    Mrs Jeanie Henderson
88-90 Miss J. Hardie, keeper, sub-Post Office
 92 James Morrison, surfaceman
    Alex. M'Farlane, labourer
    Mrs Stewart
    Mrs Eliza Marshall
    Alex. Donaldson, mason
    Miss Kate Buchanan
    John Simpson, tailor
    David M'Quiggan, smith
 96 George Christie, draper
 98 George Imrie, fishing rod maker
    Mrs Dewar
    Daniel Currie, jeweller
    David Wallace, labourer
100 William Law, grocer

CRAIGS (UPPER).

1-3 A. Penman, spirit merchant
5 John F. Ralston confectioner
Wm. Milne & Co., slaters
Robert Carlin, baker
Miss Janet Fenton
5-7-9 Jas. Gray & Co., seedsmen
11 Duncan Thomson, butcher
13 Mrs Fanny Brisbane
15 John Stewart, shoemaker
17 Mrs Janet Gordon, ironmonger
19 James Armstrong, blacksmith
Mrs Robertson
21 Mrs C. M'Kay, refresh. rooms
23 Wm. M'Innes, weaver
25 Robert Shaw, labourer
Thomas Moir, cooper
Edward M'Menemy, labourer
James Bell, waiter
27 Robert Millar, baker
29 Miss Paterson, stationer
31 James Nicol, clerk
William Reid, lorryman
Hugh Campbell, dyer
Mrs Elizabeth Robertson
John Macaulay, porter
Honor Cole, dresser
James Docherty, slater
J. Phibbs, weaver
Robert Martin, joiner
33 Wm. M'Arthur, hairdresser
Walter Balfour, slater
Mrs Jessie Kay
James Leslie, engine driver
35 J. Campbell, carpet weaver
37 Co-operative Society
‡ Craigs United Free Church—
Rev. D. D. Ormond
39 Mrs M. A. Chalmers
Alexander Mills, fireman
Miss M. Paterson, dressmaker
Mrs Alexander Short
41 Jas. Dudgeon, baker
43 John Cooper, grocer
45 Miss Sproat
47 Samuel F. Millar, baker
49 B. Di Ponio, ice-cream shop
53 Matthew Wallace, laundryman
49-55 John Mailer & Co., farm
produce merchants

2 Thomas Montgomery
Mrs Jane Campbell
Mrs Mary Crawford
Hugh Durie, mason
David Blair, carpet weaver
4 Miss E. Young, refresh. rooms
6 George Plenderleith, smith
T. L. Houston, vet. surgeon
8 Co-op. Soc.—Butchery Dept.
10 George Frame, surfaceman
Wm. Duncanson, tailor
James Pollock, signalman
Mrs Jessie Cameron
E. Gillespie, tel. linesman
John Campbell, lorryman
John Robertson, postman
Robert Goodall, cabman
John Thompson, mechanic
14 Robert Frater, plumber
Wm. Smith, carter
Arthur Greig, carter
16-18 Mrs Agnes Livingstone
18 Alexander Bean, plumber
Hally Emery, waggon inspr.
Wm. Orr, miner
20 Peter Menzies, grocer
22 Peter Reid, dairykeeper
24 James M'Kenzie, porter
Wm. M'Innes, weaver
George Owen, cycle maker
28-34 John Jamieson, printer
28 Robert Morton, clerk
J. F. Elder, compositor
36-38 Lockhart & M'Nab, electrical
engineers and smiths
36 Peter M'Nab, smith
James Duff, plumber
50 Miss J. Gillespie, spirit mer.
52 Robert Hendry, barman
54-56 John Dempster, tobacconist
60 Arch. Stewart, plumber
And. Ferguson, carpet foreman
W. Smith, engine driver
Alex. Duthie, grocer
Alfred Kenny, warehouseman
Mrs Carson
62 Miss Kenny, confectioner

CRAIGS (UPPER)—Continued.

55 J. Abercromby, warehouseman
Chas. Dingwall, railway porter
57 Walter Balfour, slater
Wm. Robertson, bus hirer
59 D. M'Diarmid & Sons, candle makers
61 Bottle Exchange
J. Gray & Co., seedsmen (stores)
Graham & Morton, ironmongers (stores)
J. & W. Ronald, builders
R Anderson & Sons, building contractors
63 J. Robertson, firewood factory

64 Samuel Fields, upholsterer
Mrs Mains
John Kay, baker
Matthew Campbell, weaver
Wm. Millar, blacksmith
Jas. Brodie, packer
Duncan M'Innes, seedsman
64A J. F. Macintosh, bootmaker
66 David Hardie, plumber
70 James Paterson, carter
Adam Graham, engine keeper
Ed. Dempsey, miner
Mrs Ritchie
72 David Millar, sexton
Miss M. M'Gibbon, dairykeeper
Mrs Eliza. Condy
Daniel Anstruther, confectioner
74 David Jamieson, wood sorter
76 Mrs M'Ewan
Mat. Wallace, laundryman
78 R. Neil, manager, Rockvale Mills
80 James Brown, wool sorter
Rockvale Mills
86 Mrs Hugh M'Adam
88 Wm. Wingate, engine driver
90 John Mitchell, kilnman
92 Robt. Duncan, labourer
Joseph Forbes, labourer
Jas. Dow, fireman
Wm. Todd, engine driver
94 Mrs M. Doig, laundress
Robt. Robertson, engine driver
98 William Robinson, vanman
Jas. Robertson, coachbuilder
Wm. Anderson, engine driver
Thos. Wingate, weaver
100 James Wylie, foreman cleaner
Alex. Rose, engine driver
Mrs Mary Christie
George Marr, pointsman
102 Thos. Carse, signalman
Mrs Agnes Smith
Peter Livingstone, fitter
Jas. M'Callum, signalman
104 And. M'Donald, engine driver
Robt. Gilchrist, weaver
J. M. Gray, weaver

CRAIGS (UPPER)—Continued.

104 Wm. Phibbs, miner
106 Andrew Wilson, grocer
    Robert Christie, clerk
    Wm. Ramsay, weaver.
    A. Leishman, crane inspector
108 David Chrystal, fitter
    Mrs Alison Blyth
    John Towers, porter
    Peter Todd, lorryman
    Mrs Agnes Ewing
    John Johnstone, lorryman

108 Duncan Marshall, weaver
110 Jas. Chrystal, fireman
    Mrs Margaret Hunter
112 Mrs And. Robertson
    Geo. Monteith, engineman
114 James M'Neil, cleaner
    Peter Wingate, engine driver
116 W. M'Beth, engine driver
    Daniel M'Donald, porter
    John Henderson, porter
    D. W. Bett, railway guard

CRAIGS (MIDDLE).

1 Alex. Kay, baker
3 Andrew Brock, joiner
    Mrs J. Coull
    John Burns, painter
5 Mrs Margaret Ferguson
    Peter Soutar, engine driver
    Robert Stevenson, weaver
    Mrs Isabella Hardie
    Jas. Brown, weaver
    Ben. Wyatt, machineman
    Mrs Ann Paterson
    Peter Duthie, hammerman
7 John Drummond, hammerman
    Adam Shepherd, labourer

4 Peter Duncanson, tailor
6 Mrs C. M'Innes
8 John W. Small, watchmaker
10 Thomas Farman, janitor
12 John Pow, fitter
    Mrs Agnes Forbes
14 Dan. M'Dougall, cooper
    Geo. Morrison, sailor

CRAIGS (LOWER).

1 Mrs Margaret Williamson
3 Geo. Aitken, cabinetmaker
5 William Mitchell, spinner
    Mrs E. Smith
7 Mrs Helen M'Killop
9 David Logan, soldier
    Frank Duncan, miner
    Mrs Margaret Deans
13 Pat. M'Geoch, miner
    Mrs Isabella M'Beth
    Thos. Kelly, miner

    R. Adam & Yates, Ltd., cork
      merchants
    James Stewart, millwright
4 Mrs Catherine Hislop
    Peter King, labourer
    Alex. Swan, bricklayer
    James Sneddon, carpet weaver
    Mrs Wm. Sneddon
6 James Bain, labourer
    James Reid, joiner
    Mrs Agnes Falconer

CRAIGS (LOWER)—Continued.

13 Mrs Flora M'Menemy
   John Gilmour, miner
   John Falconer, surfaceman
   Robt. Begg, miner
   Duncan Cramb, fireman
   John M'Menemy, miner
17 Mrs Jane Stevenson
   Walker & Paton, pram. makers
21 Mrs Margaret Millar
   Henry Kelly, gardener
   David Stanley, labourer
29 James Ramsay, tinsmith
31 David Christie, slater
   Geo. Hynde, miner
   Thos. Ross, carter
33 Craigs Mission Hall
   Wm. Gordon, labourer
   B. Di Ponio, ice-cream mer.
35 Peter Carmichael, gardener
   Issac Brooks, smith
   James M'Gibbon, baker
   Robert Munro, porter
   Wm. Scotland, smith
   James Pagan, miner
   Jas. Stewart, compositor
   Sam. Stewart, tailor
   Jas. Merrilees, compositor
   Wm. Paterson, miner
37 Thomas Mowat, flesher
   Alex. M'Kenzie, pensioner
   Frank Hailstone, engine keeper
   Thos. Mowat, jun., butcher
   Jas. Cooper, platelayer
   John Morrison, miner
   Alex. Ferguson, miner
39 Wm. Robertson, miner
   T. Dimpsey, miner
   Miss Helen Durie
   Hay Adam, carter
   John Hume, miner
41 Walter Stewart, smith
   Jas. Morrison, weaver
   John Miskell, glazier
43 Robert Kay, cellerman
   Mrs Helen Bryson

6 Mrs E. Graham
   James Lindsay, labourer
   Wm. Flowers, pensioner
   Mrs Henry Scotland
   Peter Gillespie, cooper
   Samuel Cowie, baker
8 Alexander Young, carter
   Mrs Jane Shaw
12 John Watt, labourer
   Peter M'Farlane, miner

DEAN CRESCENT.

1 Mrs M'Farlane
2 John Bruce, agent
  Peter Jamieson, Singers' agt.
3 James M'Lachlan, pensioner
4 Wm. Yule, headmaster
5 Peter Hunter, stockbroker
6 James F. Prowett, artist

7 Jas. Simpson, telegraph super.
8 Edward Meiklejohn, traveller
9 Wm. Wilson, C.R. goods agent
  Andrew Scott, ironmonger
10 George M'Ewan, grocer
11 Wm. Macpherson, joiner
12 Ralph Blackett, insurance supt.

Queenshaugh—
  Robt. Thomson, butcher
  Thos. Maxwell, slater

Shiphaugh—
  D. Barker, stair-railer
  Walter Millar, dairyman

DOUGLAS STREET.

1 James Gordon, sawyer
  Miss Etta Broadway
3 James W. Shennan, bootmaker
  Mrs Ann M'Lellan
  Thomas Mowat, porter
  Mrs Margaret M'Aree
  Mrs Mary Thomson
  Wm. Stewart, brakesman
  Alex. Stewart, labourer
  John Marriott, cabinetmaker
5 Peter Gow, tailor
  John Black, labourer
7 Wm. Dow, station clerk
  Richard Nisbet, lorryman
  Mrs Catherine Taylor
  Mrs Mary Gray
9 Robt. Clark, gardener
11 Jas. Strang, tailor
15 G. Fotheringham, river watcher
  Mrs Janet Hislop
  David Dick, boilermaker
17 Geo. Liddell, insurance agent
  J. Graham, molecatcher
  Miss Bonnelo

4 John Wright, mason
  Margaret Anderson
  Colin M'Lean, printer
  Thos. Howie, storeman
  Chas. Robertson, tailor
6 James Wright, blacksmith
  F. Anderson, engine driver
  Mrs Lockhart
  Mrs Mary Lawrie
  William Todd, railwayman
  Charles Sharp, packer
  David Ferguson, mason
8 James Watson, lorryman
  James Bryce, porter
  Robert Ramsay, fireman
  Robt. Munro, porter
  Wm. Martin, postman
  Thos. Maxwell, slater and chimney sweeper

DOUGLAS TERRACE.

1 Alex. M'Intosh, engineer
2 Andrew Dewar, grain merc.
3 James Low, teacher
4 J. J. Munro, printer
5 Thomas Reid, banker
6 Chas. Johnston, headmaster

7 Miss Cleghorn
8 Mrs Masson
9 Rev. James A. Adam (Cambusbarron U.F. Church)
10 David Buchanan, Inland Rev.
11 Alex. Moyes, headmaster
12 David Yates, cork merchant

DRIP ROAD.

Gowanbank—
1 Mrs Janet Watson
Miss M'Laren
2 Adam Thorley
Alex. Mann, brakesman
3 Joseph Bolton, rubber worker
John Watson, lorryman
4 R. Fotheringham, cabinetmaker
Thos. Neish, engineer
4½-5 Wm. Young, spirit merchant
Jas. Duncan, aerated water mak.
John A. Paterson, traveller
6 J. Duncan, aerated water manu.
Raploch Dairy—P. Stirling
Kildean Cottage—William Watson,
bootmaker

Oliver P. Derrick, auctioneer
Ellerslea—T. L. Ruddock, butcher
James Neil, butcher
Daniel M'Kerracher, farmer

Combination Fever Hospital—
Miss Clark, matron
John Francis, caretaker

Kildean—Captain Charles M'Lean, A. & S. H.

Craigforth—

James Couper, merchant

John Mitchell, overseer

DRUMMOND PLACE.

3 D. Campbell, iron merchant
5 Daniel MacEwen, grocer

2 Geo. Thomson, coachbuilder
4 James Cullens, butcher
6 David Somerville, ironmonger
8 Miss Hester E. Shand
10 Wm. Wilson, tweed manuf.
14 Miss Brown

DUMBARTON ROAD.

1 Graham & Morton, furnishers
Mrs Mary Aitken
Arch. Walls, glazier
Miss Reid
Chas. E. Johnson, traveller
Daniel Watson, grocer
3 Robertson & M'Farlane, grocers
5-13 Graham & Morton, furnishers
15 M'Luckie & Walker, architects
17-19 Drummond's Tract Depot
21 Wm. Forsyth, butcher
23 Jas. M'Ewen, iron merchant

2 Arch. Henderson (Baird & Son),
umbrella maker
Miss Young's private school
Misses M'Leod, dressmakers
Miss Margaret M'Leod
Eben. Gentleman, registrar, and
collector of rates
Wingate & Curror, writers
John G. Curror
Henry Robb
6 Mrs S. E. Hay, newsagent—
sub-Post Office

DUMBARTON ROAD—Continued.

25 Mrs Marion Reid
    Jas. Stirling, farmer
    Peter Menzies, grocer
    Alex. Graham, teacher
27 John Lamb, painter
29 J. & J. Duff, plumbers
31 Thos. Ferguson, joiner
35 Peter Stewart, gardener

King's Park Farm—
    Peter Dewar, farmer
    John Dewar, farmer
    Tom Dewar, farmer
    David Dewar, farmer
    James Ritchie, ploughman
    John M'Queen, cabinetmaker

8 M. & J. Stoddart, bootmakers
10 James M. Blair, hairdresser
    Wm. Somers, joiner
    Jas. Stewart, postboy
    G. H. Jolley, Sergeant A.O.C.
    Mrs Barbara Chelsom
    D. H. Bell, teacher
12 MacEwen & Co.'s stores
16 Thos. M'Pherson, glazier
    J. & J. Duff, plumbers
    Journal Printing Office
    D. Somerville, ironmonger
    W. & T. Marshall, blacksmiths
      and electrical engineers
Rock Terrace—
    H. Coster, piano tuner
    A. Rutherford, postal clerk
    D. B. Crockart, gunsmith
Woodside House—
    D. Crockart, gunsmith
    Allan Park U.F. Church
      Rev. Jas Purves, minister
      Rev. A. S. Andrew, assist.
    Stirling Public Hall—
      Wm. Pearson, hallkeeper
    Holy Trinity Epis. Church—
      Rev. R. Percival Brown
18 Mrs Wm. Thomson
20 Wm. Crawford, architect
22 James Currie, joiner
24 Daniel Stewart, jeweller
26 David W. Logie, writer
28 John Drew, M.D.
30 Wm. J. Moore, chemist
    Stirling Bowling Club
32 John Allan, architect
    Miss M. Allan
34 John Raffan, chemist
36 Charles Bell
38 Thos. S. Harrison, banker
40 Miss Margaret Robertson
42 Rev. Daniel Macdougall (ret.)
44 Smith Institute—
      Jas. Sword, curator
46 *Novara*—Major Collins

Clay Toll—Wm. Robertson, labourer

FORREST ROAD.

2 John M'Dougall, cashier
4 Miss Elizabeth Adamson

6 Mrs Margaret Galloway

FORTH CRESCENT.

1 H. F. Stevenson, engine kpr.
  Andrew Grainger, draper
  John Barr, sanitary inspector
  Jas. Henderson, assur. agent
2 George Begbie, cashier
  James Muir, wood manager
  David Dick
  John Weir, traveller
  Mrs Helen Buchanan
  Misses Dick, dressmakers
3 Mrs Margaret Crossen
  Miss E. M'Connachie
  Mrs Janet Watson
4 John Johnston, fish merchant
  Mrs George Nicholson
  Miss Catherine Weir
  Mrs Jane Smith
5 William A. Weir, traveller
6 James W. Paterson, traveller
7 D. G. White, town clerk depute
8 Wm. Thomson, retired draper
9 David Richardson, law clerk
10 Mrs Peter Eadie
11 Geo. Laverock, Scotch whisky
    blender
12 W. J. Clarke, seedsman
13 David Whammond, grocer
14 T. Christie, building contractor
15 Wm. Hetherington, grocer
16 John Walls, retired painter

17 Miss Susan Roberton
18 John Eadie, traveller
19 Wm. Somerville, tobacconist
20 James R. Christie, coal agent
21 Alex. Love, traveller
  Mrs Jamieson
22 Ridley Sandeman, laundryman
23 Wm. Jenkins, ret. tea dealer
24 Walter Wright, guard
25 Patrick M'Gloin, mason
  Alex. Ferguson, blacksmith
26 Mrs Christina Nelson
  James M'Guire, labourer
28 Parlan M'Farlan, grain merc.
29 William Forsyth, butcher
30 Alex. Watters, labourer
32 Mrs Marjory Greenhill
  Alex. M'Dowall
  Misses Mitchell
32-38 Wm. Gordon, newsagent
34 Devonshire Creamery Coy.—
    M'Gregor & Geddes
35 Wm. Ranger, Staff-Sgt. A.O.C.
  A. Nisbet, teacher
36 John Lennox, butcher
39 Miss Isa Marshall, dairy
40 W. E. Webb, Q.-M.-Sgt. A.O.C.
  Mrs Jessie Wilson
41 Mrs H. Bolton, general dealer
42 Cowbrough & Mercer, grocers

Forth side—

Major Stewart
Sergeant F. Robertson
Sergeant William Goits
Sergeant George Swi.t

Thomas Denham, messenger
William Crawford, foreman
John Hannah, clerk

FORTH PLACE.

1 Wm. Graham, station agent
3 R. Donaldson, clerk
5 Andrew Dick, coachmaker
7 Mrs Margaret Mitchell
9 Adam Elder, N.B. goods agent
11 George C. Cunning, clerk
13 W. Hunslow, manager, railway
   refreshment rooms
15 Mrs Christina M'Laren
17 Mrs Margaret Russell
   Mrs Isa Watson
19 Alex. Millar, coal merchant
21 James Mitchell, cellarman
23 Miss E. Reid
25 D. Forgan, musicseller

FORTH STREET.

4 Park Bros., brushmakers
6 Daniel Barker, stair-railer
  James Oliphant, confectioner
10 Campbell Drysdale, carter
16 Kemp & Nicholson, engineers
18 Robert Betts
   William Wallace, engineer
   Alex. Cruickshanks, butcher
20 John Anderson, engine driver
   Andrew Duff, engineer
20 Joseph Young, fireman
   A. F. Dewar, mine inspector
   Dun. Monteith, engine driver
   Wm. M'Pherson, joiner
   Oswald Dawson, cabinetmaker
Heathfield—D. Jamieson, ret. plmbr.
   J. & C. Steel & Co., brass works
   W. M'Naughtan, millwright and
   engineer
   Scottish Co-operative Wholesale
   aerated water manufactory

FRIARS STREET.

1 *Star Inn*—James Page
1A J. M. Page, publican (house)
   Mrs Elizabeth Smith
   Geo. Knowles, cabinetmaker
   Miss Moir
   Peter Bain, butcher
3 D. Forrester, fish merchant
3A Robert Allan, fruiterer
5-7 Matthew M'Kinlay, saddler
7 George Williams, chauffeur
   James Neil, baker
   James Stewart, millwright
9 Robert Forrest, cabinetmaker
11-13 Alex. Kerr, tobacconist
13 John Stewart, blacksmith
   Miss Robertson, dressmaker
   William Burnie, labourer
15 Miss A. Miller, milliner
17-19 Mrs J. Duffin, furniture and
   antique dealer
21 William Reid, hatter
23 Andrew Finlayson, brushmaker
   William Rogers, joiner
23 John Galloway, soldier
10 J. W. Campbell, County rates
   office
12 Mrs J. Milne
   Mrs Mary Beckett
14 John Merrilees, plumber
16 James Morrison, saddler
   Mrs M. Laidlaw, nurse
   James Stocksley, shoemaker
   Miss M'Dougall
18 J. W. Armstrong, draper
   Thomas M'Nab, joiner

FRIARS STREET—Continued.

23 John M'Innes, porter
25 J. T. Dale, hairdresser
27-31 A. Johnstone, painter
31 David Swan, jeweller
   Thomas Cowie, ostler
   William Ford, pawnbroker
33 Robert Brown, painter

33 National Telephone Co.—
   P. Edmond, manager
   W. J. Traynor, spirit merchant
35 Duncan Thomson, butcher
37 John Wright, grocer
Co-operative Society—Butchery and
   Boot Depts.

GEORGE STREET.

1 D. M'Gregor & Co., slaters
5 Miss Annie Hay, teacher
   Mrs Christina Currie
   Robert Paterson, iron turner
   William Robb, grocer
7 Thomas Arthur, clerk
11-13 W. M'Dougall & Sons, joiners
15 James Rutherford, gardener
   James M'Beth, labourer
   Wm. Bogle, colliery oversman
   John Forsyth, corkcutter
17 Mrs Grace M'Lean
   John Dennison, musician
   Robert Fairful, joiner
   Miss Agnes Halket
19 Elder's Bakery
21 William B. Elder, baker
23 James Douglas, fireman
   William Boag, gardener
   A. Thomson, corkcutter
   Jas. L. Dickson, engine keeper
   George Soutar, waiter
   Andrew Wilson, barman
   John H. Mains, weaver
   James Oliver, railway porter

2 Mrs Mary D. Roberts
   James Crawford, joiner
   William Christie, watchmaker
   Joseph Sorton, storeman
   Maxwell M'Luckie, plumber
   John Brown, labourer
   Mrs Catherine Mailley
   Adam Lindsay, cooper
   Joseph Bently, oversman
   George Marshall, postman
   Jas. C. Rawding, plumber
4 Robert Laurie, jute dresser
   James Soutar, mason
   Matthew M'Lean, tailor
   James Duguid, carter
   C. Soutar, bricklayer
   Geo. Hall, salvation army capt.
   John Strang, joiner
   Mrs Ann M'Kenzie
6 Wm. M'Dougall, joiner
   Craigs School
8 Peter Brown, shoemaker
   James Sives, linesman
   John Dow, weaver
   J. Blackwood, labourer
10 George Hogg, painter
   Wm. Horsburgh, engineer
   Mrs Jessie Alexander
   A. Wilson, mason
12 John Fisher
   James Humphries, butler
   Mrs Mary Dick
   Robert Wilson, plumber
   Robert Jenkins, compositor
14 James Gray, compositor
   A. M'Laren, engineman
   James Geddes, miner
   Murdoch Dingwall, gardener
   Thomas Marshall, smith

GLADSTONE PLACE.

1 John Orr Galloway, accountant
3 Alex. G. Graham, merchant
5 John G. Curror, Sheriff Clerk
7 J. M'Gregor, muslin manufact.
11 Mrs Ritchie
13 Mrs Emily Higginbotham
15 David B. Morris, Town Clerk
17 Mrs Geo. P. Thomson

2 Rev. John Ghalmers
4 Mrs Jessie Gray
6 Robert MacLuckie, writer
8 Miss Janet Watt
Miss Catherine Watt
Miss Isabella Watt
10 Mrs Frances Ritchie
Rev. Thomas Wright
12 Miss Mary Whitehead

GLASGOW ROAD, St Ninians.

1 William Ewing
3 Robert Hardie, painter
5 Mrs Jeffrey, confectioner
7 George M'Naughton, carter
9 Wm. M'Neil, miner
11 William Barclay, grocer
13 John Barclay, nailer
15 Miss Jane Jeffrey
Miss Annie Jeffrey
17 Robert Brown, millworker
19 Mrs Mary Crawford
21 Wm. Buchanan, vanman
23 Robert Watson, nailer
25 Alexander Dick, nailer
27 James Brodie. nailer
Mrs Agnes Dick
29 Hugh Kerr, stoker
31 Henry Drummond, ploughman
31½ Matthew Jenkins, vanman
Mrs Robert Jenkins
33 Mrs Margaret M'Farlane
35 John Livingstone, carter
37 Thomas Horne, tanner
43 Mrs Isabella Dewar
45 Robert Dick, miner
47 Mrs Margaret Paton
49 Alex. Hall, builder
Wm. Brown, colliery manager
51 Wm. Gilfillan, spirit merchant
53 Mrs Aitken
55 Robert Russell, nailer
57 Charles Machray, carriage hirer
59 Reid Irvine, bricklayer
Miss M'Farlane

South United Free Church—
Rev. Dr. Frew
Rev. D. Smith
6 David Troup, postal clerk
St Ninians Tannery—
James Grieve
8 James Lambert, contractor
10 James Cochrane, coachbuilder
George Swan, tanner
David Lockhart, tanner
12 Michael O'Brien
John Paton, tanner
14 Francis O'Brien, nailer
22 Mrs Annie Marshall
24 James Crawford, labourer
26 Robert Marshall
28 Mrs Jane Ferguson
30 Jas. Thomson, gardener
32 Mrs Euphemia Crawford
Glasgow Road House—
Alex. Jenkins, solicitor

Whins of Milton—
J. Simpson & Co., engineers, motor car builders, and makers of "Velox" high-pressure steam disinfectors

GLEBE AVENUE.

1 Patrick Murray
3 Miss Smith
5 Daniel Wylie, printer

16 Mrs Snyder
17 Rev. Mr M'Pherson (ret.)
18 Miss Margaret Stewart
19 Dr J. H. Murray

GLEBE CRESCENT.

1 Miss Elizabeth Carrick
3 Mrs Yorke
5 Miss A. L. H. Galbraith
  Miss E. Galbraith
7 Arch. G. H. Mowbray
9 Rev. George Yuille
  Wm. Cameron, coachman

2 Miss Mary Laird
  Miss Margaret Laird
  Miss Emily Laird
4 Capt. A. Linnell, A.O. Dept.
6 H. Gavin, draper
8 James Hunter, wool agent
10 A. W. Marchant, Mus. Doc.
12 Miss Mitchell
14 Mrs Susan Nisbet
   Robert Somers, retired schoolmaster
16 Mrs Janet Gourlay

GLENCOE ROAD.

1 James M'Aree, dairyman
3 Henry Haggarty, confectioner
  Mrs Margaret Young
7 Mrs Agnes Foster
9 Horace Marshall, miner
  Mrs Isabella Lennie
11 Hugh Craig, janitor
13 James Brown, barman
   James M'Kenzie, tailor
   Mrs A. M'Murtrie

13 Mrs Elizabeth Donaldson
   John Wardrop, labourer
   James Aitken, fireman
   James Hutton, fireman
   John Dow, coal carter
   Thos. Stevenson, vanman
15 Miss Maggie Nicol, dressmaker
   Arch. Stevenson, clerk
17 Joseph Williamson, dairyman
19 George Ross, potato merchant

IRVINE PLACE.

A. Simpson, carriage hirer and
  undertaker (stables)
9 John Macdonald, grocer
  R. Guiliani, confectioner
11 Wm. Simpson, pawnbroker
15 Alex. Bennie, butcher
   James Dunlop, grocer
17 Very Rev. Monseigneur Smith
   Roman Catholic School
25 Charles Hepburn, surfaceman
   James Duncanson, tailor
   Wm. Harley, painter
   Daniel M'Laren, baker
   David Robertson, barman

2 James Davie, ironfounder
4 Arch. M'Lachlan
6 Mrs Murray
8 Wm. B. Wilson, joiner
10 William Eadie, brewer
12 *The Ridge*—Mrs Janet Burden
Burden's Brewery

IRVINE PLACE—Continued.

25 Miss M. Glancy, teacher
27 Thomas Reid, brewer
   Wm. Cameron, bricklayer

27 James Smart, engine driver
   Wm. Leckie, lorryman
   Thos. B. Bannigan, traveller

JAMES STREET.

1 James Stirling, clerk
  Daniel Sinclair, joiner
  Thomas Hynd, clerk
  Hugh Campbell, labourer
3 David Dewar, tailor
  Mrs Ann Jackson
  John Forrester, coachbuilder
  William Robertson, tailor
  D. M'Naughton, ironmonger
  Mrs C. Wotherspoon
5 J. A. Kennedy, spirit merchant
  Wm. Francis, carpet designer
  Sydney Buckingham, tailor's
    manager
  John Hunter, tailor's cutter
7 Harold Cotton, clerk
  Wm. Roberts, gardener
  Wm. J. Tait, tailor's cutter
  Wm. M'Laren, tailor's cutter
33 Peter King, tailor
  David M'Nee, hairdresser
  Wm. M'Farlane, cooper
  George Gifford, carter
  Robert Hughes, fireman
  James M'Callum, clerk
  George Duncan, tailor
  Miss Catherine Maquarrie
  Bryce Philips, surfaceman
  Miss Todd

2 Miss Margaret M'Pherson
  James Dawson, traveller
  Jas. Phillips, music teacher
4 David Ferguson, inspector of
    works
6 Hugh Kirkwood, printer
8 James Sinclair, confectioner
10 George Arthur, draper
12 Miss Elizabeth Tainsh
14 Peter M'Donald, auctioneer
16 Alex. Greig, tailor
18 Jas. Ormiston, piano dealer, &c.
20 J. & W. Ronald, builders
22 Miss Mary Wright
24 Robert M'Aree, draper
26 James Struthers, cartwright
  James Oliphant, confectioner
  J. M'Millan, foreman cooper
  Oswald Dawson, cabinetmaker
32 Thomas Blair, fireman
  James Strachan, cabinetmaker
  James Todd, driver
  Mrs Jane Buchanan
  Mrs J. Brisbane
  Miss Nellie Drysdale
  James Gifford, painter
  John Harvey, tailor
  Mrs Eliz. Allardice
  Arch. Christie, joiner
  Charles Allardice, brakesman
34 James Chrystal
  Alex. P. Gray, postman
  Peter Saunders, guard
  Wm. Forbes, cabinetmaker
  Alan Watson, blacksmith
  Andrew Downie, baker
  Robert Blackwood, signalman
  Geo. Stanborough, brakesman
  Thomas Duff, law clerk
36 James Baird, blacksmith
  Peter M'Kelvie, labourer
  James Kettle, grocer
  Wm. Lindsay, labourer

JAMES STREET—Continued.

36 Thomas Gibson, joiner
Robert Petrie, cellarman
Henry Dunsmore, salesman

36 James Guthrie, compositor
James Russell, coachtrimmer
Thomas Shepherd, cooper

KING'S PARK ROAD (Allan Park).

5 John Mailer & Co., farm produce merchants

7 — Roberts, fleshers
P. D. Nairn, photographer

KING'S STABLES.

1 Mrs Minnie M'Intosh
George Cargill, mason
Wm. Kinnaird, butcher
Michael Boyle, labourer
James M'Innes, vanman

2 William Harvey, stone dresser
James Sneddon, tailor
William Millar, coachbuilder
John Page, shoemaker
H. G. Bewley, platelayer
Edward Bundy, fireman

KING STREET.

1 Hugh Gavin & Son, drapers
3 Anderson Bros., hatters
5 Tho. Lawrie, Temperance Hotel
7 Crawford & Co., booksellers
9 Jas. Hogg & Co., *Journal* Office
11 Peter Duff, plumber
People's Journal reporter's office
John Allan, architect
Mrs Wm. Rodger
Wm. Hynd, tailor
John Kennedy, joiner
J. Ewing, clothier
13 David Somerville, ironmonger
15 Duncan M'Donald, saddler
17 L. & D. Hunter, cabinetmakers
John Howat, tailor
Jas. Higgins, drain tile agent
National Telephone Co.
19 James Dow, hatter
21 T. Paterson Orr, draper
23 Royal Bank of Scotland
25 George Forsyth, cashier
David Mills, clerk
Alex. Watters, spirit merchant
27 Masonic Hall
A. M'Ewan, billiard room
John Abercromby, slater
Mrs Margaret Leitch
J. Sutherland, Glasgow carrier
29-31 A. M'Ewan, spirit merchant
33 William Bryce, cabinetmaker
David M'Gregor, lorryman
James Haney, labourer

2 British Linen Bank
Arthur Brown, banker
4 North of Scotland Bank
Hill & Whyte, solicitors
6 R. S. Shearer & Son, booksell.
8-10 Golden Buffet and Golden Lion
Hotel—Stevenson Bros.
12-18 Co-operative Society, Ltd.
16 Eben. Simpson, architect
Thomas Currie, burgh assessor
Mrs Margaret Harold
John Merrilees, plumber
Miss Wedderspoon, dressmaker
Cargill & Thomson, painters
20-22 Union Bank of Scotland
22 Robert MacLuckie, banker
Mathie, MacLuckie & Lupton, solicitors
24 Robert Cairns, accountant
26 Mrs P. Comrie, refresh. rooms
28 J. Jamieson & Co., tailors
32-34 S. Collier, Ltd., bootmakers
36 Thos. Menzies & Co., drapers
38 Robert Boyd, miner
40 Robert Liddel, grocer, &c.
42-44 James Paterson, draper
46 Peter M'Ronald, upholsterer
James M'Indoe
Miss Agnes B. Taylor
Mrs Agnes Taylor
48 James Minty, clothier
52 James W. Campbell, banker
54 Bank of Scotland

KING STREET—Continued.

33 Archibald Angus, painter
P. Campbell, Glasgow carrier
Mrs Agnes Wordie
Mrs John Wordie, cooper
H. M. Kirkwood, printer
Duncan M'Lachlan, mason
35 D. Crockart & Son, gunmakers
37 Mrs J. Dewar
Andrew Dewar, gardener
John S. Mair, bootmaker
James Cannon, labourer
James M'Laren, plumber
Michael Murray, surfaceman
Mrs G. Smith
Mrs Agnes Hislop
39 Alex. Keir, fruiterer
41 The Smith Shoe Coy. (John
   S. Mair)
43 G. R. Jenkins, draper
45 F. Grogan, basket maker
Wm. Livingstone, cabinetmaker
James M'Nab, clerk
A. Stevenson, hotel proprietor
Adam Johnstone, painter
Miss Ann Younger, dressmaker
47-51 Graham & Morton, ironm'grs

49 James Stewart, clerk
John M'Gregor, smith
Robert Crawford, tinsmith
John Sinclair, compositor
53 Harvey & Hunter, jewellers
55 Robert Christie, Sun Inn
Hutchison & Co., dressmakers
Andrew Harley, ironmonger
Mrs Orr
57-59 M'Aree Bros., drapers
Clydesdale Bank, Ltd.—
   W. M. Reyburn, banker
Town Council Chambers
67 Walker & Skinner, chemists
69 James Nicol, clothier
71 Mrs Crocket, stationer
73 Wm. Goudie, refresh. rooms
75 Robert Barnett, engine driver
George Wilson, coachman
Wm. Condie, traveller
Alex. Williamson, lorryman
Mrs Wordie, cooperage
Mrs Campbell
John Hill, machineman
77 Norwell's Boot Shop
79 M'Culloch & Young, drapers

KIRK WYND, St Ninians.

2 James Gray, miner
3 John Galloway, blacksmith
5 James Archibald, beadle
Peter Harvey, sexton

St Ninians Parish Halls—
   Mrs Ewing, caretaker
St Ninians Parish Church—
   Rev. Dr. Robertson

LAURELHILL PLACE.

1 Miss Anita Turner
2 Mrs Alison Morris
5 Rev. David Smith

7 James Gray, seedsman
9 A. J. M'Dermont, cashier
11 Miss Jane Galbraith

LINDEN AVENUE.

Burnbank—Miss M'Farlane
   P. Skinner, cutter
Elmbank—Robert Morrison, tailor
Rowanlea—W. Ferguson, traveller
The Linden—R. Foster, plasterer

Thistlecroft — R. Tennent Smith,
   produce merchant
Woodbank—R. Marshall, residenter
   Robert Maclaurin
   W. Towers, electrician

MAIN STREET, St. Ninians.

1 Mrs Nicol
Jacob Dick, painter
John Gray, seedsman
P. Brown, plumber
Wm. Thomson
1A J S. Louden, seedsman
James Walls, blacksmith
Alex. Calder, joiner
3A Alexander Mills, gardener
William Rae, baker
Charles Barclay, tailor
John Johnstone, plumber
Thomas M'Murdo, miner
Richard Gibb, miner
3B George Ewing, plumber
John Evans, baker
James Muirhead, painter
Michael O'Brien, mason
Thomas Stevenson, vanman
Patrick Glancy, miner
John Watson, miner
3·5 William Aitken, baker
7-9 Miss Anderson, draper
11 James Oliver, spirit merchant
13 James Napier, plasterer
15 Andrew M'Donald, nailmaker
William Napier, joiner
James Dick, miner
Mrs Helen Dick
Robert Smith, blacksmith
17 Marion Wright, confectioner
19 Janet Leighton, confectioner
21 David Honeyman, engineman
23 John Horn, fitter
North United Free Church—
Rev. C. Mackenzie
31 John Johnston, broker
33-35 John Corser, grocer
37 Richard Martin, miner
Fred. Palombo, ice-cream mer.
39 Alexander, Ure, labourer
41 John Young, carter
45 Samuel Dixon, miner
47-49 James Forsyth, bootmaker
51 Mrs Margaret Stewart
Robert Davidson, miner
James Hill, miner

4 S. Reid, inspector of poor
6 Mrs Mary Welsh
Mrs Jane Monteath
8 James Kay, tanner
10 Miss E. M'Farlane, confect.
12 Miss Margaret Stevenson
Mat. Paton, gardener
14 Jas. Whytock, labourer
16 Alex. M'Donald, wine mer.
18 Mrs Margaret Colston
Miss Barbara Brown
Miss Jane Hackney
20 Robert Gemmel, miner
Joseph M'Ivor, miner
John Muir, miner
William M'Lachlan, miner
22 John Gemmel, miner
24 David Taylor, insurance agent
Donald Scott, mason
Thos. Carmichael, engineman
Mrs Helen Lithgow
Thomas Nichol, valet
26 William Paton, compositor
William Andrew, baker
Hector Robertson, miner
Alexander Thomson, nailer
Wm. Wilson, boot salesman
Alexander M'Callum, miner
32 U.F. Church Mission Hall
34 J. Somerville, manufacturer
36-42 John & Wm. Somerville,
nail manufacturers
44-46 Mrs Margaret Glen, grocer
48-50 Robt. M'Lean, china mer.
52 Thomas Leighton, tailor
54 James Nokes, greengrocer
56 James Gillespie, nailworker
James Lindsay, miner
58 James Nokes, grocer
60 Mrs Isabella Walker
62 Andrew Simpson, miner
64 Thomas Caldwell, labourer
Chas. Denovan, tailor
Mrs Elizabeth Paton
Alexander Harvey, tanner
66 Mrs Ann Muirhead
70 Alex. Baxter, labourer

MAIN STREET—Continued.

51 Alexander Coldwell, miner
Thomas Morrison, miner
Hugh Campbell, scavenger
55 Mrs C. Thompson, grocer
57 William Paterson, labourer.
59 David Aitken, slater
John Aitken, slater
Robert Graham, residenter
Miss M'Laren
61 Mrs Janet Barclay
63 William Stocksley, carter
Thomas Rough, carter
65 Robert Taylor, carter
67 Thomas Harper, miner
69 James Hendry, miner
William M'Naughton, traction
engine driver
Mrs Jane Crawford
71 Alex. Fitzpatrick, miner
James Frail, miner
Mrs Graham
73 Robert Davidson, shoemaker
75 Luke Heally, miner
77 Miss Margt. Gillespie, confect.
79 Robert Somerville, baker
Frank Mason, miner
James Holdan, miner
David Quin, miner
81 Mrs A. Nash, grocer
83 Alexander Lamond, saddler
85 R. Robertson, candlemaker
David Hughes, traveller
Robert Morgan
John Brodie, nailer
M'Diarmid & Sons, candle-
makers
87 A. Tortolano, confectioner
89 Mrs Jane Martin
93 David Thomson, miner
95-97 David Jenkins, fruiterer
99 James Gilfillan, plasterer
101 John Bateman, telephone linesman
103 John Gemmell, weaver
George M'Callum, miner
John Barr, miner
Edward M'Kenstrie, engineman

70 George Bowie, carter
Andrew Brown, carter
John Laird, roadman
Henry Paul, soldier
72 F. Palombo, ice-cream mer.
74 James Brown, pensioner
David Pollock, fireman
Wm. M'Kendrick, miner
Donald Martin, miner
Mrs Annie Sneddon
Mrs Euphemia Campbell
76 John Crawford, nailer
Mrs Christina Lowther, hawker
William Adams, tanner
Alex. Ramage, miner
78 John Hart, newsagent
80 Alex. Paterson, labourer
Edward Moir, steeplejack
John Cooper, joiner
82 John Buchanan, butcher
84-86 John B. Taylor, stationer, Post
Office
88 Peter Morrison, labourer
90 Police Station—
Alex. Legge, policeman
92 John M'Lachlan, miner
100 George Fleming, miner
Matthew Reynolds, miner
Robert Lessels, miner
102 Alex. Welsh, ironmonger
104 Alex. Welsh, boltmaker
Mrs Agnes Gillespie
110 Mrs Greig Crawford
James Crawford, nailer
112 John Denovan, bootmaker
114 Mrs M'Gowan, refresh. rooms
116 James Hoggan, miner
118 Robert Duff, miner
James Burnett, miner
John Agnew, painter
David Jenkins, carter
John Don, labourer
120-122 J. D. Simpson, butcher
124 Miss Agnes Ewing
126 Mrs Scott
Robert Dick, miner
William Steel, miner

MAIN STREET – Continued.

126 Robert Fraser, miner
128 J. Scott, plumber and electrician
130 George Denison, confectioner
132 Alex. Kerr, engine driver
    Wm. Martin, nailer
134 William Paton, nailer
142 Stirling Co-op. Society Branch
    William Bishop, miner
    James Murphy, miner
    George Wallace, baker
    Robert Menzies, miner
    James Menzies, miner
144 Andrew Watt, pitheadman

144 George Cunningham, miner
    Robert Hunter, miner
    George Denison, confectioner
    James Copeland, miner
    Sinclair Gair, labourer
144-146 Jas. Burnett, wine merchant
148 George Powrie, coachbuilder
150 Mrs Helen Muirhead
    Robert Thorburn, carter
    Mrs Eliz. Berrie
    William Wright, miner
152 William Martin, nailer
154 Robert Barclay, bootmaker

MANSE CRESCENT, St. Ninians.

1 Miss Mary Brown, milliner
3 L. Saunders, In. Revenue officer
5 George Paterson, cashier
7 John Wright, grocer
9 Alexander Walls, plasterer
11 Alexander Keir, fruiterer
13 Miss Wares
15 Rev. Wm. M'Lellan
17 Miss Agnes Oswald

4 A. S. Third, science master
8 Thomas Graham
10 J. R. Neilson, quarrymaster
12 Miss Ann Storrier
14 Archibald Thomson, law clerk
16 Miss Jane Frater
18 Jas. Monteith, colliery director
The Manse—
    Rev. John M. Robertson, D.D.

MAR PLACE.

2 Fred. Meston, Q.-M. Sergeant
    John M'Culloch, Col.-Sergeant

2 J. Bertram, Col.-Sergeant

Snowdon House—Hamilton G. Henderson

MAXWELL PLACE.

Stirling Post Office
3 Miss M. Gowans, tobacconist
4 Wm. M'Laren, painter
5 Mrs M. Ewing
6 D. R. M'Kenzie, dancing master
7 Mrs Jessie Robertson
8 Miss Helen Taylor
    Chas. Moyes, goods guard
9 Colin M'Lean, stableman

9 Robert Smith, vanman
    James Duncan, fishmonger
10 John Wright, plumber
    Stevenson Bros., potato merchts.
12 B. D. Shennan, bootmaker
13 Miss Jamieson, confectioner
15 James Gray, tile layer
    John Hunter, labourer

MELVILLE TERRACE.

1 David Marshall, dentist
2 Miss Margaret Cummings
3 G. T. Drummond, jeweller
  Peter Memorial Church
4 Miss Hogg's Ladies' School—
  Mrs M'Laren, caretaker
5 Robert Willis, iron merchant
6 Dr James Moorhouse
7 Wm. J. Stevenson, chemical
  manufacturer
8 Miss Agnes Anderson
  Miss Helen Anderson
9 George Jardine
10 Miss Elizabeth Stewart
  Hamilton Stewart
11 Wm. Somerville, iron merchant
12 Rev. Dr. Robert Frew
13 Jas. Johnston, wood merchant
14 James Dow, hatter
15 James Gray, seedsman
16 Dr. F. J. Greig
17 Mrs Rosabella Blakey
18 Miss Jessie Gilchrist
19 Miss Mary Robson
20 Miss M'Diarmid

MILLAR PLACE.

1 James R. M'Elfrish, traveller
  Staff Q.-M.-Sergt. Basil, A.O.C.
  Miss Helen Marshall
3 Miss E. Farquharson
  Rev. Alex. S. Andrew
  John M'Kay, traveller
  Miss J. Coutts, teacher
  Miss M. Ferguson
5 Sergt.-Major T. Bryant, A.O.C.
  Archd. Menzies, teacher
  Mrs Jane M'Kean
  John Ferguson, cashier
9 Duncan M'Ewan, grocer
11 Ralph Dawber, traveller
13 Rev. Jas. M'Lachlan, M.A.
15 Mrs Janet Pye
17 Rev. Thomas Skeoch
19 J. I. Wilson, dentist
21 John Sim, bank teller
23 John A. Gordon, chemist
25 Miss Janet Wilson
27 Charles Munro, traveller
29 L. Hunter, cabinetmaker
31 Alex. Park, brush manufacturer
33 Alex. Roxburgh, manager of
  carpet works.
35 Mrs Margaret Allan
39 James Stevens, hairdresser
41 Mrs M. Lister, dressmaker
6 John Malley, fireman
  Thomas Wright, fireman
  Mrs Elizabeth Fisher
  James Stewart, gardener
8 Miss Isa Hay
12 Geo. R. Jenkins, draper
14 Mrs Mary Laing
16 Wm. Johnstone, painter
18 James Sinclair, traveller
20 Henry D. M'Lellan, solicitor
24 Jas. Park, brush manufacturer
26 Q.-M.-Sergt. Chivers, A.O.C.
28 Charles Threlfall, traveller

MURRAY PLACE.

3 John Craig, fruiterer
5 R. Drummond & Sons, jewellers
7 Alloa Coal Company—
    John Dewar, agent
    Mrs A. Grieve, shopkeeper
    Miss M'Naughton
    George Jeffrey, carriage hirer
    W. J. Anderson, S.P.C.C. inspec.
9 Mrs Agnes Grieve, Berlin wool
    warehouse
11 Lambert Hepting, jeweller
13 W. Drummond & Sons, Ltd.,
    seed merchants
15 James Sinclair, confectioner
15½ Maypole Dairy Co, Ltd.
17 James Millar & Sons, bakers
    Samuel F. Millar
19 Geo. Horsburgh, confectioner
    Geo. M'Lean, corkcutter
    Mrs M. M'Rorie
    Fred. Chappel, traveller
    Mrs M. Dewar, picture dealer
    Golden Lion Hotel stables
21 Wm. Crawford, china merchant
23 Thomas Lamb, cycle agent
25 Davidson & Co., Ltd., boot
    manufacturers
27 Davidson & Stevenson, writers
    J. F. Mackie, solicitor
    T. C. Darling, solicitor
    Peter Douglas, solicitor
    Crawford & Fraser, architects
    Jas. H. Hastings, teacher
    Mrs Isabella Mackay
    Miss Jane Hill
    Mrs Margaret Ritchie
29 R. D. Waddell, sausage mer.
31 James M. Blair, hairdresser
33-35 Cooper & Co., tea merchants
37 Wann & Condie, accountants
    Prudential Assur. Co.'s office
    —R. Blackett, supt.
    James Robertson, wood mer.
    Miss J. Stevenson, dressmaker
    Mrs Jessie M'Robbie
    Charles Steel, brassfounder
    Mrs M. Hart, dressmaker

2-4 P. M'Alpine, Waverley Hotel
6 Sowdan & Forgan, piano sellers
8-12 M'Lachlan & Brown, milliners
12 Mrs Margaret Stanborough
    Mrs Joanna Osborne
14 Virtue & Co. ironmongers
16 J. Robertson & Sons, clothiers
18 M. O. Thomson, jeweller
20 David W. Logie, writer
    John Keir, clerk
    A. M. Lupton, architect
22 John Steel, plumber
24 Wm. J. Moore & Son, chemists
26-30 Virtue & Co., cabinetmakers
    and house furnishers
28 County Temperance Hotel—
    Donald M'Killop
32 Misses E. & J. Reid, baby linen
    warehouse
34 George Alexander, jeweller
36 Mrs Deans—Temp. Hotel
38 A. D. Henderson, umbrella
    maker (Baird's umbrella
    warehouse)
44 North Parish Church Hall
    Andrew Simpson, joiner
    Oddfellows' Lodge Room
    Robt. Anderson & Son, building
    contractors' office
46-48 North Parish Church—
    Rev. D. P. M'Lees
48 Alex. Skene, church officer
50 Baptist Church—
    Rev. G. Yuille
52 Thomas Millar, labourer
54-56 Mrs Lennox, Station Hotel
    The County Club—
    John Sloan, steward
60 M. & J. Stoddart, bootmakers
62 Stirling Gaslight Co. showrooms
64 David Chrystal, writer
    J. S. Henderson, writer
    Mrs Watt
    Mrs D. Hodge
    Don. Cox, County road surveyor
    Robert Goldie, County assist.
    sanitary inspector

MURRAY PLACE—Continued.

39 James Smith, tobacconist
 P. Macnaughton
41 H. Gardner, fancy goods mer.
43 Eneas Mackay, bookseller
45 Thomas Lamb, cycle maker
 Hutton & Turnbull, printers
 Archibald Robertson, waiter
 John M'Kinlay, clerk
 John Lyon, cartwright
47 Thomas Muir, spirit merchant
49 J. M. Stewart, veterinary surgeon
51 John Brown, grocer
53 M'Lean & Henderson, stock-
 brokers
 Soutar & Co., clothiers
 Robert Dobbie, engineer
 R. Smith, joiner
 Queen's Nurses' Home—
 Stirling Nursing Association
53-55 Alex. Norris, restaurateur
57 Crowe & Rodgers, photo-
 graphers
59-63 J. M'Kinlay & Son, tailors
 South United Free Church—
 Rev. J. Arnott
 Congregational Church—
 Rev. J. C. M'Lachlan
 Inland Revenue Offices—
 Mrs Aitken, caretaker
 Commercial Bank—
 H. S. Robson, banker

64 William Condie, Sheriff officer
66 John Sloan, cigar merchant
68 Templeton's restaurant
72 John M. Stewart, veterinary
 surgeon (tel. No. 0170)
 Mrs Helen M'Donald
74 Platt & Common, surgeon
 dentists
80 Daniel Ferguson, banker
82 National Bank of Scotland

Station Road—

Thomas Ross, sculptor
Stirling Railway Station—
 North British, Caledonian, and
 Forth and Clyde Railways
Jas. Samuel, stationmaster
N.B. Agent—Wm. Graham

Mrs Lennox, Station Hotel bar
Caledonian Railway Goods
 Station and Offices—
W. Wilson, goods agent
Wm. Muir, head porter

NELSON PLACE.

1 David Pate, shoemaker
3 John Cooper, vanman
 Mrs Margaret Mirk
 Wm. M'Arthur, plumber

2 Rich. Gordon, coachwright
8 Alex. Brown, barman
 C. T. Chisholm, upholsterer
 John Adams, art metal worker

4

NELSON PLACE--Continued.

3 Miss Maggie Pate
5 Nicol M'Laren, carter
7 Albert Held, hairdresser
  Jas. Richardson, engine driver
  James Young, pointsman
  E. Jeffrey, insurance agent
9 John Crawford, joiner
11 Alex. Learmonth, clerk
13 P. M'Nab, electrical engineer
15 Mrs Jessie Langmuir
17 John Donaldson, joiner
19 Mrs Janet Whyte
21 Mrs Hugh Paterson
23 Mrs Nicholas Baxter
25 William Currie, seedsman
27 Wm. Sanderson, yardsman

10 J. Kenny, printer
12 Mrs M'Laren
14 Matthew Finlayson, joiner
16 David Thomson, seedsman
  William Thomson, clerk
18 Miss Mary Liddell
20 Mrs Elizabeth Menzies
22 Peter Lindsay
24 Jas. D. Valentine, ironmonger
26 Mrs M'Callum
28 Robert Scott, engine driver
30 Alex. Fraser, gardener
32 William S. Fraser, grocer
34 Miss Margaret Connall
  W. Barclay, telephone linesman

NEWHOUSE.

1 Wm. Porter, spirit merchant
3 G. Forbes Forsyth, organist
5 John Brown, grocer
5½ Archibald Duncan, printer
7 John Ferguson, joiner
  Wm. White, clerk
  J. M'Diarmid, candlemaker
  Alex. M'Gibbon, baker
  John M'Farlane
9 H. Chalmers, French polisher
  Mrs Jane Jaffray
  James Lister, clerk
  Mrs Jane Balfour
  Miss Joan Baird
  Miss Jane Alexander
11 William Dow, hatter
  Peter Aitken, builder
  Mrs William Muirhead
  Miss Inglis
  Andrew Gray, residenter
13 Mrs C. Drummond, grocer
15 Charles Wood, grocer
  Jas. Cambridge, boot salesman
  Miss Mary Croall
  R. C. Forbes, teacher of short-
    hand
  Miss Margaret M'Arthur
  John Dewar, joiner
17 Miss Brown, teacher

8 John T. Roberts, spirit mercht.
12 Joseph Robertson, miner
  James Morgan, lorryman
  Thomas Bell, miner
14 T. Davidson, market gardener
16 Mrs James Wright
18 Jas. Lindsay, coachsmith
20-22 Charles Wood, grocer
  Miss Reid
24 John Ferguson, gardener
  Alex. M'Graw, groom
  Robt. Auchinvole, pit sinker
  Mrs Jessie M'Laren, nurse
26 Mrs Margaret Low
28 Miss M. Corbett, millworker
  Robert Dewar, labourer
  Mrs Mary Miller
  Mrs Mowatt
30 James Richardson, millworker
32 Mrs Mary Monteath
34 Mrs Dodds
36 Jas. Gray, lorryman
  P. M'Gibbon, ropespinner

NEWHOUSE –Continued.

17 D. Lindsay, editor, *Observer*
    James Dick, blacksmith
19 Mrs Margaret M'Queen
21 Mrs Annie Dougall
23 Robert B. Philp, schoolmaster
25 Henry Stevens, law clerk
    David Burgess, cabinetmaker
    Geo. Christie
    Arthur Burness, upholsterer
    David Pegler, electrician
    Alexander Crawford, joiner
29 Mrs Robert Kemp
31 Miss Margaret Baird
33 James Farish, baker
35 David M'Callum, tailor
37 G. R. Paton, wood carver
39 Daniel Paterson, joiner
41 Hugh M'Bride, painter
    Mrs Mary Cameron
43 Ninian M'Allister, coachbuilder
45 Mrs Jane Loch
    Mrs Ann Crichton
47 Thomas Glen, mason
49 Daniel Sinclair, sawyer

49 Andrew Don, lorryman
51 Archibald Black, roadman
    George Dick, carter
53 Geo. M'Intosh, hairdresser
55 Henry M'Diarmid, baker
    M. Duncan, surfaceman
57 Eben. Robertson, gasworker
    Wm. Anderson
59 Wm. Brisbane, labourer
    Robert Jenner, coachman
63 Mrs Reid
    Mrs Jane Cameron
    Peter Alexander, joiner
    George Muir, labourer
    James Barclay, nailer
65 James Paton, traveller
67 J. Duncan, professional golfer
69 James Drummond, seedsman
71 And. Thomson, gas collector
73 Wm. Murdoch, storeman
    Mrs Margaret Glen
    Joseph Petrie, viceman
    Arch. Ewing, painter
75 Jas. Somerville, nailmaker

ORCHARD PLACE.

1 Wm. Cairns, plumber
12 Chas. Campbell, ostler
    Thos. Robertson, coal agent
14 John Robertson, vanman
16 George Sewell, porter
16 Wm. Beveridge, miner
    Alex. Penman, miner
    John Stewart, tinsmith
    John White, mason
    Somerville & Valentine, iron-
        mongers
    Mrs Lennox, carriage hirer

16 Mrs Margaret Littlejohn
22 John Martin, smith
    Hugh M'Donald, carter
24 Mrs Agnes M'Gregor
    John Scott, lorryman
24 Miss Martin
    Alexander Donald, labourer
    Virtue & Co., ironmongers
26-28 James Davie & Sons, iron-
        founders
30-32 George Thomson, coach-
        builder
    W. R. Gall, contractor (office)

PARK AVENUE.

1 Dr. D. M'Fadyen
3 Miss Helen M'Donald
4 Miss Margaret Greig
5 Dr. R. C. Highet
6 Rev. J. P. Lang

7 Mrs Annie M'Donald
9 Simon M'Leod, hosiery manu-
    facturer
10 John Gillespie, grocer
11 W. Stevenson, live stock agent

PARK LANE.

3 Mrs Helen M'Ewen
Arch. Paterson, tailor
Geo. Ross, tailor
Alex. Stewart, lorryman
D. Petrie, ret. police constable
Hugh M'Master, foreman carter
5 Wm. Samson, engineer
John Murray, joiner
Mrs A. Buchanan
Mrs Reid
Joseph Mackieson, hairdresser
Alex. Mackintosh, iron turner
7 Wm. Laird, warehouseman
John M'Dougall, baker
Hugh Murnin, miners' agent
Peter Dunn, seedsman
John Simpson, signalman
Adam Lennox, cattle dealer

2 Dalgetty Bros., joiners
4 W. Miller, blacksmith
14 James Bett, railway guard
James Hall, mason
Peter Henderson, waiter
16 D. & J. M'Ewen & Co., stores
18 Arch. M'Lachlan, Son & Co.,
cement, lime amd coal mercs.

PARK PLACE.

2 T. Ronald
5 Lambert Brown, traveller
6 George Alexander, jeweller
Miss C. Alexander
12 Alexander Colville
13 C. P. Stevenson, musicseller
14 Geo. Lowson, LL.D., Rector
15 William Alexander
16 James Jackson, clerk

Roseville—Misses Robertson
Glenelm—
    Mrs Jane C. Drummond
Ashfield—W. J. Milne Menzies
Park Villa—Mr Brodie
Sunnyside—J. W. Roberts
Rockdale Cottages—
    Geo. Shearer, nurseryman
    J. Smith, gardener
Rockdale Lodge—Miss A. Paton
The Shieling—
    M. H. Paterson, stockbroker
    John M'Donald, gardener
Killorn Villas—John M'Lean
            Wm. Cassels, mer.
Killorn Cottage—
    Thomas Bradford
Cliffside—
    Geo. Murdoch, stockbroker
Mossbank—
    William Cochrane, draper
Coney Park Nursery—
    Geo. Shearer, manager

PARK TERRACE.

1 Robert Frater, plumber
2 Andrew Auld, spirit merchant
3 Dr W. A. Mackintosh
6 Thos. Brisbane, wood merchant
7 Miss Campbell
8 Wm. Donaldson, solicitor
9 William Dawson
10 Jas. B. Kidston
11 Mrs Gibson
12 Rev. John Arnott, M.A.
13 Miss Dobbie
14 Neilson Bird
15 Charles Wilson
16 Mrs Mary Speirs
17 John A. Sinclair MacLagan
18 Wm. Cuthbert, cooper
   James Dewar, coachman
19 Robert Taylor, writer
20 Thomas Todd
21 Theodore Keyden, stockbroker
22 Dr. D. Cuthbertson
23 Henry Kinross, seedsman
24 Robert Maclaurin
25 Mrs Agnes Jane Leishman
26 Mrs Christina Harvey
27 Miss Christian Morrison
   Geo. Petrie, gardener
28 Miss Frances Bolton
   Alex. Buchanan, coachman
   R. M'Donald, gardener

Laurelhill—Miss A. E. Speirs
Alex. M'Lennan, gardener
Thomas Bowes, coachman

PITT TERRACE.

1 David Morton, ironmonger
2 James Mailer, traveller
3 Mrs J. C. B. Johnston
5 John T. Dale, hairdresser
6 Miss Buchanan
7 Mrs Isabella Forsyth
8 John Duff, plumber
9 Robert K. Common, dentist
10 Mrs M'Nicol
11 Dr D. P. M'Farlane
12 Miss Annie Flint
13 Miss J. P. Stronach

POLMAISE ROAD.

Batterflats—Mrs M'Gregor
Batterflats Cottage—
   Peter Thomson, gardener
Penroseville—R. Raines
Llewellyn—C. Fuge, iron merc.
Polmaise Castle—James Murray
Bearside—J. T. M'Laren, factor
Springwood—Patrick Welsh, writer
Deroran—C. Buchanan, stockbroker
Deroran Lodge—
   And. Shearer, gardener
   Peter Graham, coachman

PORT STREET.

1-5 W. Somerville & Valentine, ironmongers
3 Philp & Dobbie, solicitors
   Mrs Sharp
7 W. & J. Cullens, fleshers
21 R. Adam, china merchant
23 James Cullens, flesher
25 Miss M. Gray, servants' registry
   Charles Gray, clerk
   John Lamb, painter
   Mrs Janet Stevenson
   Thomas Denovan, traveller
   J. C. Duncan, electrician
   Miss Mary Bain
   Mathieson Bros., engravers
27 W. Hetherington, grocer
29 Robert Thomson, butcher
31 J. Johnston & Son, fish mercs.
35 Alex. Troup, coachtrimmer
   Thomas Moore, coachwright
   Alex. M'Arthur, fireman
37-39 Kinross & Sons, coachbuilders
41 The Burgh Club—J. Dunk
43 T. Henderson & Son, joiners
   Robt. M. Currie, cab proprietor
   Archd. M'Callum, postboy
45 B. D. Shennan, bootmaker

2 H. Ferguson & Son, bootmakers
4 T. & J. Muirhead, solicitors
   Stirling Savings Bank
   Mrs Mary Blair
   Robt. Anderson, cabinetmaker
   Jas. G. Kinnaird, tailor
6 John Dempster, tobacconist
8 A. & R. Swan, jewellers
10 Keith & Ralston, purveyors
12 I. Stoddart, bootmaker
   Miss Rebecca Hardie
14 Cowbrough & Mercer, grocers
16 John Raffan, chemist
18 James Banks, jeweller
20 John Bennett, tailor
   George Blair, cabman
22 D. & J. Stewart, jewellers
24 Dunn & Wilson, milliners
26 Fleming & Buchanan, writers
   Mrs E. Meikle
   Mrs Jane Stewart
   William M'Leish, joiner
28 H. P. Tyler, boot manufacturer
30 John T. Dale, hairdresser
32 Alex. Chrystal, engine fitter
   Mrs M. Crawford
   Alex. Denovan, mason
34 Peter Brodie, baker
36 Wm. Christie, jeweller
38 Duncanson, chemist
40 D. & J. MacEwen & Co., grocers
42 Robertson & Macfarlane, grocers
44-46 W. S. Palmer, umbrella maker
48 David Berrie
   Miss Margaret M'Ewan
   Mrs Helen Barclay
50 Mrs Johnston, fish merchant
52 Thos. Elder & Sons, bakers
54 Stirling Liberal Assoc. Rooms
   Wm. Carson & Sons, painters
   George Owen, motor agent
   Thomas Taylor, clerk
   Miss Margaret M'Ewan
56 F. Spite & Co., Ltd., chemists
58-68 George Starkey, grocer
60-62 George Riddle, tobacconist
62 Alex. Paterson, solicitor

PORT STREET—Continued.

47 William Banks, residenter
James A. Gibson, solicitor
Dan. M'Diarmid, postboy
Mrs Janet Beveridge
Miss Maggie Robertson
Miss Carter
49 John M'Kay, clothier
51 John Gillespie, grocer
53 Archibald & Brown, solicitors
Thos. J. Y. Brown, Session
Clerk for St. Ninians
Miss I. M'Leod, dressmaker
Mrs Janet Sutherland
John Lindsay, joiner
55 John King, spirit merchant
57-59 Wm. Low & Co., grocers
61 A. Penman, Port Customs
63 Wm. Porter, spirit merchant
65 Alexander Keir, fruiterer
67-67½ George Morgan, draper
67½ The Gospel Hall
Hugh Ferguson
R. M'Donald, butcher
William Gilmour, gardener
69 George Owen, cycle maker
71 Mrs B. Crichton, glazier
73 Robert Frater, plumber
75-77 Robt. Stevenson, fancy goods
merchant
77 Mrs Susan Hay
Miss Jane Brown, shopkeeper
77-81 Robt. B. Wallace, upholsterer
79 J. A. Hogg, chemist
81 Fairful, Wilson & Somers, joiners
G. Owen, motor garage
Miss Charlotte Hood
James Finlayson, plumber
Alex. Fletcher, plumber
83 William Shirra, bookseller
85 Wm. Templeton, tobacconist
87 Miss Bethia Finlayson
J. B. M'Ewan, clerk
Miss Frances Murdoch
Miss C. Sutherland
Miss M. Sutherland
89 Robert Wallace, draper
91 J. Pullar & Sons, dyers

62 W. H. Young, accountant
W. S. Stephen, bootshop mangr.
Robert Roberts, butcher
A. W. Stewart, seedsman
R. Sugget
64 S. Collier, Ltd., boot manuftrs.
66 Robert Walls, miller
68 Mrs Catherine Borrowman
Miss Margaret Pitblado
Thomas Buchan, baker
Donald Connell, postboy
James Darragh, contractor
70 Fleming, Reid & Co., Greenock
wool store
72 Dun. Soutar, warehouseman
John Walker, mill foreman
James Wilkie, plumber
Peter Kerr, mattressmaker
D. B. M'Gill, traveller
David Russell, baker
Frank Rae, grocer
Miss Ann Leonard, nurse
David Soutar, cabman
And. Robertson, painter
John Simpson, painter
Miss Carrey
Miss Grace Hodge
Charles Robb, baker
John Harley, painter
Miss Hay, cook
Thomas Lindsay, cabman
J. Milne, clerk
James Orme, hairdresser
Alex. Stevenson, miner
Mrs Agnes Clark
Miss Nora Dunn, dressmaker
— M'Gill, surfaceman
74 Miss J. M'Arthur, baby linen
shop
76 Brown & Wilson, surg. dentists
78 Alex. Keir, fruiterer
80 A. & J. Jenkins, solicitors

PRINCES STREET.

1 Mrs Paterson
Peter Gray, seedsman
Miss Millar, dressmaker
E. W. Simpson, solicitor
Peter Watt, grocer
John Fyfe, sanitary inspector
5 William Strang, draper
9 Miss Mary Ballantyne
11 Mrs C. Macfarlane
Henry Valentine
John Watt, seedsman
13 John Kirkwood, printer
Miss Janet Stuart
G. B. Crockart, gunsmith
15 Rev. Walter Scott
17 Rev. D. D. Ormond
19 Miss Susan M'Farlane
21 D. Cowan, Sheriff-Clerk depute
23 Mrs Christina Muirhead
Thos. Muirhead, solicitor
J. Muirhead, solicitor
25 Lambert Hepting, watchmaker
27 Wm. Simpson, auctioneer

2 John Hunter, spirit merchant
10 Wm. M. Brown, house factor
12 James Samuel, stationmaster
14 Thomas Ferguson, joiner
16 Andrew Cumming, grocer
18 Simpson's Furniture Stores
24 Peter Bell, joiner
Elizabeth Robertson
Mrs Margaret Leitch
John Mackay, traveller
Mrs Jane Thompson
John Skinner, chemist
G. C. Gray, cashier
James M'Arthur, seedsman
Volunteer Drill Hall—
L. G. Watters, Sgt.-Major

QUEEN'S ROAD.

1 John E. Shearer, bookseller
Miss L. E. Shearer
Miss C. Shearer
2 James H. Johnston
3 C. Gartshore, seedsman

4 Robert Liddell, grocer
5 Roderick Reid, postmaster
6 Thomas M'Nab, joiner
7 Mrs E. M'Farlane

QUEEN STREET.

3 Adam Turnbull, printer
John Wright, plumber
Miss Margaret M'Combie
5 H. Pearson, fruit merchant
Wm. Robertson, tanner
7 Mrs Jessie Fairley
David Hill, ironmonger
9 Wm. Bethune, porter
Miss Catherine Ritchie
11 Mrs Agnes Walker
13 Andrew Bowie
John Lawrie, newsagent
15 Miss E. Peter, dressmaker
17 Mrs Ann Crombie
Miss Catherine Henderson

2 Alex. Macandrew, traveller
4 Robert Wallace, draper
Miss M. M'Elfrish, music teacher
6 Wm. Leslie, insurance super.
8 Miss Annie Robertson
10 Miss Miller
14 John Blyth, insurance agent
Mrs Jessie M'Luckie
18 Gilbert Henderson, painter
David Mundell, joiner
22 Mrs L. Reid, laundress
24 Miss Ferguson
Mrs Margaret Hendry
26 Mrs Hogan, furniture dealer
28 W. T. Henderson, cabinetmkr

QUEEN STREET—Continued.

17 C. W. Sorton, postal clerk
19 Miss Janet Lennox
   Mrs Janet Brown
   Wesleyan Methodist Church
21 Rev. John Cartwright
23 Wm. Burns, coal agent
   Wm. Hay, piano tuner
   John Robertson, vanman
   Miss Marion Brown
25 Mrs Helen Lindsay
   Robt. M'Kenzie, boot salesman
   D. B. M'Diarmid, grocer
   John Pride, insurance agent
27 James M'Kay, compositor
   Andrew Black, painter
   Alex. M'Kay, Officer S.P.C.A.
   Mrs Margaret M'Gregor
   James Nicol, joiner
29 John Webster, vanman
   Andrew Campbell, miner
   David Milton, tailor
31 Mrs Janet Johnston
33 James Campbell, butcher

28 Mrs Robert Brown
30 Wm. Battison, town's foreman
   Mrs C. Crocket, bookseller
32 James Thompson, traveller
   David Gilmour, bootmaker
36 Miss Taylor
   Miss S. M. M'Donald
   Miss Anderson
   John Brewster, clerk
38 J. A. Chrystal, C.R. auditor
40 Miss Margaret Middleton
42 Francis Coleman, tailor
44 Robert Gray, ironmonger
48 Robt. Yellowlees, leather merc.

RANDOLPH ROAD.

1 Thomas Muir, spirit merchant
3 Mrs Margaret Laidlaw
5 Rev. John A. Arnold
7 Miss Margaret Cowbrough
   Miss Jane Cowbrough
9 William Easson, grocer
11 Miss Jane Johnston
13 David Forgan, traveller
15 James F. Mackie, writer
17 Mrs Isabella Bald
21 T. Paterson Orr, draper
29 E. M. Stewart, fireclay goods
   manufacturer
31 T. J. Y. Brown, solicitor

2 James D. Smith, gas manager
4 Mrs Margaret Gall

Bellfield Road—

Tordarroch House—
   Jas. F. Macintosh, bootmaker
   Miss Stewart
Auchencrieff House—
   R. T. Paul, draper
   Miss Cook

7 W. Bain, photographic artist
9 James Paterson, draper

RANDOLPH TERRACE.

1 Mrs Hunter	2 Rev. Colin M'Kenzie
3 Samuel Reid, inspector of poor	E. W. Simpson, solicitor
5 Miss Isabella M'Grouther	4 Dr. Alexander Chalmers
7 John Somerville, nail maker	
9 Mrs Margaret Rae	
11 David B. Nicoll, stationer	
13 Dr. Archibald B. Laidlaw	
15 Miss Isabella Hay	
17 W. S. Palmer, umbrella maker	
19 Miss Elizabeth Hay	
21 Rev. Gabriel Smith	
23 John Oswald, stationer	
25 Mrs Crichton	
27 Bernard Reynolds, builder	

RAPLOCH.

1 John Taylor, nurseryman
Charles Smith, dairyman
2 Mrs Cannon
Mrs Margaret Malley
3 Peter Kenny, labourer
4 Mrs Nora Connelly
5 Mrs Catherine Coan
6 James Culley, mason
James Welsh, labourer
James Hughes, miner
Thomas Quigley, bricklayer
7 Austin Ging, labourer
William Culley, bricklayer
8 William Howieson, yardsman
9 Thomas Ging, labourer
Michael Marry, labourer
10 Patrick Kaney, labourer
10½ John Scullion, miner
11 John Cannon, engine driver
12 John Condroy, labourer
Mrs Joyce
Mrs M'Kendrick
13 Michael Joyce, labourer
Raploch School
15 R. Dickson, School Board officer
16 John Joyce, labourer
16½ Mrs Mary Manson
17 Mrs Janet Drummond
18 Mrs Mary Thornton
19 James Dawson, joiner
20 James Bee, electrician

21 Thos. Derrick, general dealer
Norman White, miner
Mrs Stewart
22 Hugh Murray, miner
John Cassell, labourer
James Wilson, miner
James Thomson, carter
23 Thomas King, labourer
24 Charles Laing, fireman
25 James Boland, labourer
John Malley, wood cutter
26 Michael Conaboy, labourer
27 Thomas Kenny, quarryman
Thomas Joyce, labourer
29 James Bissett, painter
30 John Philliban, labourer
31 Daniel Moody, labourer
Thomas Brannan, labourer
33 John Welsh, miner
37 John Dow, blacksmith
David Morrison, cycle agent
38 John Monteath, surfaceman
39 Patrick Murphy, labourer
40 Mrs Milroy
James Ging, labourer
William White, labourer
45 John Coyne, gatekeeper
46-47 Alex. Sands, joiner
48 Duncan Hamilton
50 William Bain, painter
51 George Zeller, labourer

ROSEBERY PLACE.

1 A. H. Goudie, master of works
2 Mrs Helen M'Kean
3 Gordon Grant, police super.
4 Misses Drummond ,
5 A. M'Kenzie, assist. postmaster

6 William Gourlay, builder
9 Henry Webster, assist. registr.
11 Mrs E. Carmichael
13 Mrs Mary A. Thomson

ROYAL GARDENS.

1 Charles G. Atha
2 Miss Ann H. Lang
3 George Adam, china merchant
4 Mrs Elizabeth Russell
5 Miss K. P. Henderson
6 James MacLuckie, writer

7 John Dickson Steel, C.A.
8 Miss Emily Colquhoun
9 George Hepburn, ret. engineer
10 Misses A. and I. M'Gowan
11 Mrs Adams

SHORE ROAD.

G. Jeffrey, cab proprietor
Herbert Leathley, fish merc.

Wordie & Co., contractors

Seaforth Place—

1 Mrs Helen Wylie, tea rooms
3 Mrs Margaret Murray
   Alex. Hall, baker
13 George Scorgie
   Mrs Christina Cruickshanks
15 Mrs Winks
   David Hunter, wool carder
   William Davidson, clerk
   George Graham, traveller
   Henry Brown, insurance agent
   James Napier, labourer
17 Thomas M'Donald, carter

17 Walter Ross, vanman
   Walter Moran, brakesman
   Peter Campbell, lorryman
   John Allardyce, porter
   Wm. Davidson, signal fitter
   Peter Kilpatrick, cab driver
   Robert Easton, miner
   John Brisbane, porter
   Finlay M'Martin, labourer
   David Smith, porter
19 Mrs Elizabeth Robertson
21 David Buchan, lathsplitter

SNOWDON PLACE.

1 John Jack, cartwright
3 Alex. Meiklejohn, ironmonger
5 Wm. Templeton, tobacconist
5A Peter Fraser, miner
7 Mrs Jessie M'Alpine
9 Mrs Christie
   Robert King, coachman
15 John Risk, distiller
17 Miss Struthers

4 Robert D. Fraser, C.A.
12 Miss Mary Murray
14 Miss C. H. Aitken
16 James Grieve, tanner
18 James Henderson
20 Robert Alex. Smith
22 Miss Griffiths Buchanan
24 Miss Agnes Buchan
26 C. Sandes, Lieut.-Col. A.P.C.

SNOWDON PLACE - Continued.

19 William Cowbrough
21 Mrs Thomson Aikman
23 Miss Jane Faulds
25 Mrs Christie
27 John King, spirit merchant
29 Mrs Mary Archibald
31 David Marshall, dentist
33 Miss M. Hogg
   Miss H. Hogg
35 Miss Buchanan
37 John R. Ure, iron founder

28 R. T. Neilson, writer
30 Miss Catherine Forrester
34 Miss Murrie
   Stewart Murrie, banker
36 Misses Logan

SOUTHFIELD CRESCENT.

3 Mrs Thomson

Woodville—
   John M'Dougall
   Adam Ferguson, gardener
Ochilview—
   Miss MacLellan

SPITTAL STREET

13 Mrs Hogg
   William Melville, plumber
15 John Fyfe, Sanitary Inspector's
   office
17 Donald M'Kinnon, engineman
19 Alex. R. Campbell, joiner
   J. Stevenson, tailor
21 James Stocksley, tailor
25 Mrs Emily Hiuves
25-27 Mark Hodgson, china mer.
   Allan's School—
      C. Johnston, headmaster
   Girls' Industrial School—
      Miss A. Mitchell, matron
   Royal Infirmary—
      Miss J. Peebles, matron
29 Geo. M'Fadyen, fireman
   Duncan Cameron, porter
   Robert Watt, contractor
   Stirling High School—
      Alexander Scott, janitor

2 Miss R. Stirling, confectioner
8 Thomas Campbell & Co.,
   plumbers
10 Peter Callinan, labourer
12 James Chrystal, fireman
   William Brown, platelayer
   James Cherry, tailor
14 A. M'Callum, smith and bellhanger
16 J. F. Lorimer, cabinetmaker
20 James Brodie, carter
22 Mrs Crocket, leather cutter
32 Andrew Soutar, ostler
   Neil M'Millan, fish salesman
   R. Adams, tailor
   Wm. Hamilton, miner
   Alexander Laird, plumber
   John Hamilton, insur. agent
   Robert Taylor, plumber
38 Salvation Army hall
40 Miss Isabella Oswald
42 Alex. Cameron, insurance agent
46 Mrs Ann Welsh
48 Patrick Kaney, labourer

SPITTAL STREET—Continued.

50 John M'Kenzie, postman
John M'Laren, surfaceman
54 Patrick Cavanagh, labourer
62 Thomas Gordon, fireman
William Murray, cooper
David Wishart, lorryman
Nicol Reid, waiter
64-66 James M'Culloch, slater
66 Robert Smith, slater
Mrs Janet Barnes
P. M'Gibbon, ropespinner

66 Mrs Neilson
74 East Church Institute
76 Joseph Wilson, miner
James M'Ilroy, cabman
Hugh Watson, gardener
Mrs Clementina Buchanan
Christopher Mowat, butcher
82 Robert Oswald, slater
Mrs Jessie Scott
Mrs Margaret Mack
84 Mrs A. Sangster, china mer.

SPRINGFIELD PLACE.

Rose Cottage—Mrs Jessie Mitchell
Geo. Hutton, joiner
1 James Chalmers, mason
Peter Taylor, wright
Wm. Holmes, weaver
Mrs Helen Henderson
David Johnstone, platelayer
Wm. Hughson, hairdresser
James Crook, fireman
Mrs Mary Goodbrand
3 Wm. M'Farlane, labourer
James Smith, porter
Thos. Haining, engine driver
James Lithgow, labourer
5 Mrs Jane Gilchrist
James Wilkie, railway inspector
Geo. Donaldson, granite cutter
Wm. M'Pherson, boilermaker

2 David Gilchrist, weaver
William Junior, guard
David Finlayson, joiner
Robt. Morrison, engine driver
James Campbell, bottler
John Chisholm, wire fencer
Robert M'Gregor
4 John M'Gregor, carter
Mrs Charlotte Campbell
Mrs Annie Thomson
James M'Gregor, fireman
M. Finlayson & Sons, joiners

ST. JOHN STREET.

1 Mrs Janet Kilpatrick
Miss Janet Sharp
John Steven, hawker
Robt. Colquhoun, hawker
James Gavin, miner
John M'Kenzie, lorryman
James Mulhearn, labourer

2 Mrs Katherine Kelly
John Meiklejohn, baker
Thomas Fairley, telephone
linesman
Patrick Coyne, mason
Patrick Hunt, mason
Thomas Gow, joiner

ST. JOHN STREET—Continued.

1 James Johnstone, labourer
  Mrs M'Kenzie
3 John Yates, dealer
5 Mrs T. Kelly
  George Meikle, surfaceman
  Mrs M'Kenzie
  Miss Janet Chalmers
  Patrick Philliban, miner
  Charles Ross, labourer
  Wm. Anderson, labourer
  James Wyllie, quarryman
  Alex. Robertson, labourer
7 Mrs Taylor, spirit merchant
9 James Millar, mason
  John Henley, labourer
  John Chrystal, coachbuilder
9-11 A. Bermingham, gen. dealer
13 Wm. Clark, miner
  Mrs W. Forrest
  James Ellery, stoker
  A. M'Ewan, blacksmith
  A. M'Donald, coachbuilder
  Alex. Heggie, shoemaker
  Robert Forrest, cabinetmaker
15 Hugh Lawless, gardener
17 James Wright, engine driver
  Mrs Anne Legge
  Mrs Lawson
  David Wotherspoon, labourer
  John Taylor, coachbuilder
23 James Bellingham
25 Mrs Margaret Calder
  John M'Kenzie, tanner
  Mrs Elizabeth M'Aulay
  James Simpson, brushmaker
  James Milgrew, slater
  Charles Duncan, carter
  Mrs Margaret Wilson
  Mrs M'Nee
27 J. Bellingham, coach hirer
  Erskine U.F. Church—
    Rev. T. Wright
Military Prison—
    Sergt. Wm. Jenkins
    Sergt. Edward Spittal
    Staff-Sergt. Jordan
    David Holmes, chief warder

6-8 John Conoboy
10 Wm. M'Callum, tailor
  James Findlater, labourer
  John Douglas, labourer
  Charles M'Ewan, labourer
  Joseph Knox, wireman
  Thomas Convery, mason
12 John Yates, broker
14 Mrs Mary Hunter
14½ James Yates, hawker
  Angus M'Lellan, labourer
  Alex. Todd, labourer
  Hugh Walbanks, miner
  Mrs Mulherron
  Thomas Mulherron, carter
  Arch. Hodge, baker
  Miss M'Laren
18 Wm. Flannigan, labourer
  James Lavin, labourer
  Thomas Cannon, labourer
20 Arch. Campbell, shoemaker
24-26 William Newton, hawker
32 Casual Sick Home—
    Frank M'Ginlay, keeper
  Headquarters, 13th Coy., 1st
    Fife Vol. R.G. Artillery
  East and West Churches—
    J. Fowler, church officer
  Guild Hall—
    Wm. M'Naughton, keeper

ST MARY'S WYND.

1-3 Alexander Riach
7 Robert Allison, craneman
9 W. & J. Aitken, bakers
11 Mrs Bella M'Donald
11A Mrs C. M. Ryan, broker
13 Peter Morrison, carter
15-17 Robt. Allan & Son, bakers
19 Bernard M'Coll, labourer
   David Mitchell, labourer
   Robert Henny
   Mrs Catherine Tully
21 Wm. Kelso, miner
25 Robert Hoggan, miner
   Mrs Young
31 Mrs Marion Mulherron
35-37 Chas. M'Lachlan, joiner and
   undertaker
39 Richard Docherty, labourer
41 Hugh Newlands, labourer
   Wm. D. Melville, hawker
   Alex. Reid, labourer
   Francis Harvey, labourer
45 Philip Brady, labourer
47 Mrs Lizzie M'Kenzie
   James Wordie, labourer
   John M'Farlane, miner
   James M'Coll, miner
51 Thomas Mullen, labourer
53 Marykirk Parish Church—
   Rev. T. Skeoch
73-75 Mrs Taylor, spirit merchant
81 Episcopal School—
   John W. Herron, headmaster
85-87 Arch. Dougall, grocer
87 Walter Dick, labourer
   Walter Dick, jun., lorryman
89 Mrs Henderson, confectioner
91 Wm. Johnston, spirit merchant

2 Michael Kerr, labourer
   Mrs Donnachie
   Mrs Sarah Heally
   John M'Kenna, miner
   Andrew Roy, miner
   Charles Devine, labourer
   Mrs Bridget Mailley
   Miss Jane Simpson
   Thomas Quin, labourer
4 W. J. Traynor, spirit merchant
6 Mrs Callary
   James Machar, bricklayer
   James Duggan, hawker
8 Alex. Cameron, millwright
   Colin M'Lachlan, carter
   James Henderson, labourer
   Hugh Cassidy, labourer
   Hugh M'Guire, miner
   James M'Vey, labourer
   John M'Nulty, carter
   Mrs Margaret M'Ardle
   Wm. M'Phee, hawker
   Jas. M'Quillan, engine driver
   Joseph Cook, labourer
   James Neilson, labourer
   Mrs Rabbit
   Mrs Stevenson
   Mrs Ann Kane
   John M'Callum, labourer
   Thomas Connelly, labourer
   David Muir, labourer
10 Mrs Ann Cormack, broker
12 Mrs Ellen Buchanan
   Mrs Cambie
   James Kerr, platelayer
16 Mrs Reynolds, general dealer
18 John Barton, labourer
   John Niven, miner
   Wm. M'Callum, labourer
   Jesse Leathley, fish hawker
   Mrs Reid
   Wm. M'Callum, hawker
   James Soutar, labourer
   Hugh Barrie, hawker
   Adam Henderson, labourer
   Samuel Wilson, labourer
24-30 C. Oram, general dealer

ST. MARY'S WYND—Continued.

26 Chas. Henderson, pit sinker
John Macher, labourer
28 Joseph Murphy, labourer
Mrs Ann Duncan
Mrs Martha Cassidy
Wm. Muir, labourer
Mrs Marshall
John M'Ewan, stonebreaker
John Wotherspoon, labourer
Henry Alridge, labourer
34 Geo. F. Williamson, moulder
Edward Philiban, platelayer
Wm. Henderson, rubber worker
36 A. V. Kennedy, spirit merchant
38 Miss Ina Gow
Thos. M'Lellan, labourer
John Conway, labourer
Wm. Reid, hawker
Frederick Hensbay, tailor
Charles Devine, labourer
Stewart M'Lean, miner
John Flannigan, labourer
James Galloway, labourer
James Craig, miner
Peter M'Donald, miner
Wm. Blackadder, labourer
Ralph Hall, labourer
Charles Campbell, miner
Mrs Helen Coan
Laurence Donahoe, butcher
Robert Muir, labourer
Mrs Eliz. Hewitt
John Muir, labourer
Martin Leyden, labourer
John Devine, labourer
James Mungall, labourer
John M'Kay, labourer
Mrs Sylvia Lundie
Mrs Ann M'Graw
Mrs Catherine Flannigan
Rev. Joseph B. Hare
40 Wm. Oliver, labourer
44 James M'Lauchlan, labourer
Patrick Duffy, miner

46 Michael Peebles, labourer
50 John Sheridan, labourer
52-56 Mrs C. M'Ilvean, grocer
60 Mrs Jane Gray
Wm. Preston, engine driver
Laurence Gaerty, shoemaker
Patrick Gallacher, labourer
Thomas Cully, labourer
Cornelius M'Garvie, labourer
64 Thomas M'Ewan, labourer
68 Hugh Robb, carter
Robt. Lindsay, police sergt.
(retired)
70 Charles Nisbet, labourer
72 Wm. Johnstone, miner
74 Frank Smith, labourer
David Wylie, engine driver
Mrs Ann Cannon
76 Andrew Smeaton, baker
78 Mrs Finlayson
M. Hare, insurance agent
Mrs Stewart
Patrick Quigley, labourer
80 Henry Mullan, labourer
82 Miss Maggie O'Neil
84-86 Richard Kane, shoemaker
86 Peter Comrie, baker
Wm. Bruce, timekeeper
Michael Hennachen, labourer
J. Tracey, mason
88 Thomas Burgoyne, tailor
90 Michael Collins, insur. agent
Catholic Young Men's Institute
92 Mrs F. Ross, confectioner
94 Michael Scoffield, painter
John Coan, labourer
Thomas Boyle, platelayer
Thomas Stewart, brushmaker
George M'Queen, clerk
96 Patrick Scoffield, labourer
98 Geo. Gilmour, police constable
Michael M'Mannes, labourer
James Jack, platelayer
100 J. Scott, tobacconist

ST. NINIANS ROAD.

Viewforth—
　George Pearson, gardener
Langgarth—
　William Renwick, residenter
　George M'Call, gardener
Springbank—
　Alister J. Dickson, stockbroker
　James Meston, gardener
Annfield—
　Robert Lawson
　D. M'Isaac, gardener
Brentham Park—
　T. Alexander, chemical manuf.
　John Birse, gardener
　John Dow, coachman
Woodlands—
　John D. M'Jannet, residenter
Benarty House—
　Robt. B. Tennant, ironfounder
Easter Livilands—
　Mrs L. Geddes
　John Smith, gardener
Westerlands—
　Jas. W. Drummond, seedsman
Vineburgh Cottage—
　Neil M'Intyre, gardener

Thrushville—
South Lodge—
　John M'Ewen, grocer
　Miss M. M'Ewen
　Miss C. M'Ewen
Randolphfield—
　Alexander Hadaway, residenter
　Dan. Smith, gardener
Clifford Park—
　John Brown Smith, residenter
　Wm. Wallace, coachman
　John M'Nally, gardener
Williamfield—
　James Reid, residenter
　Robert Muir, gardener
Beechwood—
　Alexander M'Grigor, writer
　Robert Burns, gardener
　Thos. Godden, coachman
Braehead Farm—
　Thomas M'Farlane
Calton Cottages—
　1 Allan Hughes, platelayer
　3 Robert Brown
　4 John Wilson, miner
Calton House—Wm. Forsyth, miner

SUNNYSIDE, St. Ninians.

1 Robt. Tait, confectioner
3 James Shaw, miner
5 George Jenkins, nailer
7 Mrs Mary Brisbane

2 Thomas Baird, ploughman
4 James Laurie, engineman
　Thomas Brisbane, smith
6 John Blewitt, nailer

THISTLE STREET.

1 T. Robertson, coal merchant
　Wordie & Co., carting contract.
5 Thos. Muir, Son & Patton, Ltd.,
　coal merchants
7 D. M'Kerracher & Son, coal
　merchants and contractors
　C.R. Ambulance Hall
　Stirling Gas Company
21 Alexander Bean, gas worker
　Macdonald & Fraser, Ld., auctrs.
　J. & J. Cunningham, merchants
　Wm. M'Donald, auctioneer

10 Mackintosh & Mackintosh,
　whisky blenders
12 Daniel Sinclair, joiner
14 Thos. Lamb, motor car store
18 Stirling Unionist Club
20 Casey & Darragh, contractors
22 Robert Jeffrey
　Mrs Elizabeth M'Nab
24 William M'Laren, carter
28 Alexander Walls, plasterer

5

THISTLE STREET – Continued.

May Day Yard—

John Drummond, porter
James M'Laren, porter

James Simpson, porter

TORBREX, St. Ninians.

The County Cricket Club Ground
1 Alex. Muirhead, bricklayer
3 Hugh Brooks, millworker
5 Hector Henderson, joiner
7 James Gillies, coachwright
9 Wm. Stevenson, miner
11 Miss Ann Finlayson
13 Joseph Dalziel, glazier
15 Mrs Catherine Yeaman
17 John Scott, joiner
19 Mrs Helen Stewart

2 Robert Reid, labourer
4 John Wright, tailor
12-14 Alexander Millar
16 Wm. Paton, stonebreaker
18 Mrs Elizabeth Paton
20 Mungo Chapman, nurseryman
22 Mrs Elizabeth Stewart
24 John Watson, tanner
26 David Thompson
 James Thompson, slater
 Miss Catherine Gorrie
 Miss Janet Robertson
Polmaise Cottages—
 George Hardie, joiner
 Alex. Stenhouse, forester
 Wm. M'Gregor, forester

Coxithill—

Coxithill Farm—
 James Christie, farmer

Torbrex House—
 J. R. Buntine, Hon. Sheriff-Substitute for Stirlingshire
 Robert Syme, gardener
 John Armour, coachman
 John Barclay, butler

Stripeside—

1 Miss A. Murdoch, saleswoman

2 Miss Janet Craig

UNION STREET.

8 Wm. Horn, carter
 George Fisher, residenter
 Wm. Gibb, auctioneer
 Alex. Logie, joiner
 Mrs Jane Alexander
 Walter Walton, waiter
10 John Comrie, clerk
 Archd. Angus, blacksmith
 T. Finlayson, police inspector

10 David Scott, reporter
12 Alex. Anderson
 George Christie, draper
14 David Bayne, grocer
16 Mrs Jane Lindsay
 John Bell, bottler
 Alex. Cameron, tailor
 John Stewart, mason
18 Charles Robertson, cooper

UNION STREET—Continued.

18 J. M'Rae, Supt. Forth Fisheries
    James Hunter, railway guard
    H. M'Beath, Singer's salesman
20 H. M'Donald, Singer's salesman
    Geo. Christwood, insur. agent
    David Dickie, joiner
    Wm. Law, grocer
22 Mrs Gilfillan
    Robert M'Laren, bellhanger
    John Johnston, tailor
    Alex. Scott, engine driver
24 Miss Helen Wilson
    Mrs Torrance

24 Henry James, butcher
    Mrs Campbell
26 Peter Macrae, insurance agent
    James Martin, joiner
    Mrs Mary Hall
    John Weir, draper
28 A. Carruthers, laundry mangr.
    T. L. Finlayson
    James Chisholm
    Wm. Linsell, A.O.C.

Stirling Combination Poorhouse—
    Don. M'Millan, governor

VICTORIA PLACE.

1 John Paterson, poor inspector
2 Mrs Margaret Henderson
3 John M'Kenzie, M.A., teacher
4 Mrs Paton
5 Mrs Agnes Walker
6 John Denholm, captain
10 Frederick Tod, banker
12 Miss Hunter
    Wm. Hunter, iron merchant
15 Mrs Macnie
16 Mrs Janet Paterson
17 Robt Morton, ironmonger
18 Major Oliver, R.A.
19 Robert A. Brown, merchant
20 Horatio Cave, manufacturer
21 Leon J. Platt
22 Mrs Agnes M'Nair
    Miss Christie

23 Mrs Elizabeth Philp
24 Miss Mary Ann Kidston
    Miss Martha Kidston
    Miss Isabella Kidston
25 John M'Lauchlan, draper
26 Miss Isa Murray Wright
    Miss Jane Wright
27 Mrs M'Farlane
Stirling Golf Club-house—
    John Duncan, professional
Victoria Golf Club-house
Margate—Robt. Whyte, solicitor
Margate—Miss Margaret Easson
    Miss Isabella Easson
Parkgate—Thomas Weir, traveller
Queensgate—A. F. M'Kenzie, Col.,
    A. & S. H.

VICTORIA SQUARE.

1 A. D. Millar, H.M. Inspector
    of Schools
3 Rev. James Purves
5 Miss Robertson
7 Mrs Agnes Steven
9 Mrs Lawson
13 Wm. Rodgers, photographer
15 David Chrystal, writer
17 Miss Jessie Fraser
    Miss Jean Fraser
19 Mrs Cameron

2 Mrs Nicholson
4 George Kinross, coachbuilder
6 Robert Yellowlees, tanner
8 W. S. Morrison
10 Thos. D. Paton, auctioneer
12 James Nimmo, coal merchant

VIEWFIELD PLACE.

County Buildings—
  John G. Curror, Sheriff Clerk
  Patrick Welsh, procurator-fiscal
  Wm. M'Pherson, caretaker
  Headquarters of Stirlingshire
    Constabulary
  John D. Sempill, chief-constable
  Sergeant John M'Farlane
  Jas. Rodger, police constable
  Office of Inspector of Weights
    and Measures
    John M'Donald, inspector

Viewfield U.F. Church—
  Rev. Walter Scott
Wm. Donaldson, sculptor
Barnton House—
  Duncan Johnston, traveller

1 Dr. Wilson
  Thomas Wilson
2 John M'Ewen, grocer
3 James Eadie, traveller
4 William Somerville, dentist
5 Wm. Smellie, photographer
6 Robert Dawson, teacher
7 Robert Menzies, grocer
8 John M'Gregor, spirit merc.
9 Miss M'Kay, dressmaker
10 Miss J. Johnstone, dressmaker
11 Miss Morrison, dairy, &c.
12 John Lawrie, newsagent
13 Donald M'Kenzie, traveller
  Mrs M'Intyre
  Alex. Milne, saddler
  J. M'Donald, police inspector
14 John Wright, grocer

VIEWFIELD STREET.

1 Mrs Agnes Dumbreck
  A. Mackechnie, cabinetmaker
5 Miss Margaret M'Rae
  Mrs Janet Dowell
  J. P. Aitken, ironmonger
  Miss Malcolm, dressmaker
  Peter M'Arthur, residenter
  John Robertson, gardener
13 William Allan, clerk
  Robert Andrew, miner

10 James Brown, goods clerk
  John Morris, labourer
  Angus M'Lean, postboy
  Arch. M'Lachlan, Son & Coy.,
    cement merchants
  James Ferguson, lorryman
  Duncan Fraser, postboy
12 Alex. Moodie, mechanic
  Miss Margaret Jarvie
  Wm. Morris, butcher
  James Shaw, printer
  Mrs W. Carnegie, dressmaker
  James Ewing, engine fitter
  Thomas Dunn, painter
  John Duncan, shoemaker
14 Mrs J. C. Robertson, dairy
16-18 J. Thomson, watchmaker
18 Mrs Annie M'Kerchar
  Miss Isabella Hart
  Mrs Mary Maltman
  Wm. Williamson, gardener
  Miss Jane Leckie
20 G. Henderson, painter
22 J. F. Macintosh, bootmaker

WALLACE STREET.

1 John M'Gregor, spirit merchant
3 Peter Eadie, vanman
  Mrs Jane M'Donald
5 John Menteith, labourer
  Jas. Webster, insurance agent
13 Mrs Christina Cameron
  Mrs Jessie Rowan
  Mrs Helen Paterson
21 Mrs Isabella M'Kenzie
  Miss Elizabeth Turnbull
  Mrs Jane Mitchell
  Mrs E. Paterson, music teacher
  William Braes, engineer
  James M'Pherson, reporter
23 Miss Mary Paton
  Mrs Ferguson
  David M'Intosh, traveller
  William Currie, traveller
  P. Edmond, telephone super.
  Mrs Janet C. Hamilton
25 Mrs Helen Lawrence
  Wm. Hunter, insurance agent
  John Gordon, salesman
  George Davidson, architect
  Mrs Elizabeth Campbell
  Mrs Robertson
  Louis Robertson, clothier
27 James Speirs, grocer
  Robert Robertson, clothier
  John Scott, contractor
  Mrs Banks
  John Forbes, traveller
  J. D. Smith, engineer
35 Cowbrough & Mercer, grocers
37 Miss Drysdale, music teacher
  Miss Mary Johnstone
  Mrs Crocket
  Wm. Miller, blacksmith
39 David Williams, engine driver
  Mrs Helen Rutherford
41 Donald Gunn, cashier
  Ben. Salter, Sergt.-Major, R.E.
43 J. Thomson, ret. watchmaker
  Robert M'Intyre, printer
45 Mrs Elizabeth Dow
  Mrs M. Nicol
47 Duncan Taylor, tailor

2 Peter Schoffield, ret. postman
  James Livingstone, ret. porter
  W. Livingstone, cabinetmaker
  Chas. Begbie, photographer
8 W. A. Finlayson, joiner
  David Hain, signalman
  James P. Crawford, clerk
  Cameron Harley, ironmonger
  Arch. Frederick, mason
  J. R. Good, tailor and clothier
10 Miss Margaret Robb
  Miss Isabella Trotter
  Miss Isabella Robertson
  F. L. Pearson, warehouseman
  David Beath, traveller
  Miss Grace Fraser, dressmaker
14 Speedie Brothers, auctioneers
  George Muirhead, shepherd
16 T. Brisbane, wood merchant
18 The Alloa Coal Company—
    John Dewar, agent
  R. W. Smith & Co., coal and
    fireclay goods merchants
  W. Burns, coal merchant
Bridge Cottage—
  Thos. Nelson, loco. foreman
Bridge Custom—John M'Lean

WALLACE STREET—Continued.

47 Arch. Ferguson, grocer
49 Peter Marshall, contractor
  Thos. Moyes, insurance agent
  A. C. Moyes, insurance agent
51 Miss Jeannie Wilson
  Peter Edmond
  B. D. Shennan, bootmaker
  Duncan Ferguson, draper
53 Miss Margaret Borthwick
  Miss M'Donald
  Alex. Marshall
  Mrs William Hay
55 George Owen, retired smith
  Charles Hawdon, engineer
  Misses Kyle
  Mrs Margaret Meiklejohn
57 John M'Kay, clothier
  Matthew Struthers, draper
  James Bett, carter
  Miss I. Pollock

59 Mrs Dunlop
  Wm. M'Naughtan, engineer
  Miss M'Naughtan, dressmaker
  Wm. J. Nicol, postal clerk and
    Session clerk for Marykirk
  Wm. C. Nicol, postal clerk
61 Duncan Campbell, butcher
  Mrs Isa Green
  Miss Frances Garrett
  Wm. M'Shean, clerk
63 Robert Watt, ironmonger
  William Thompson
  Mrs Isabella M'Ginnigal
  Mrs Macdonald
65 Mrs Mary Kane
67 David Soutar, clothier
69 John M'Laren, joiner
  John Wright, draper
  Chas. Coutts, tailor's cutter
  John Duff, clerk

WEAVER ROW, St. Ninians.

5 James M'Kee, miner
7 James Glencross, miner
7½ Mrs Jane Corsar
  Archibald Young, joiner
  David Ferguson, labourer
  Mrs Thomas Brown
9 Thomas Morgan, candlemaker
  John Murdoch, labourer
9½ Mrs Elizabeth Brown
  James Brown, bolt maker
12 Mrs Agnes Campbell
13 James Couper, blacksmith
  James Smith, miner
15 George Murray, miner
  Robert Leyden, nailer

17 James Scobbie, miner
19 Francis M'Gill, miner
  James Baird, roadman
  David Ferrier, miner
  Mrs Agnes Brown
  James Harper, miner
  Miss Harper
  Wm. Brown, baker
21 William Brown
23 Miss Agnes Corser
25 Alex. Thomson, tanner
  Henry Brisbane, tailor
  St. Ninians Public School—
    R. B. Philp, headmaster
27 Robert Denovan, tailor

WELL GREEN.

1 Donald Richardson, platelayer
  Mrs Mary Walker
  Charles Currie, joiner
  Walter Thomson, weaver
3 James Taylor
  James Corr, vanman
  Mrs Elizabeth Cameron
  James Mortimer, traveller
5 George Douglas, engine driver
  David Sharp, barman

6 Joseph Strang, coachman
  Murdoch Imrie, labourer
  Andrew Murrie, engine driver
  Robert Young, dairyman
  Laurence Ferrier, cabinetmkr.
  John Hunter, overseer
12 Alex. Cochrane, smith
14 William Samson, fitter
  Thos. M'Pherson, glazier
  Robert Devlin, miner

WELL GREEN—Continued.

5 James S. Philp, insur. agent
James M'Farlane, tailor
7 J. Imrie, engine driver
Jas. Young, engine keeper
David M'Kinnon, joiner
John Millar, plumber
9 Andrew Fulton, storeman
James Moffat, vanman
Eben. Hutton, storeman
Thos. Kirkpatrick, labourer
11 Alex. M'Gregor, cooper
Andrew Munro, warper
James Stewart, pitsinker
Robert Samson, engineman
13 Duncan M'Gibbon, postman
John Carmichael, blacksmith
Ralph Cross, weaver
Alexander Robertson, carter
15 George Watson, slater
Wm. Campbell, miner
Wm. Brunton, bootmaker

15 Alex. M'Laren, gardener
17 H. C. Andrews, cabinetmaker
George Jamieson, glazier
Mrs Margaret Gordon
Mrs Nicol
19 Miss Jessie M'Lachlan
W. M. Lockhart, grocer
James Gray, colour mixer
21 Donald Livingstone, shepherd
James Milne, salesman
Alex. Johnstone, labourer
Robert Myles, miner
23 James Carnegie, traveller
Mrs Mary Ramsay
R. Roberts, warehouseman
Colin Lennox, grocer
25 Thomas Jack, weaver
Mrs Jane Crawford
Mrs Agnes Symons
Mrs Janet M'Intosh

WINCHEL PLACE.

3 James Stewart, signalman
4 Andrew Scobie, mason
5 Robert Armstrong, guard
6 Walter Shirra, postman
7 Peter Sharp, labourer
8 John Lawrie, cellarman
B.W.T.A. Hall
9 Thomas Lawrie, engine driver
10 Thomas Power
Mrs Elizabeth Adams
Mrs Isa Sandeman

11 Wm. Allan, brushmaker
Martin O'Neil, cardriver
Frank Young, shoemaker
James Kinnaird, joiner
12 James Telfer, labourer
13 John Border, labourer
14 Wm. Wylie, carting contractor
15 Sam M'Adam, fisherman
17 Peter Duffy, labourer
John Newsome, labourer

WINDSOR PLACE.

1 Peter M'Naughton, tobacconist
3 Misses C., I., and J. Stewart
5 David Kinross, traveller
7 J. Wilson, inspector of schools
9 Angus M'Ewan, spirit merc.
11 James Brown, solicitor
13 James Kemp Smith, engineer

2 Duncan M'Donald, saddler
4 James Mitchell
Miss Jessie Lister
6 Alex. D. Stevenson
8 Miss Grace Campbell
10 J. L. Macdonald, confectioner
12 Mrs Dunsmore
Michael Dunsmore
Enclosure House—
T. W. R. Johnston, editor, *Journal*

YORK PLACE.

1 Mrs Jane Jamieson
2 Samuel Ferguson, tailor

3 Miss Mary Hodge
4 Mrs Joan Carnie
Dr. Alexander Flett

CAUSEWAYHEAD ROAD.

(West side.)

Allandale—Miss Wright
Auchendoune—H. P. Watt, auctr.
Ravenswood—Mrs J. J. Thomson
Dunard—J. Marshall, Organising
    Secy., County Council
Ravenna Cottage—T. Hutchinson,
    gardener
Miss Margaret B. Davidson
Menmuir Villa—Mr Beattie
Armadale—A. Oliphant, confectr.
Mooivue—Mrs C. Howieson
Riversdale—Mrs Forbes
Lyngarth—
    Mrs Thomson
    W. D. Forbes, ironfounder
Tramway Company's Stables
Forthview—
    J. Scott, tram. foreman
    A. Anderson, car driver
Cressington—Miss Macfarquhar
Ardenlea—George Porteous
Gowanlea—Mrs A. Cottle
Tweedbank—A. Milne, guard
Spittal Villa—T. Walker
Hildontree—Mrs Bennett
Causewayhead Police Station—
    Constable J. Fraser
Blair-Uallais—W. B. Cook, editor
    Stirling Sentinel
Dunvegan—Miss M. C. Robertson
St. Margaret's—Robert Ferguson,
    photographer
Lizville—Miss Jessie Burns

———

Togneri Bros., ice-cream vendors

(East side.)

Tramway Company's Stables
Causewayhead Station
T. Muir, Son & Patton, coal agents
J. Strang, coal agent
Oil Works—James Shand & Co.
Craiglea—Mrs Anderson
Ben View—
    Alex. Fowler, stationmaster
Cornton Cottage—Mrs Headridge
Muirlands Cottage—
    Lieutenant Dickson
Sheriffmuirlands—
    A. Bean, engineer
Abbey Craig Laundry Company
Beechwood—
    Wm. Stirling, draper
Inverardran—
    E. Munro, gardener
Grange House—
    R. Thomson, clerk
    J. Clark, journalist
    Miss Archibald
    Walter Harkness, clerk
St. Leonard's—
    Mrs Parshall
    John Brown, law clerk
    J. Kinross, retired farmer
    Mrs Seaton
Garscube—
    Miss Walker
    J. R. Henderson
Craigroyston—
    Miss Roy, dressmaker
Causewayhead Cottage—
    W. Miller, blacksmith
Woodside Cottage—
    W. Wallace, signalman
    W. Allison, roadman
    A. M'Gowan, cartwright
Jessamine Cottage—
    Mrs Rutherford
Viewfield—
    J. Craigie, retired clergyman
    Mrs J. Mackie
    A. Deans, painter
    T. Deans, painter

CAUSEWAYHEAD.

Bridge of Allan Road.

Wallace Arms Inn—Mrs. Harris
Robert Neil, joiner
A. Headridge, builder
Miss M. Stewart, confectioner
Andrew Stewart, carrier
Lily Cottage—
  David Flockhart, coal agent
  Wm. Hunter
  J. Dent, labourer
  M. M'Bean
  Richard Lawrie

Holly Cottage—
  E. Mavor, tailor
  Mrs Campbell
  Alex. Jeffrey, plumber
  Miss Jeffrey
Rose Cottage—
  James Livingstone, carpenter
  Alex. Anderson, joiner
Craigview—
  Alex. Young, J.P.
  Mrs Watson
Spittal Farm—James Lucas

Alloa Road.

Frank Young, bootmaker
A. C. Deans, painter
Mrs A. Petrie
Miss M'Caully
Elderslie—
  Mrs Gibb
  John Macfarlan, driver
  Alex. Braidwood, ret. merc.
  James Strang, coal agent
Logie Parish Mission Hall—
  James Neil, caretaker

Victoria Villa—
  Mrs T. Ferguson
  R. B. Wood, com. trav.
Craigfoot Cottage—
  Mrs Archibald Brown
  David Paton
Hole Cottage—
  Fred. Trench, gardener
  Wm. Morland, coachman
Holehead House—
  William Lucas

Causewayhead School and Schoolhouse—A. Dalziel, headmaster

Hunter's Buildings—
  John Frater, carter
  Mrs Hall
  A. Ewing, draper
  Miss Louden
  James Miller, carter
M'Ewen's Buildings—
  J. Raeoch, carter
  T. Caddell, waiter
  J. M'Fadyen, blacksmith
  Wm. Ralston, rubber worker
  Wm. M'Dougall, mason

Craig Wallace View—
  George Robertson, labourer
  Reading Room
  Sub-Post Office—Miss Bean
  R. Grindlay, carriage maker
  W. Bean, blacksmith
  James Marshall, car driver
  James Walker, painter
  Miss Headridge
  W. Miller, painter
  Miss M'Millan, laundrymaid

CAUSEWAYHEAD—Continued.

Spittalfield Cottage—
   Mrs J. Robertson
Spittal Cottages—
   A. Oliver, car conductor
   J. Hamilton, gardener

Abbey Craig Park—
   A. Macdowall
Wallace Monument—
   W. Middleton, custodian

Towers Place—
   1 A. Sutherland, mason
   3 George Miller, carter
     W. Donaldson, carter
   5 John Sutherland, mason
   6 Mrs John M'Kerracher
   7 D. Marshall, car driver
   8 W. Donaldson, carter
   9 Mrs M'Lean
   10 Peter Miller
   11 A. Scott, carter
   12 A. Graham, carter
   13 D. Buchanan, painter
   14 M. Thornton, labourer
   15 Miss M'Laren
      M. M'Allister, labourer
Broadloan—
      J. M'Intyre, gardener
      G. Miller, labourer
      Mrs M'Laren
Craigbank—
      J. Lewis, painter
      C. Petrie, vanman
      J. Miller, labourer
      P. Johnston, labourer
      R. Blackwell, builder
      Adam Brown
Rosemount—Mrs Menzies
Hillside—
      Wm. Cunnison, cashier
      Mrs Mitchell
Abbeyview—

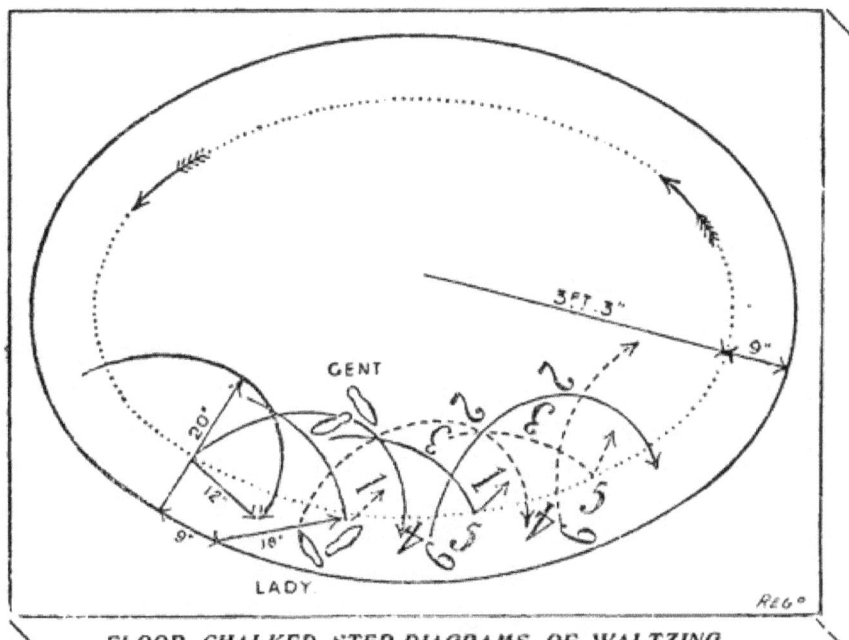

BUSINESS DIRECTORY.

Aerated Water Manufacturers.

Andrew Buchanan, 9 Baker st
James Duncan, Drip rd
Robert Liddel, 40 King st
J. & J. Miller, Burghmuir
Scottish Co-operative Society, Forth
street

Agricultural Implement Makers.

Finlayson & Son, Kerse
Kemp & Nicholson, Forth st
W. M'Naughtan, Forth st

Architects and Surveyors.

John Allan, 11 King st
Crawford & Fraser, 27 Murray pl
A. M. Lupton, 20 Murray pl
M'Luckie & Walker, 15 Dumbarton
road
Eben. Simpson, 16 King st

Art Dealers.

Mrs. Dewar, 35 Arcade
Adam Johnstone, 30-34 Arcade
John Walls, Maxwell pl

Artists and Engravers.

Mathieson Brothers, 25 Port st

Auctioneers.

O. P. Derrick 43 Baker st
Macdonald, Fraser & Co., Ltd.,
Thistle street
Andrew Simpson, 44 Barnton st
Speedie Brothers, Ltd, Wallace st
Henry P. Watt, 22 Baker st

Bakers.

W. & J. Aitken, 3 and 54 Baker st;
45 Barnton st; 9 St Mary's
Wynd; 3 and 5 Main st,
St Ninians
R. Allan & Sons, 17 St Mary's
Wynd
Peter Brodie, 34 Port st and 5-7
Seaforth Place
Mrs. Mary Boreland, 82 Baker st
Co-operative Society, Barnton st
Thos. Elder & Sons, 52 Port st
W. M. Goudie, 73 King st
Keith & Ralston, 10 Port st
J. Millar & Sons, 17 Murray pl and
45 Upper Craigs
Wm. M'Callum, 19 Broad st
William Mitchell, 3-5 Bannockburn
rd., St Ninians
James Neil, 15 Baker st and 15
Broad st

Bank Agents.

British Linen Bank, 2 King st—
Arthur Brown
Bank of Scotland, 54 King st—
James W. Campbell
Clydesdale Bank, 61 King st—
W. M. Reyburn
Commercial Bank, Murray pl—
Hugh S. Robson
Great North of Scotland Bank, 4
King st—Hill & Whyte
National Bank, 68 Murray pl—D.
Ferguson
Royal Bank, 23 King st—T. L.
Reid
Union Bank, 22 King st—Robert
M'Luckie

Basket Maker.

F. Grogan, 45 King st and 25 Broad st

Billiard Rooms.

A. M'Ewan, 27 King st

Berlin Wool and Baby Linen.

J. W. Armstrong, 18 Friars st
Miss A. Danskin, 12 Arcade
Mrs A. Grieve, 9 Murray pl
Miss Kate M'Farlane, 33 Arcade
Miss M'Arthur, 74 Port st
Misses E. & J. Reid, 32 Murray pl
Miss L. White, 22 Arcade

Billposters.

Stirling Billposting Co., Craigs

Booksellers and Stationers.

Cook & Wylie, 9 Barnton st
Crawford & Co., 7 King st
Mrs Crocket, 71 King st
John H. Craig, 15-21 Arcade
Drummond's Tract Depot, 17-19 Dumbarton Road
Eneas Mackay, 43 Murray pl
R. S. Shearer & Son, 6 King st
William Shirra, 83 Port st

Boot and Shoe Makers.

Alex. Adam, 106 Baker st
William Boswell, 18 Baker st
Robert Barclay, 154 Main st, St Ninians
Co-operative Society, Friars st
Simon Collier Ltd., 34 King st and 64 Port st
Davidson & Co., Ltd., 25 Murray place

John Denovan, 112 Main st, St Ninians
James Dickson, 38 Baker st
Hugh Ferguson & Son, 2 Port st
James Forsyth, 49 Main st, St Ninians
David Gilmour, 57 Barnton st
Mrs Galashan, 31 Arcade
Michael Hannan, 22-24 Arcade
Richard Kane, 84 St Mary's Wynd
James F. Macintosh, Viewfield Buildings (Chiropodist), and 64a Craigs
Norwells, 77 King st
T. O'Brien, 1 Bow st
B. D. Shennan, 45 Port st and 12 Maxwell place
James Shennan, 49½ Cowane st
John Stewart, 15 Upper Craigs
The Smith Shoe Co., 41 King st
M. & J. Stoddart, 8 Dumbarton rd and 60 Murray pl
John Shaw, 37 Cowane st
H. P. Tyler, 28 Port st
William Watson, 15 Barnton st
Frank Young, Causewayhead

Brewers and Maltsters.

Peter Burden's Trustees, Irvine pl
J. & J. Miller, 29 Burghmuir

Brokers and Furniture Dealers.

John Brown, 79 83 and 112-114 Baker st
Wm. Brown, 86 Baker st
James Balloch, 96 Baker st
Mrs Cormack, 5 Bow st
John Corser, 35 Main st, St Ninians
Mrs Duffin, 17 Friars st
W. Galloway, 49 Baker st
Wm. Ging, 27 Broad st
Mrs Hogan, 64 and 64½ Baker st
John Holland, 109 Baker st

J. Johnston, 31 Main st, St Ninians
A. J. Mullen, 6 and 8 Bank st
Mrs M'Gonville, 100 Baker st
P. M'Kay, 99-101 Baker st
C. Nealus, 59 Baker st
James Peebles, 16-18 Bow st
Thomas Ryan, 6 Bow st
William Simpson, 32 Bow st
R. Taylor, 65 Main st, St Ninians
Edward Welsh, 16 Broad st
J. Yates, 3 St John st

Builders.

Anderson & Son, Murray place
F. & W. Aitken, Newhouse
J. Fotheringham, 45 L. Bridge st
Wm Gourlay, Rosebery pl
A. Headridge & Sons, Causeway-
    head
Jas. Headridge, Causewayhead
B. Reynolds, 27 Randolph terrace
J. & W. Ronald, 20 James st

Butchers.

Alexander Benme, 65 Barnton st
John Buchanan, 82 Main st, St
    Ninians
Donald Campbell, 20 Baker st
W. & J. Cullens, 10-12 Baker st and
    7 Port st
James Cullens, 23 Port st
Christie & Macdonald, 34 Bow st
Co-operative Society, 8 Up. Craigs,
    45 Cowane st, and 12 Friars st
Eastmans Limited, 46½ Baker st
Wm. Forsyth, 21 Dumbarton rd
R. & J. Greenhorn, 16 Up. Bridge
    street
Mowat & Sons, 77 Baker st
J. Lennox, 30 Forth cres
C. Mowat, 91 Baker st
James Neil, 3 Bow st
Robert Roberts, Allan Park
J. W. Simpson, 122 Main st, St
    Ninians
Duncan Thomson 35 Friars st
    and 11 Upper Craigs
Robert Thomson, 29 Port st

Brush Manufacturers.

Park Brothers, 4 Forth st

Candlemakers.

D. M'Diarmid & Sons, 59 Up. Craigs
    and 85 Main st, St Ninians

Carriage Hirers.

Jas. Bellingham, 27 St John st
Robert M. Currie, 43 Port st
Thos. Hathaway, Cambusbarron
George Jeffrey, 2 and 4 Shore rd
Mrs Lennox, Station Hotel
Stevenson Bros., Golden Lion Hotel
Andrew Simpson, 44 Barnton st

Cabinetmakers and Upholsterers.

William Bryce, 33 King st
Oswald Dawson, 26 Forth st
Robert Forrest, 9 Friars st
Graham & Morton, 37 Burghmuir
    (Showrooms, Dumbarton rd)
T. Henderson & Son, 43 Port st
Lawsons Limited, Baker st
John Lorimer, 63 Cowane st and
    Spittal st
Wm. Livingstone, 45 King st
Wm. Mailer, 70 Baker st
Virtue & Co., Murary pl
H. P. Watt, 22 and 32 Baker st
Robt. B. Wallace, 81 Port st

Carrier (Glasgow.)

P. Campbell, 33 King st

Cement and Tile Merchants.

Arch. M'Lachlan, Son, & Co., 16
    Viewfield st

Carriers, Carters, and Contractors

Cowan & Co. (N.B. Railway)
W. R. Gall, 20 Orchard pl
Hunter & Co., Abbey rd
James Lambert. 8 Glasgow rd, St Ninians
D. M'Kerracher & Son, 7 Thistle st
James M'Arthur, 59 Bannockburn rd, St Ninians
Muir, Son, & Patton, Thistle st
Stirling and Bridge of Allan Tramways Company (secretary, A. Wardlaw, Bridge of Allan); Stirling agent, W. Somerville, 2 Barnton st
Jas. Taylor, St Ninians
Wordie & Co. (Caledonian Railway)

Chemists and Druggists.

Duncanson, 38 Port st
John A. Gordon, 12 Barnton st
J. A. Hogg, 79 Port st
John Livingstone, 58 Baker st
W. J. Moore & Son, 24 Murray pl
John Raffan, 16 Port st
F. Spite & Co., Ltd., 56 Port st
Walker & Skinner, 67 King st

Chimney Sweeps.

Hector Henderson, Baker st
J. M'Culloch, 66 Spittal st
T. Maxwell, Douglas st

Coachbuilders.

W. Kinross & Sons, 37-39 Port st
George Thomson. 30-32 Orchard pl

Coalmasters and Agents.

The Alloa Coal Company, Wallace st—John Dewar, agent ; town office, 7 Murray pl
William Burns, Wallace st
Miss Gardner, 41 Murray pl
Jas. Headridge, Causewayhead
Alex. Millar, N.B. Goods Station
Muir, Son, & Patton, Cal. Ry. Stn. and Causewayhead
Peter Murray, 7 Clifford rd
D. M'Kerracher & Son, 7 Thistle st
A. M'Lachlan, Son & Co., 10 Viewfield st
Thos. Robertson, 1 Thistle st
R. W. Smith, & Co., Wallace st
Jas. Strang, Causewayhead

Confectioners.

W. & J. Aitken, 3 and 54 Baker st, 45 Barnton st, and 9 St Mary's Wynd
Mrs Angus, 14 Lower Bridge st
R. Anstruther & Son, 54-60 Cowane st
J. Cameron, 42 Spittal st
J. Cattanach, 13 Bow st
K. Darmody, 27 Broad st
G. Denison, 130 Main st, St Ninians
Thomas Gasser, 38 Barnton st
M. George, 69 Barnton st
Mrs Jane Gray, 62 St Mary's Wynd
Miss Hamilton, 40 Arcade
G. Jamieson, 13 Maxwell pl
Charles Jeffrey, 3 Glasgow rd
Alex. Keir, 39 King st, 65 and 78 Port st
Keith & Ralston, 10 Port st
Kennedy & Co., Old Bridge (manufacturing)
Miss Kenny. 62 Upper Craigs
Miss J. Leighton, 19 Main st, St Ninians
Thomas Marshall, 14 Arcade
P. M'Glennon, 12 Broad st
Wm. M'Innes, 23 Upper Craigs
A. M'Pherson, 10 Lower Bridge st

Mrs W. Brown, 87 Baker st
Mrs P. Comrie, 26 King st
Jas. Millar & Sons, 17 Murray pl
Mrs B. M'Donald, 9½ St Mary's Wynd
Miss E. M'Farlane, 10 Main st, St Ninians
J. Oliphant, 6 Forth st (wholesale)
A. Oliphant, 14 Bayne st (wholesale)
A. Oswald, 42-44 Arcade
Miss J. Roxburgh, 7 Barnton st
Mrs F. Ross, 92 St Mary's Wynd
James Sinclair, 15 Murray pl
Miss Stirling, 2 Spittal st
Miss Stevenson, 26 Arcade
Mrs Sutherland, 36 Abbey rd
E. Suttie, 78 Cowane st
R. Tait, Sunnyside, St Ninians
Charles Wood, 20 Newhouse
Miss M. Wright, 17 Main st, St Ninians

Coopers.

Haldane & Co., 32 Abbey rd
P. Harvey, 53 Main st, St Ninians
John Wordie, 33 King st

Cork Merchants.

Adam & Yates, Ltd., Lower Craigs

Curriers, Leather Merchants, and Skinners.

Mrs Crocket, 22 Spittal st
James Grieve, St Ninians
D. Yellowlees & Sons, 30 Queen st

Cycle Agents.

John Anderson, 12 Albany cres
D. Cuthiell, Drip bridge
Thomas Lamb, 23 Murray pl
D. Morrison, Raploch
George Owen, 69 Port st
Shakespeare & Chalmers, 32 Barnton street

Dairykeepers, Cowfeeders, and Milk Purveyors.

And. Buchanan, 40 Low. castlehill
Miss Christie, 22 Cowane st
James Christie, Coxithill ¾ Farm, St Ninians
Mrs Cruikshanks, 36 Lr. Castlehill
J. Duguid, 80 Baker st
Miss C. Finlayson, 26 Bow st
F. R. France, 11 Broad st
Miss J. Fraser, 28 Abbey rd
James Fullarton, 32 Baker st
Mrs Gilvear, 22 Lower Castlehill
John Henderson, 6 Cowane st
James Hay, 16 Borestone pl
Jas. D. Kemp, 23 Bannockburn rd
Alex. Lucas, Craigton
John Lucas, Ladysneuk
Mrs A. Livingstone, 16 Up. Craigs
P. Meiklejohn, 51 Cowane st
Walter Millar, Shiphaugh
M. Morrison, 10 Viewfield pl
Miss I. Marshall, 39 Forth crescent
James M'Aree, Glencoe rd
Neil M'Caffer, Crofthead
Wm. M'Callum, 19 Broad st
Miss M'Farlane, 28 Abbey rd
T. M'Farlane, Braehead Farm, St Ninians
Miss M. M'Gibbon, 72 Up. Craigs
Jas. M'Kenzie, Seaforth pl
D. M'Kerracher, Raploch Farm
Hugh Nisbet, 8 Barnton st

6

D. Robertson, North Kersebonny
P. Reid, 22 Up. Craigs
Mrs Robertson, Viewfield bldgs
P. Stirling, Drip rd
A. Tritton, 21 Broad st
Arch. Watt, Whitehouse Farm
C. S. Wood, 20 and 22 Newhouse
Robert Young, Well Green Dairy

Dentists.

Brown & Wilson, 76 Port st
David Marshall, 1 Melville terrace
Platt & Common, 64 Murray pl
J. W. Somerville, 4 Viewfield pl

Drapers.

G. Arthur & Sons, 14 Barnton st
John Brown, 37-39 Baker st
George Christie, 96 Cowane st
Ferguson & Struthers, 4 Baker st
A. Fisher, Barnton st
P. M. Forfar, 33 Barnton st
Hugh Gavin & Son, 1 King st
Mrs Jane Hall, 40 Abbey rd
G. R. Jenkins, 43 King st
W. & A. Johnston, 42-48 King st
Lawsons Limited, 34 Baker st
Thos. Menzies, 36 King st
D. Mackenzie, 13 Viewfield pl
M'Aree Brothers, 57-59 King st
M'Culloch & Young, 1 Baker st
    and 79 King st
David M'Intosh, 23 Wallace st
Peter M'Neil, 29 Lower Bridge st
George Morgan, 67 Port st
T. Paterson Orr, 21 King st
A. T. Paul, 5-7 Arcade
Wm. Strang & Co., 67 Barnton st
Robert Wallace, 89 Port st
Thomas Wylie, 13 Lower Bridge st
John Wright, 40 Cowane st

Dressmakers.

Miss Bain, Kildean
Miss Baldie, 6 Allan Park
Miss Bett, 51 Wallace st
Mrs Carnegie, 12 Viewfield st
Mrs Agnes Collis, 74 Cowane st
Misses Dick, 2 Forth Crescent
J. B. Donaldson, 25 Dumbarton rd
Miss Danskin, 12 Arcade
Miss Davidson, 40 Barnton st
Miss Dumbreck, Viewfield st
Miss Ferguson, Forth cres
Misses Finlayson, 24 Baker st
Miss Fraser, 10 Wallace st
Miss Hardie, 12 Port st
Mrs Mary Hart, 37 Murray pl
Mrs Hume, 52 Barnton st
Hutchison & Co., 55 King st
Miss Johnstone, 10 Viewfield pl
Mrs Lister, 41 Millar pl
Mrs Mackenzie, 21 Wallace st
Miss Macnaughtan, 59 Wallace st
Miss Marshall, 49 Wallace st
Miss A. Millar, 15 Friars st
Miss M. Millar, 1 Princes st
Miss Milner, 12 Cowane st
Miss M'Gloin, 25 Forth cres
Miss J. M'Leod, 53 Port st
Misses M'Leod, 2 Wolf Craig
Miss M'Rae, 47 Cowane st
Miss M. Paterson, 39 Upper Craigs
Miss Peter, 15 Queen st
Miss Quarrie, 33 James st
Miss Janet Robb, 28 Newhouse
Miss Roy, Craigroyston, C'wayhead
Miss J. Stevenson, 37 Murray pl
Miss Ellen Turner, 52 Broad st
Miss Wedderspoon, 16 King st
Miss Younger, 45 King st
Miss White, 22 Arcade

Dyers and Cleaners.

J. Pullar & Sons, 91 Port st
Stirling Steam Laundry, Abbey rd
M. Wallace, 53 Upper Craigs

Drysalter, &c,

Parlan Macfarlan, 10 Abbey rd

Electric Wiring Contractors.

J. & J. Duff, Dumbarton rd
Lockhart & M'Nab, 34-38 Craigs
W. & T. Marshall, 16 Dumbarton rd
John Scott, 128 Main st, St Ninians
Graham & Morton, 47 King st
John Steel, 22 Murray pl

Fancy Goods and Toys

Mrs Bolton, 40 Forth cres
J. H. Craig. 15-21 Arcade
Miss Donaldson, 35 Baker st
Miss Gardner, 41 Murray pl
J. Gordon, 17 Upper Craigs
Misses E. & B. Kyle, 6 Baker st
J. Lawrie, Viewfield pl
E. Millar, 74 Baker st
Robert Stevenson, 75 Port st

Farm Produce Merchants.

John Mailer & Co., Up. Craigs and
    37 Allan pk. (Tel. No. 5Y3.)
R. Tennent Smith, Thistlecroft

Fishmongers.

Andrew Buchanan, 13 Barnton st
Sutherland Bremner, 24 Barnton st
Mrs A. Forrester, 42 Barnton st
David Forrester, 3 Friars st
John Johnston, 31 Port st
Mrs Johnstone, 50 Port st
Mrs H. Leathley, 14-16 Shore rd
Stirling Fish Mart Co., 67 Baker st

Florists, Fruiterers, and Greengrocers

Robert Allan, 3A Friars st
S. Bremner, 24 Barnton st
Mrs Eliza Brown, 6-8 Arcade
Richard Copley, 59 Barnton st
John Craig, 3 Murray pl
M. Hodgson, 25 Spittal st
D Jenkins, 95, 97 Main st, St Nin
Alex Keir, 65, 78 Port st, 39 King st
Miss M. Morrison, 62 Upper Craigs
H. Pearson, 12 Upper Bridge st
Mrs Templeton, Murray pl
T. Young, 56 Baker st

Gamedealers (Licensed).

Andrew Buchanan, 13 Barnton st
S. Bremner, 24 Barnton st
Mrs A. Forrester, 42 Barnton st
David Forrester, 3 Friars st
John Johnston, 31 Port st
Mrs Johnstone, 50 Port st

Gardeners.

M. Chapman, Torbrex
Murdoch Dingwall, 14 George st
R. Copley, 59 Barnton st
R. Crawford, 1 Borestone cres
William Gilmour, 67½ Port st
Wm. Gow, 12 Torbrex
T. Hutchison, Causewayhead rd
Henry Kelly, 21 Lower Craigs
J. Lamont, 7 Borestone pl
T. M'Rorie, Upper Bridge st
A. Morgan, Whins of Milton
E. Munro, Causewayhead
W. Roger, Upper Bridge st ; house
    --13 Albany cres
John Robertson, Seaforth pl
Jas. Thomson, Barnsdale Gardens,
    St Ninians

Girls' Schools.

Misses Hogg, 4 Melville Terrace
Miss Graham, Abercromby pl
Miss Young, 2 Dumbarton rd

Glass and China Merchants

Robert Adam, 21 Port st
William Crawford, 21 Murray pl
Mark Hodgson, 27 Spittal st
Robert M'Lean, 48 Main st, St
    Ninians
Mrs Robertson, 17 Barnton st
Mrs A. Sangster, 56 and 86 Spittal st

Glaziers and Glass Merchants

W. G. Crichton, 71 Port st
Thos. M'Pherson, 16 Dumbarton rd

Grocers (Licensed).

John Brown, 51 Murray pl
Andrew Buchanan, 9 Baker st
John Buchanan, 7 Broad st
Christie & M'Donald, 34 Bow st
Cowbrough & Mercer, 14 Port st
    and 35 Wallace st
Andrew Cumming, 28 Baker st
Dunlop & Co., 12 Bow st
Wm. Easson, 102 Baker st
Ferguson Brothers, 62 Baker st
John Gillespie, 51 Port st
W. Hetherington, 27 Port st
David Hunter, 57 Baker st
Robert Liddel, 40 King st
Wm. Low & Co., 57-59 Port st
D. & J. MacEwen & Co., 40 Port
    st and 12 Dumbarton rd
MacEwen Bros., 16-18 Barnton st
Duncan M'Ewan, 36 Barnton st
R. Menzies & Co., 22 Bow st
Peter Menzies, 20 Upper Craigs
Mrs C. M'Ilvean, 56 St Mary's Wynd
Agnes Nash, 81 Main st, St Ninians
James Nokes, 54 and 58 Main st,
    St Ninians
Robertson & Macfarlane, 42 Port st
    and Dumbarton rd
Peter Watt, 6 Broad st

J. Corser, 33 Main st, St Ninians
Arch. Dougall, 85 St Mary's Wynd
Mrs C. Drummond, 13 Newhouse
Mrs Glen, Main st, St Ninians
Mrs Jane Hall, 40 Abbey rd
R. Hardie, 3 Glasgow rd, St Ninians
Mrs C. Henderson, 110 Baker st
Wm. Law, 100 Cowane st
Lipton Limited, Barnton st
Wm. Low & Co., 25 Arcade
Maypole Dairy Co., 15½ Murray pl
D. B. M'Diarmid, 9 Low Bridge st
D. M'Donald, 71 Baker st
D. M'Alpine, 4-6 Borestone pl
Mrs Noble, 39 Lower Bridge st
James Speirs, 49 Cowane st
G. Starkey, 58 Port st
C. Thompson, 55 Main st, St Nin
Mrs Tritton, 21 Broad st
R. D. Waddell, 29 Murray pl
Chas. Wood, 20 and 22 Newhouse
John Wright, 37 Friars st and 14
    Viewfield pl

Gun and Fishing Tackle Makers.

D. Crockart & Son, 35 King st

Grocers, Tea, and Provision Merchants.

T. Adamson & Co., 29 Arcade
D. Bayne, 73 Wallace st
Wm. Barclay, 11 Glasgow rd
Miss Christie, 14-16 Cowane st
Cowbrough & Mercer, 42 Forth cres
Co-operative Society, Ltd, 12-14
    King st, 1 Broad st, 37 Upper
    Craigs, 36 Cowane st, 3 Barnton
    st, and St Ninians
Cooper & Co., 33-35 Murray pl
J. Cooper, 43 Upper Craigs

Hairdressers.

Geo. Aimer, 26 Baker st
George Barr, 2 Bow st
James Blair, 31 Murray pl
John T. Dale, 30 Port st and 25
    Friars st
Joseph Mackieson, 6 Barnton st
Wm. M'Arthur, 33 Upper Craigs
E. Millar, 74 Baker st
John M'Dougall, 61 Baker st
James Stevens, 34 Barnton st
Wm. Stewart, 78½ Main st, St
    Ninians

Hatters and Hosiers.

Anderson Brothers, 3 King st
William Brown, 2 Arcade
James Dow, 19 King st
J. Dowell, 56 Barnton st
H. G. Mathie, 4 Barnton st
James Nicol, 69 King st
William Reid, 21 Friars st
Salmond, 53 Barnton st

Horseshoers and Farriers.

W. Bean, Causewayhead
Geo. Plenderleith, 6 Upper Craigs
John M. Stewart, 49 Murray pl
John Stewart, 13 Friars st
Thomas Walls, 11 Bannockburn rd, St Ninians

Hotels (Licensed).

Castle Hotel—Mrs Hamilton, Esplanade
Crown Hotel—P. W. Stevens, 41 Arcade
Douglas Hotel—Mrs R. Morgan, 2½-4 Arcade
Golden Lion Hotel—Stevenson Brothers, 10 King st
Station Hotel—Mrs Lennox, 54-56 Murray pl
Sun Inn—R. Christie, 55 King st
Wallace Arms Hotel—Jas. Oliver, St Ninians

Hotels (Temperance).

Arcade Temperance Hotel — D. M'Killop
County Temperance Hotel — D. M'Killop, 28 Murray pl
Laurie's Temperance Hotel—Thos. Laurie, 5 King st
Miss Deans, Temperance Hotel— 36 Murray pl
Waverley Temperance Hotel—P. M'Alpine, 2-4 Murray pl

House Furnishers.

J. Creagh, Barnton st
Robert Forrest, 9 Friars st
Graham & Morton, 1-15 Dumbarton road
Lawsons Limited, 17-25 Baker st
Virtue & Co., 14 Murray pl
Andrew Simpson, 44 Barnton st

Ice Cream Vendors.

R. Corieiri, 45 Baker st
Giannandrea, 40 and 93 Baker st and 10 Broad st
R. Giuliana, 31 Baker st and 4 Cowane st
D. Giovanelli, 45 and 88 Baker st
B. de Ponio, 47 Upper Craigs
P. Togneri, 116 Baker st
A. Tortolano, 87 Main st, St Ninians

Importers of Feeding Stuffs.

J. & J. Cunningham, Thistle st
James Gray & Co., Craigs
D. & J. M'Ewen, 40 Port st
Parlan M'Farlan, Shore
Drummond & Sons, Ltd., 13 Murray pl

Incorporated Accountant.

W. H. Young, 62 Port st

Ironfounders.

Walker & Paton, Burnside Foundry, Lower Craigs
J. Davie & Sons, 26-28 Orchard pl

Iron Merchants.

Daniel MacEwen, 23 Dumbarton rd
Somerville & Valentine, 1-5 Port st
David Somerville, 13 King st

Ironmongers.

Co-operative Society, Barnton st
Mrs J. Gordon, 17 Upper Craigs
Graham & Morton, 47-51 King st
Cameron Harley, 26-28 Barnton st
    and Taylor's bldgs, Ba'ckburn
Somerville & Valentine, 1-5 Port st
David Somerville, 13 King st
Archibald Speed, 5 Broad st
Virtue & Co., 14-26 Murray pl

Jewellers and Watchmakers.

George Alexander, 34 Murray pl
Bankrupt Stock Realisation Co.,
    10 Arcade
James Banks, 18 Port st
Wm. Christie, 36 Port st
R. Drummond & Son, 5 Murray pl
J. T. Drummond, 39 Arcade
J. F. Fenton, 11 Bruce st
Harvey & Hunter, 53 King st
Lambert Hepting, 11 Murray pl
Wm. M'Kenzie, 7 Baker st
John W. Small, 8 Middle Craigs
D. & J. Stewart, 22 Port st
A. & R. Swan, 8 Port st
M. O. Thomson, 18 Murray pl
J. Thomson, 16 Viewfield st

Joiners

Anderson & Son, Murray pl
James Currie, 16 Dumbarton rd
Dalgetty Bros., 2 Park lane
Fairful, Wilson, & Somers, 81 Port st
Thos. Ferguson, 14 and 31 Dum-
    barton rd
M. Finlayson & Son, Springfield
John Gardner, B'nockburn rd, St Nin
T. Henderson & Son, 43 Port st
J. Meiklejohn, Craigmill
W. M'Dougall & Son, 11-13 George st
C. M'Lachlan, 37 St Mary's wynd
Thomas M'Nab, 20 Friars st
Wm. M'Pherson, 24 Forth st
A. Sands, Raploch
Andrew Simpson, 44 Murray pl
D. Sinclair, 12 Thistle st
Robt. Smith, 11 Barnton st

Lathsplitter.

David Buchan, 21 Seaforth pl

Laundries and Laundresses.

Abbey Craig Laundry Co., Cause-
    wayhead.
Mrs Doig, 94 Upper Craigs
Misses Fotheringham, 65 Bannock-
    burn rd, St Ninians
J. S. M'Rorie, Upper Bridge st
Mrs Reid, 22 Queen st
Miss E. Thompson, 19 Seaforth pl
Stirling Steam Laundry—Wyllie,
    Sandeman & Co., 52 Abbey rd
Upper Craigs Laundry Coy.—(M.
    Wallace) 53 Upper Craigs
Mrs Young and Miss Hall, 14
    Park lane

Manufacturers.

Messrs Templeton, Rockvale Mills,.
    Craigs
Bannockburn Hosiery Company,
    Abbey rd pl
Caledonian Carpet Co., Forthbank
The Rubber Company of Scotland,
    Ltd. (india rubber and asbes-
    tos manufacturers), Forthvale
    Works
John E. Thurman & Co. (wool,
    waste, and flock), Bridgehaugh
    Mill

Manure Merchants.

Jas. Gray & Co., Upper Craigs
Parlan M'Farlan, Shore
A. M'Lachlan, Son & Co., View-
    field st

Millers and Grain Merchants.

D. & J. M'Ewen & Co., 16 Park lane
R. Walls, 66 Port st

Medical Practitioners and Surgeons

Alex. Chalmers, surgeon, 4 Randolph terrace
John Drew, M.D., Rudecroft, 28 Dumbarton rd
Alex. Flett, 4 York pl
Lt.-Col. Greig, surgeon general, 16 Melville ter
R. C. Highet, 5 Park avenue
A. B. Laidlaw, 13 Randolph ter
J. E. Moorhouse, M.D., 6 Melville terrace
J. H. Murray, 19 Glebe crescent
D. M'Fadyen, M.D., C.M., 1 Park avenue
Peter M'Fadyen, M.D., 1 Park av
P. F. M'Farlan, 11 Pitt terrace
W. A. Mackintosh, 3 Park ter
Graham Skinner, Allan Park House
A. F. Wilson, surgeon, 1 Viewfield pl
A. Whytt, 20 Clarendon pl

Mill and Wheel Wrights.

M. Finlayson & Son, Springfield
Kemp & Nicholson, Forth st
W. M'Naughtan, Forth st
James Stewart, 44 Lower Craigs
Robertson & M'Laren, Craigmill

Milliners.

Mrs Borrowman, 43 Barnton st
Co-Operative Society, 18 King st
Dunn & Wilson, 24 Port st
Miss J. Gardner, 63 Barnton st
G. R. Jenkins, 43 King st
James Paterson, 42 King st
Miss Jollie, 36 Arcade
T. Menzies & Co., 36 King st
M'Aree Bros., 57-59 King st
M'Culloch & Young, 1 Baker st
Miss Mills, 9 Main st, St Ninians
Miss A. Millar, 15 Friars st
M'Lachlan & Brown, 8-10 Murray pl
T. Paterson Orr, 21 King st
Miss Rutherford, 46 Arcade
Misses Thomson, 9-11 Arcade
R. Wallace, 89 Port st

Musicsellers and Piano Tuners.

James Phillips, 19 Nelson pl
Sowdan & Forgan, 6 Murray pl
C. P. Stevenson, 23 Arcade

Music Teachers.

Mrs J. M. Brown, 19 Queen st
Miss Davie, Irvine pl
Miss D. Dawson, 6 Viewfield pl
J. Dawson, James st
J. Dennison, 17 George st (violin)
W. H. Dobson, 9 Albert pl
Miss Fergusson, 24 Queen st
G. F. Forsyth, 3 Newhouse
Wm. Hay, 23 Queen st
Miss Henderson, 28 Up. Bridge st
D. Burns Jamieson, 87 Port st
C. Lennox, 17 Bruce st (violin)
A. W. Marchant, Mus. Doc. 10 Glebe crescent
Miss M'Elfrish, 4 Queen st
Miss M'Ewen, 87 Port st
Miss Nisbet, 10 Barnton st
Miss Oliphant, Causewayhead rd
Miss Owen, 55 Wallace st
Mrs Paterson, 21 Wallace st
Miss Samuel, 12 Princes st

Nail and Bolt Makers.

Arch. Jenkins, St Ninians
Arch. M'Lachlan, Whins of Milton
Jas. Somerville, St Ninians
J. & W. Somerville, St Ninians
J. Brown, Stripeside, St Ninians

Newsagents.

Mrs Annie Collins, 54 Barnton st
Miss Allan, 55 Barnton st
Bookstall, Railway Station
J. Cattanach, 13 Bow st
Mrs Crocket, 71 King st
Miss Donaldson, 35 Baker st
P. Fallin, 100 St Mary's Wynd
Wm. Gordon, 118-120 Baker st and 34 Forth crescent
Miss Gowans, 3 Maxwell pl
J. Hardie, 90 Cowane st

Mrs S. E. Hay, 6 Dumbarton rd (post office)
A. Henderson, 28 Bow st
Miss Kenny, 62 Upper Craigs
J. Lawrie, 12 Viewfield pl
Miss J. Leighton, 19 Main st, St Nin
P. Mackintosh, 50 Baker st
Mrs Marriott, 62 Cowane st
Miss C. M'Bain, 25 Arcade
E. Millar, 74 Baker st
Mrs Paterson, 39-41 Cowane st
Miss A. Paterson, 29 Upper Craigs
W. L. Shirra, 83 Port st
W. Somerville, 2 Barnton st
T. Stevenson, 13 Baker st
J. B. Taylor, Post Office, St Ninians
Miss C. Thomson, 55 Cowane st
A. Ure, 39 Main st, St Ninians

Nurses.

Miss M. Elliott, 61 Barnton st
Mrs A. Ewing, 108 Upper Craigs
Mrs Finlayson, 8 Lower Bridge st
Mrs Kerr, 12 Bayne st
Mrs Lockhart, 6 Douglas st
Mrs Jessie M'Laren, 24 Newhouse
Mrs M'Nee, Woodside pl, Cambusbarron
Miss M. Pow, 52 Cowane st
Mrs C. Scotland, 3 Burghmuir
Mrs Smith, 102 Upper Craigs
Mrs Welsh, 76 Baker st

Oil Merchants.

J. Walker & Co, 61 Upper Craigs

Opticians.

M. O. Thomson, 18 Murray pl
J. A. Gordon, 12 Barnton st
Walker & Skinner, 67 King st

Pawnbrokers.

Mrs Cormack, 8 St Mary's Wynd
A. J. Mullen, 16-18 Bow st
William Simpson, 32 Bow st

Painters.

Robert Brown, 33 Friars st
Cargill & Thomson, 16 King st
Wm. Carson & Sons, 54 Port st
A. Deans, Causewayhead
A. Douglas & Sons, King's Park rd
G. Henderson & Son, 20 Viewfield street
Adam Johnstone, 30-34 Arcade
John Lamb, 27 Dumbarton rd and 25 Port st
T. Scotland, 25 Broad st
John Walls, 5 Maxwell pl

Perambulator Makers.

Walker & Paton, Burnside Works, Lower Craigs
M'Ewen & Co., Abbey Road Works
D. Sinclair, 12 Thistle st

Photographers.

Charles Begbie, 2 Wallace st
Morton, 48 Arcade
P. D. Nairn, Allan Park
Crowe & Rodgers, 57 Murray pl
Wm. Smellie, 5 Viewfield pl
F. E. Bussell, Castle Esplanade

Plasterers.

Robert Foster, Burghmuir
Alexander Walls, Thistle st and Forth st

Plumbers, Gasfitters, and Brassfounders.

William Cairns, 1 Orchard pl
Thomas Campbell & Co, 8 Spittal st
J. & J. Duff, 16 and 29 Dumbarton road

Robert Frater, 73 Port st
David Hardie, 66 Upper Craigs
John Johnstone, St Ninians
John Merrilees, 14 Friars st
John Scott, 128 Main st, St Ninians
John Steel, 22 Murray pl
J. & C. Steel, Stirling Brass Works, Forth st
John Wright, 10 Maxwell pl

Potato Merchants.

Thomas Callum, Orchard pl
John Corser, St Ninians
Donald Ferguson, 76 Upper Craigs
D. Jenkins, St Ninians
Stevenson Bros., 40 Barnton st

Printers (Letterpress).

Cook & Wylie, 9 Barnton st— Telephone No. 0169
James Hogg & Co., 9 King st
Hutton & Turnbull, 45 Murray pl
H. M. Kirkwood & Sons, 33 King st
John Jamieson, 28-34 Upper Craigs

Publicans.

David Brock, 18 Broad st
John Brimber, 2-4 Bannockburn rd
R. Christie, Sun Inn, 55 King st
Clark Donaldson, 46½ Baker st
Janet Gillespie, 50 Upper Craigs
William Gilfillan, 51 Glasgow rd., St Ninians
A. S. Greig, 42 Broad st
J. Burnett, 144-146 Main st, St Ninians
A Hunter, Lorne Tavern, Castle Wynd
John Hunter, 51 Barnton st
Wm. Johnstone, 91 St Mary's Wynd
A. V. Kennedy, 36 St Mary's Wynd
John King, 55 Port st

Mrs Laurie, 66-68 Baker st
Mrs Lees, 94 Baker st
Mrs Lennox, Station rd
G. Milne, Abbey Inn, Cam'kenneth
Andrew Murdoch, 55 Baker st
Alex. M'Donald, 16 Main st, St Ninians
Angus M'Ewan, 29-31 King st
John M'Gregor, 1 Wallace st
John M'Lean, Wallace st (Bridge Custom)
John Mitchell, 14-16 Baker st
Thomas Muir, 47 Murray pl
Jas. Oliver, 11 Main st, St Ninians
James Page, 2 Baker st
Andrew Penman, 61 Port st (Port Custom)
Andrew Porter, 2 Lower Bridge st
William Porter, 63 Port st
Public - House Trust, Corn Exchange road
Alex. Roberts, 29 Baker st
A. Roberts, 8 Newhouse
Stevenson Brothers, 8 King st
Mrs M. Taylor, 75 St Mary's Wynd
Mrs Taylor, 7 St John St
W. J. Traynor, 4 St Mary's Wynd
Alex. Watters, 65 Baker st
Mrs Young, 61 Lower Bridge st
Wm. Young, 5 Drip rd

Restaurants and Tea Rooms.

W. & J. Aitken, Barnton st
John Blyth, 30 Baker st
Mrs Bremner, 105 and 115 Baker st
Mrs Peter Comrie, 26 King st
Mrs M'Gowan, 114 Main st, St Nin.
Thomas Elder & Sons, 52 Port st
Thomas Gasser, 38 Barnton st
Miss Kinnaird, 69 Barnton st
Mrs Gill, 45 Cowane st
William Goudie, 73 King st
Miss G. Jamieson, 12-13 Maxwell place
Keith & Ralston, 10 Port st .

P. M'Alpine, 4 Murray pl
Miss M. M'Culloch, 42 Baker st
Angus M'Ewan, 29-31 King st
Donald M'Killop, 51-53 Baker st
J. Millar & Sons, 17 Murray pl
Mrs C. M'Kay, 21 Upper Craigs
M'Lachlan & Brown, 12 Murray pl
Miss Morrison, 11 Viewfield pl
Alex. Norris, 55 Murray pl
Miss Agnes Oswald, 42-44 Arcade
Palace Tea Rooms, Castle Wynd
George Scorgie, 9-11 Seaforth pl
Miss R. Stirling, 2 Spittal st
Miss Templeton, Murray pl
Mrs H. Wylie, Seaforth pl
Miss Eliza Young, 4 Upper Craigs

Saddlers.

T. Gentles & Son, 50 Barnton st
A. Lamond, 83 Main st, St Ninians
Duncan M'Donald, 15 King st
Matthew M'Kinlay, 5 Friars st
A. Milne, 2 Park lane

Sculptors.

William Donaldson, Viewfield pl
Thomas Ross, Station rd

Seedsmen.

John Craig, 3 Murray pl
William Drummond & Sons, Ltd.,
    13 Murray pl
Jas. Gray & Co., 5-9 Upper Craigs;
    stores, 69 Craigs

Slaters.

J. & D. Aitken, 59 Main st, St
    Ninians
Walter Balfour, 31 Upper Craigs
A. Blair, 4 Port st
J. & W. Gentles, 40 Barnton st
T. Maxwell, Douglas st
Milne & Co., 5 Upper Craigs
J. M'Culloch, 66 Spittal st
D. M'Gregor & Co., 1 George st
Oswald & Son, 82 Spittal st

Sewing Machine Manufacturers.

The Singer Sewing Machine Co.,
    22 Barnton st

Smiths, Engineers. and Implement Makers.

W. Bean, Causewayhead
Walker & Paton, Lower Craigs
Andrew Davidson, 32 Baker st
J. Davie & Sons, 26-28 Orchard pl
Kemp & Nicholson, Forth st
Lockhart & Macnab, 34 Craigs
W. & T. Marshall, 16 Dumbarton rd
W. Miller, 4 Park lane
R. Miller & Son, 64 Upper Craigs
W. M'Naughtan, Forth st
John Scoular & Co., Crook
John Simpson & Co, motor car
    builders and makers of
    "Velox" steam coil disin-
    fectors, Whins of Milton
John Syme, 20 Abbey rd

Solicitors.

Archibald & Brown, 53 Port st—
    Jas. Archibald, T. J. Y. Brown
Brown & Murray, 10 Barnton st—
    James Brown, J. G. Murray
David Chrystal, 64 Murray pl
Davidson & Stevenson, 27 Murray
    pl—J. F. Mackie, T. C. Darling
P. Douglas, Murray pl
Fleming & Buchanan, 26 Port st—
    J. S. Fleming, A. C. Buchanan
Ebenezer Gentleman, 2 Wolf Craig
James A. Gibson, 47 Port st
J. S. Henderson, 64 Murray pl
Hill & Whyte, 4 King st—R. A.
    Hill, R. Whyte
A. & J. Jenkins, 80 Port st
D. W. Logie, 20 Murray pl
Mathie, MacLuckie, & Lupton, 22
    King st—R. MacLuckie, J. M.
    MacLuckie, Thomas Lupton

Morrison & Taylor, 46 Barnton st
  —Eben. Morrison, R. Taylor,
  William Donaldson
T. & J. Muirhead, 4 Port st
H. D. M'Lellan, 48 Barnton st
Alex. Paterson, 62 Port st
Philp & Dobbie, 3 Port st—James
  Dobbie
E. W. Simpson, 1 Princes st
Wingate & Curror, 2 Dumbarton rd
  —John G. Curror, Sheriff
  Clerk; Henry Robb

Saw Trimmer.

William Ritchie, 21 Seaforth pl

Stair Railer.

Daniel Barker, 6 Forth st

Stockbrokers.

M'Lean & Henderson, 53 Murray pl

Tailors and Clothiers.

William Brown, 2 Arcade
John Bennett, 20 Port st
Co-operative Society, Barnton st
John Cuthbert, 60 Baker st
James Dalgetty, 95 Baker st
James Dowell, 56 Barnton st
John Ewing, 11 King st
Thos. Ferguson & Son, 2 York pl
Jas. Forsyth, 14 Upper Bridge st
John R. Good, 8 Wallace st
Harvey & Harris, Barnton st
John Howat, 17 King st
William Hynd, 11 King st
Jas. G. Kinnaird, 4 Port st
J. Jamieson & Co., 28 King st
Lawsons Limited, 32-36 Baker st
James Minty, 48 King st
M'Aree Brothers, 57-61 King st

M'Culloch & Young, 79 King st
Jas. Mackenzie, 50 Cowane st
John M'Kay, 49 Port st
J. M'Kinlay & Son, 59-63 Murray pl
James Nicol, 69 King st
J. Robertson & Sons, 16 Murray pl
P. Robertson, 55 Lower Bridge st
Soutar & Co., 53 Murray pl
W. Strang & Co., 67 Barnton st
John Young, 62 Port st

Teachers (Private).

Miss J. Algie (painting), c/o John-
  ston, Arcade
J. D. Black, 59 Cowane st (bagpipes)
Miss Buchan, 1 Esplanade
Miss Carter, 47 Port st (needlework)
Mrs Crossen, 3 Forth cres (dresscut.)
J. C. Dobbie (elocution), 53 Port st
J. Ferguson (elocution), 5 Millar pl
R. C. Forbes, 15 Newhouse (short-
  hand, &c.)
J. Gordon, 24 Bruce st (dancing)
Miss N. Harvey, Gowanbrae (paint.)
J. H. Hastings, Murray pl (shorth'nd)
D. R. Mackenzie, 6 Maxwell pl (danc.)
Mrs Morley, Whins of Milton
  (decorative metal work)
John M'Kenzie, 3 Victoria pl
Miss Paul, 18 Viewfield st (sewing)
Miss C. Stewart, Torbrex (sewing)

Telephone.

National Telephone Coy, Ltd.—
  District Office and Public Call
  Office, 33 Friars st.; Public
  Call Office, 17 King st

Tile Layers.

Gray & Co., Shore rd

Tinsmiths.

A. M'Callum, 14 Spittal st
Graham & Morton, King st

Tobacconists

Miss Nellie Allan, 55 Barnton st
J. Cattanach, 13 Bow st
Mrs Annie Collins, 54 Barnton st
John Dempster, 6 Port st
P. Fallin, 100 St Mary's Wynd
Miss Gowans, 3 Maxwell pl
W. Gordon, 118-120 Baker st and
   32-38 Forth cres
Alex. Kerr, 11 Friars st
J. Lawrie, 12 Viewfield pl
Miss C. M'Bain, 28 Arcade
P. Mackintosh, 50 Baker st
Miss A. Paterson, 29 Upper Craigs
George Riddle, 60 Port st
John Sloan, Murray pl
James Smith, 39 Murray pl
W. Somerville, 2 Barnton st
W. Templeton, 85 Port st
A. Ure, 39 Main st, St Ninians

Tobacco Manufacturer.

John Dempster, 54-56 Upper Craigs

Threshing Mill Proprietors

Raines & Co., Ltd., Bridgehaugh
Andrew Bean, Causewayhead

Umbrella Makers.

A. D. Henderson (successor to A.
   Baird & Son), 38 Murray pl
W. S. Palmer, 44-46 Port st, and
   Barnton st
R. W. Salmond, 53 Barnton st

Undertakers.

Jas. Currie, 16 Dumbarton rd
John Durham, Bannockburn
Robert Forrest, 9 Friars st
T. Henderson & Sons, 43 Port st
Fairful, Wilson, & Somers, 81 Port st
Thos. Ferguson, 14 Dumbarton rd
Mrs Lennox, Station Hotel
J. F. Lorimer, 16 Spittal st
C. M'Lauchlan, 37 St Mary's Wynd
Stevenson Bros., Golden Lion Hotel
Andrew Simpson, 44 Murray pl
   and 8 Bow st
H. P. Watt, 22 Baker st

Valuators.

Thomas Currie, 16 King st
T. Henderson & Sons, 43 Port st
J. & W. Ronald, 20 James st
Andrew Simpson, 44 Barnton st
H. P. Watt, 22 Baker st

Venetian Blind Maker.

John Murray, 32 Baker st

Veterinary Surgeons.

T. L. Houston, 6 Upper Craigs
John M. Stewart, 72 Murray pl

Waterproof and Rubber Goods.

Stirlingshire Rubber Co., 1-3 Arcade

Whisky Blenders.

Mackintosh & Mackintosh, 10
   Thistle st

Wood Merchants.

Thomas Brisbane, 16 Wallace st
Dunn Brothers, 16-18 Abbey rd
James Johnston, 28-30 Abbey rd

Wood Carver.

George R. Paton, 17 Lower Craigs

Wool Merchants.

Robert Gilfillan, 17 Burghmuir
William Hunter, 8 Glebe crescent

Woollen Merchants.

Fleming, Reid & Co., 70 Port st

Miscellaneous

Bottle Exchange Co., 61 Up. Craigs
H. Dalgetty, clog maker, 97 Baker st
Wm. Hill, bird dealer, 47 Broad st
D. Rennie & Co., Drip rd (fire-
   wood, &c.)
Scottish Guild of Handicraft, Ltd.,
   Burghmuir—art metal workers,
   &c.
A. Wilson, public analyst, Whins of
   Milton

GENERAL DIRECTORY.

(Alphabetically Arranged.)

A

Abercrombie, Mrs, 59 Cowane st
Abercromby, James, plumber, 7 Bruce st
Abercromby, John, slater, 27 King st
Abercromby, J., warehouseman, 55 Upper craigs
Adam, Geo., china merchant, 3 Royal gardens
Adam, Hay, carter, 39 Lower craigs
Adam, Rev. James A., 9 Douglas st
Adam, R., china merchant, 21 Port st
Adam, Alex., shoemaker, 106 Baker st
Adam & Yates, Ltd., cork merchants, Lower
    craigs
Adams, J., coal merc., Aitken's bldgs., B'burn rd
Adams, John, art metal worker, 8 Nelson pl
Adams, Mrs, 11 Royal gardens
Adams, Mrs Elizabeth, 10 Winchel pl
Adams, R., tailor, 32 Spittal st
Adams, William, labourer, 58 Cowane st
Adams, Wm., tanner, 76 Main st, St. Ninians
Adamson & Co., T., grocers, 29 Arcade
Adamson, Miss Elizabeth, 4 Forrest rd
Adamson, Robt., goods clerk, Causewayhead
Agnew, John, painter, 118 Main st, St. Ninians
Agnew, Rev. W., editor, Tract Depot, 24 Allan pk
Aikman, William, joiner, 3 Bayne st
Aimer, George, hairdresser, 23-26 Baker st
Aird, Miss Agnes, 50 Arcade
Aitken, Adam, labourer, 82 Cowane st
Aitken, Miss C. H., 14 Snowdon pl
Aitken, David, slater, 59 Main st, St. Ninians
Aitken, Geo., cabinetmaker, 3 Lower craigs
Aitken, John, slater, 59 Main st, St. Ninians
Aitken, Alex. J., signalman, 10 Bayne st
Aitken, J., upholsterer, 24 Bow st
Aitken, James, fireman, 13 Glencoe rd
Aitken, James, labourer, 48 Cowane st
Aitken, J. P., ironmonger, 5 Viewfield st
Aitken, Mrs Mary, 1 Dumbarton rd

Aitken, Mrs M., 2 High st, Cambuskenneth
Aitken, Mrs, 53 Glasgow rd, St. Ninians
Aitken, Mrs, caretkr. Inl. Rev. offices, Murray pl
Aitken, Mrs, 24 Bow st
Aitken, Mrs M., 23 Baker st
Aitken, Peter, builder, 11 Newhouse
Aitken, Thomas, vanman, 24 Baker st
Aitken, William, baker, 52 Baker st
Aitken, Wm., baker, 3-5 Main st, St. Ninians
Aitken, W. & J., bakers, 45 Barnton st, 3 and 54
    Baker st, and 9 St Mary's wynd
Aikman, Mrs Thomson, 21 Snowdon pl
Alexander, George, jeweller, 31 Murray pl
    house—6 Park pl
Alexander, Miss C., 6 Park pl
Alexander, Miss Jane, 9 Newhouse
Alexander, Mrs Jane, 8 Union st
Alexander, Mrs Jessie, 10 George st
Alexander, Peter, joiner, 63 Newhouse
Alexander, T., chemical manufacturer, Brentham
    Park
Alexander, William, 15 Park pl
Allan, George, 44 Broad st
Allan, John, miner, Waterloo house
Allan, John, architect, 32 Dumbarton rd;
    office—11 King st
Allan, Peter, hairdresser, 45 Broad st
Allan, Robert, fruiterer, 3a Friars st
Allan, Thomas, labourer, 24 Lower castlehill
Allan, Miss, tobacconist, 55 Barnton st
Allan, Mrs Janet, 13 Burghmuir
Allan, Miss M., 32 Dumbarton rd
Allan, Mrs Margaret, 35 Millar pl
Allan & Son, R., bakers, 35-17 St. Mary's wynd
Allan, Wm., clerk, 13 Viewfield st
Allan, Wm., brushmaker, 11 Winchel pl
Allardice, Charles, brakesman, 32 James st
Allardice, Mrs Elizabeth, 32 James st
Allardice, Mrs, 16 Lower Bridge st
Allardyce, John, porter, 17 Seaforth pl
Allison, Robt., craneman, 7 St. Mary's wynd
Allison, W., roadman, Woodside Cot., C'wayhead
Alloa Coal Co.—J. Dewar, agent, 7 Murray pl;
    depôt—Wallace st
Allsworth, William, labourer, 48 Lower castlehill
Alridge, Henry, labourer, 28 St. Mary's wynd
Anderson, A., joiner, Rose Cot., Causewayhead
Anderson, A., car driver, Forthview, C'wayhead
Anderson, Alex., labourer, 35 Cowane st
Anderson, Alex., 12 Union st

GENERAL DIRECTORY.

Anderson Bros., hatters, 3 King st
Anderson, F., engine driver, 6 Douglas st
Anderson, Geo., labourer, 8 Broad st
Anderson, James, tacklemaker, 66 Cowane st
Anderson, John, engine driver, 20 Forth st
Anderson, John, engine driver, 9 Bruce st
Anderson, John, blacksmith, 12 Albany cres
Anderson, John, blacksmith, 24 Cowane st
Anderson, John, painter, 46 Cowane st
Anderson, J., cabinetmaker, 4 Upper Bridge st
Anderson, Miss Agnes, 8 Melville ter
Anderson, Miss Helen, 8 Melville ter
Anderson, Miss, draper, 7-9 Main st, St. Ninians
Anderson, Miss, 36 Queen st
Anderson, Margaret, 4 Douglas st
Anderson, Mrs, Craiglea, Causewayhead
Anderson, Mrs Margaret, 23 Broad st
Anderson, Robert, plumber, 59 Cowane st
Anderson, Robt., cabinetmaker, 4 Port st
Anderson, W. J., S.P.C.C. insp., 7 Murray pl
Anderson, Wm., engine driver, 98 Upper craigs
Anderson, Wm., 57 Newhouse
Anderson, Wm., labourer, 5 St. John st
Anderson & Sons, R., building contractors, 61
    Upper craigs and 44 Murray pl
Andrew, Rev. Alex. S., 3 Millar pl
Andrew, Robert, miner, 13 Viewfield st
Andrew, Wm., baker, 26 Main st, St Ninians
Andrews, H. C., cabinetmaker, 17 Well Green
Angus, Arch., blacksmith, 10 Union st
Angus, Arch., painter, 33 King st
Angus, Rev. Jas., 11 Upper Bridge st
Anstruther, Daniel, confectioner, 72 Upper craigs
Anstruther, Mrs, confectioner, 54 Cowane st
Arbuthnot, D., engineer, 9 Clarendon pl
Archibald, John, baker, 13 Broad st
Archibald, Miss, Grange House, Causewayhead
Archibald, Mrs Mary, 29 Snowdon pl
Archibald, Jas., beadle, 5 Kirk wynd, St. Ninians
Archibald & Brown, solicitors, 53 Port st
Armour, John, coachman, Torbrex House
Armstrong, Alex., vanman, 47 Cowane st
Armstrong, James, blacksmith, 19 Upper craigs
Armstrong, J. W., draper, 18 Friars st
Armstrong, Robt., guard, 5 Winchel pl
Armstrong, Robt., blacksmith, 9 Bannockburn rd
Arnold, Rev. John A., 5 Randolph rd
Arnott, Rev. John, M.A., 12 Park ter
Arthur, Thomas, clerk, 7 George st
Arthur, Thomas, joiner, 43 Cowane st

Arscott, Conductor W. H., A.O.C., 1 Millar pl

Arthur & Son, George, drapers, 14 Barnton st;
    house—10 James st
Ashby, Rev. A. (Baptist assist.), 22 Bruce st
Atha, Chas. G., 1 Royal gardens
Auchinvole, R., pitsinker, 24 Newhouse
Auld, And., spirit merchant, 2 Park ter
Aytoun, Major, D.S.O., The Castle

B

Bailey, James G., traveller, 11 Coburg av
Baillies, James, rubber worker, Cambuskenneth
Bain, James, labourer, 6 Lower craigs
Bain, Miss Margaret, 5 Balmoral pl
Bain, Miss, dressmaker, 52 Barnton st
Bain, Miss Mary, 25 Port st
Bain, Peter, butcher, 1A Friars st
Bain, Thomas, residenter, 81 Baker st
Bain, Thomas, mason, 69 Baker st
Bain, Mrs William, 30 Barnton st
Bain, W., photographic artist, 7 Bellfield rd
Bain, Wm., painter, 50 Raploch
Baird, J., roadman, 19 Weaver row, St. Ninians
Baird, James, blacksmith, 36 James st
Baird, Miss Joan, 9 Newhouse
Baird, Miss Margaret, 31 Newhouse
Baird, T., ploughman, 2 Sunnyside, St. Ninians
Baird, William, retired farmer, 13 Abbey rd
Baker, Edmund, art master, 21 Clarendon pl
Baker, Leonard, ret. art master, 22 Albert pl
Bald, Mrs Isabella, 17 Randolph rd
Baldie, Miss M. A., dressmaker, 6 Allan pk
Balfour, Mrs Jane, 9 Newhouse
Balfour, Peter, draper, 13 Abbey rd
Balfour, Walter, slater, 33 and 57 Upper craigs
Ballantyne, Miss Mary, 9 Princes st
Balloch, John, hawker, 4 Bow st
Banks, Mrs, 27 Wallace st
Banks, James, jeweller, 18 Port st
Banks, Wm., residenter, 47 Port st
Bannigan, T. B., traveller, 27 Irvine pl
Bannockburn Hosiery Co., 11 Abbey rd pl
Bankrupt Stock Realisation Co., 10 Arcade
Barclay, Andrew, miner, 48 Baker st
Bardsley, Mrs C., 4 Barn rd
Barclay, Chas., tailor, 3A Main st, St. Ninians

Barclay, James, nailer, 63 Newhouse
Barclay, John, butler, Torbrex House
Barclay, John, warehouseman, 76 Cowane st
Barclay, J., nailer, 13 Glasgow rd, St. Ninians
Barclay, Mrs Helen, 48 Port st
Barclay, Mrs Janet, 61 Main st, St. Ninians
Barclay, R., bootmaker, 154 Main st, St. Ninians
Barclay, W., grocer, 11 Glasgow rd, St. Ninians
Barclay, W., telephone linesman, 34 Nelson pl
Barker, Daniel, stair-railer, 6 Forth st; house
    —Shiphaugh
Barnes, Mrs Janet, 66 Spittal st
Barnett, Robt., engine driver, 75 King st
Barr, George, hairdresser, 2-20 Bow st
Barr, John, surveyor of taxes, 2 Clarendon pl
Barr, John, county san. inspec., 48 Barnton st;
    house—1 Forth cres
Barr, John, miner, 103 Main st, St. Ninians
Barrat, Thomas, miner, 44 Baker st
Barrie, Hugh, hawker, 18 St. Mary's wynd
Barton, John, labourer, 18 St. Mary's wynd
Basil, Staff Q.-M.-Sergeant, A.O.C., 1 Millar pl
Bateman, J., tel. linesman, 101 Main st, St. Ninians
Battison, Alex., porter, 31 Lower Bridge st
Battison, P., gilder, 61 Cowane st
Battison, William, 32 Upper Bridge st
Battison, Wm., town's foreman, 30 Queen st
Bauchop, Mrs E., Cambuskenneth
Baxter, Alex., labourer, 70 Main st, St. Ninians
Baxter, Mrs Nicholas, 23 Nelson pl
Baxter, Alex., market gardener, Cambuskenneth
Baxter, John, joiner, 1 Bayne st
Baxter, Robt., engine driver, 10 Upper Bridge st
Bayne, David, grocer, 73 Wallace st; house—
    14 Union st
Bayne, Louis, joiner, 5 Bruce st
Bayne, William, labourer, 47 Cowane st
Bean, A., engineer, Sheriffmuirlands, C'wayhead
Bean, Alex., gas worker, 21 Thistle st
Bean, Alexander, plumber, 18 Upper craigs
Bean, David, tailor, 19 Abbey rd
Bean, Miss, sub-Post Office, Causewayhead
Bean, W., blacksmith, Causewayhead
Beath, David, traveller, 10 Wallace st
Beaton, Alex., engine driver, 24 Bruce st
Beattie, Captain A., The Castle
Beattie, Peter, Menmuir Villa, C'wayhead rd
Beckett, Mrs, 12 Friars st
Bee, James, electrician, 20 Raploch
Begbie, Chas., photographer, 2 Wallace st

Begbie, George, cashier, 2 Forth cr
Begbie, John, clerk, 23 Cowane st
Begg, Robert, miner, 13 Lower craigs
Bell, Charles, 36 Dumbarton rd
Bell, D. H., teacher, 10 Dumbarton rd
Bell, James, waiter, 25 Upper craigs
Bell, John, bottler, 16 Union st
Bell, Peter, joiner, 21 Princes st
Bell, Thomas, miner, 12 Newhouse
Bell, William, Lieut.-Colonel, 26 Albert pl
Bellingham, J, coach hirer, 23 St. John st
Bennett, Mrs Anne, 108 Baker st
Bennett, Mrs, Hildontree, Causewayhead
Bennett, Mrs, residenter, 22 Bruce st
Bennett, John, tailor, 20 Port st
Bennett, Robert, grocer, 22 Bruce st
Bennett, William, labourer, 69 Bannockburn rd
Bennie, A., butcher, 12 Friars st
Bennie, Alex., flesher, 65 Barnton st; house
    —15 Irvine pl
Bennie, John, draper, 10 Bruce st
Bently, Joseph, oversman, 2 George st
Bermingham, A., dealer, 9-11 St John st
Bermingham, J., general dealer, 22 Broad st
Bermingham, Thomas, hawker, 20 Broad st
Bertram, Colour-Sergeant, Military hospital,
    Castle wynd
Berrie, David, 18 Port st
Berrie, Mrs Eliz., 150 Main st, St. Ninians
Bethune, F., ret. coachman, 51 Lower Bridge st
Bethune, Wm., porter, 9 Queen st
Bett, D. W., railway guard, 116 Upper craigs
Bett, James, carter, 57 Wallace st
Bett, James, railway guard, 14 Park lane
Betts, Robert, 18 Forth st
Beveridge, Arch., checkweigher, 8 William pl
Beveridge, Mrs Janet, 47 Port st
Beveridge, Wm., miner, 16 Orchard pl
Bewley, H. G., platelayer, 2 King's stables
Bibbie, Lance-Sergt. A. & S. H., 10 Bayne st
Binnie, Henry, cooper, 5 Abbey rd pl
Binnington, J., prison warder, 24 Upper castlehill
Bird, Neilson, 11 Park ter
Birrell, Geo., rubber worker, 6 Lower Bridge st
Birse, John, gardener, Brentham Park
Bishop, Wm., miner, 142 Main st, St. Ninians
Bissett, James, painter, 29 Raploch
Black, Alex., painter, High st, Cambuskenneth
Black, Andrew, mason, 80 Cowane st
Black, Andrew, painter, 27 Queen st

Black, Andrew, shoemaker, 24 Lower castlehill
Black, Arch., roadman, 51 Newhouse
Black, James, plasterer, 44 Cowane st
Black, Mrs Janet, 10 Lower Bridge st
Black, John, labourer, 5 Douglas st
Black, R. B., managing director, Forthvale Works,
    Cornton rd
Black, Thomas, blacksmith, 24 Broad st
Black, Tom, glazier, 58 Cowane st
Blackadder, John, draper, 14 Bruce st
Blackadder, Wm., labourer, 38 St. Mary's wynd
Blackburn, Miss Mary, 20 Allan pk
Blackett, Ralph, insurance supt., 11 Dean cr
Blackwell, R., builder, Craigbank, Causewayhead
Blackwood, J., labourer, 8 George st
Blackwood, Robert, signalman, 34 James st
Blair, Mrs Ann, 24 Broad st
Blair, David, carpet weaver, 2 Upper craigs
Blair, George, cabman, 20 Port st
Blair, James M., hairdresser, 31 Murray pl;
    house—10 Dumbarton rd
Blair, Jas., miner, 6 William pl
Blair, Mrs Mary, 4 Port st
Blair, Thomas, fireman, 32 James st
Blakey, John Wood, 48 Lower castlehill
Blakey, Mrs Rosabella, 17 Melville ter
Blennie, R., lorryman, Aitken's bldgs., B'burn rd
Blewitt, John, nailer, 6 Sunnyside, St. Ninians
Blyth, Mrs Alison, 108 Upper craigs
Blyth, John, insurance agent, 14 Queen st
Blyth, John, caretaker Y.M.C.A. Inst., 2 Allan pk
Blyth, John, confectioner, 30 Baker st
Boag, Mrs, 23 Cowane st
Boag, Wm., gardener, 23 George st
Bogle, Wm., colliery oversman, 15 George st
Boland, James, labourer, 25 Raploch
Bolton, Miss Frances, 28 Park ter
Bolton, Mrs Helen, general dealer, 41 Forth cr;
    house—27 Abbey rd
Bolton, Joseph, rubber worker, 3 Drip rd
Bonnelo, Miss, 17 Douglas st
Booth, John, stableman, 8 Upper Bridge st
Boreland, Miss, saleswoman, 10 Barnton st
Boreland, Mrs Mary, pastrycook, 36-82 Baker st
Border, John, labourer, 13 Winchel pl
Borrowman, Mrs, milliner, 43 Barnton st; house
    —68 Port st
Borthwick, Mrs Margaret, 53 Wallace st
Boswell, William, bootmaker, 18 Baker st; house
    —13 Albert pl

Bowes, Thomas, coachman, Laurelhill, Park ter
Bowie, Alex., clerk, 19 Cowane st
Bowie, Andrew, 13 Queen st
Bowie, Geo., carter, 70 Main st, St. Ninians
Bowie, John, cooper, 69 Lower Bridge st
Bowie, Thomas, joiner, 17 Cowane st
Boyd, Robert, miner, 38 King st
Boyes, E., maltman, 20-24 Upper Bridge st
Boyle, Michael, labourer, 1 King's stables
Boyle, Thomas, platelayer, 94 St. Mary's wynd
Braes, Wm., engineer, 21 Wallace st
Braidwood, A., ret. merc., Elderslie, C'wayhead
Bradford, Thos., Killorn cottage, Park pl
Bradley, John, labourer, 5 Bayne st
Brady, James, mason, 12 Bayne st
Brady, Philip, labourer, 45 St. Mary's wynd
Brannan, Michael, labourer, 8 Broad st
Brannan, Peter, stoker, 36 Broad st
Brannan, Thomas, labourer, 31 Raploch
Bremner, Alex., tailor, 23 Cowane st
Bremner, Mrs C., restaur., 105-107 Baker st
Bremner, Sutherland, fish merc., 20-24 Barnton st
Bremner, Thomas, painter, 4 Upper Bridge st
Bremner, William, restaurateur, 113 Baker st
Brewster, John, clerk, 36 Queen st
Brimber, John, spirit merc., 2-4 Bannockburn rd
Brisbane, Mrs Fanny, 13 Upper craigs
Brisbane, H., tailor, 25 Weaver row, St. Ninians
Brisbane, John, porter, 17 Seaforth pl
Brisbane, Mrs J., 32 James st
Brisbane, Mrs Mary, 7 Sunnyside, St. Ninians
Brisbane, T., smith, 4 Sunnyside, St. Ninians
Brisbane, Thos., wood merchant, 16 Wallace st
      house—6 Park ter
Brisbane, Wm., labourer, 59 Newhouse
Broadway, Miss Etta, 1 Douglas st
Brock, David, spirit merc., 18 Broad st ; house—
      48 Broad st
Brock, Andrew, joiner, 3 Middle craigs
Brodie, ——, Park Villa, Park pl
Brodie, James, packer, 61 Upper craigs
Brodie, James, carter, 20 Spittal st
Brodie, James, nailer, 27 Glasgow rd, St. Ninians
Brodie, John, nailer, 85 Main st, St. Ninians
Brodie, P., baker, 34 Port st ; house—1 Clifford rd
Brogan, John, rubber worker, 5 Bayne st
Brooks, H., millworker, 3 Torbrex, St. Ninians
Brooks, Issac, smith, 35 Lower craigs
Brooksby, Mrs Barbara, 111 Lower Bridge st
Brown, Allan, butcher, 13 Bruce st

Brown, Andrew, 24 Bruce st
Brown, Adam, Craigbank, Causewayhead
Brown, Mrs Agnes, 19 Weaver row, St. Ninians
Brown, Alex., barman, 8 Nelson pl
Brown, And., carter, 70 Main st, St. Ninians
Brown, Archibald, waiter, 107 Lower Bridge st
Brown, Arthur, banker, 2 King st
Brown, Miss Barbara, 18 Main st, St. Ninians
Brown, Mrs Catherine, 4 Bow st
Brown, Mrs E., fruiterer, 6-8 Arcade; house—
   Causewayhead
Brown, Mrs Eliz., 9½ Weaver row, St. Ninians
Brown, Henry, insurance agent, 15 Seaforth pl
Brown, James, barman, 13 Glencoe rd
Brown James, goods clerk, 10 Viewfield st
Brown, James, weaver, 5 Middle craigs
Brown, James, wool sorter, 80 Upper craigs
Brown, James, solicitor, 11 Windsor pl
Brown, Jas., pensioner, 74 Main st, St. Ninians
Brown, James C., clerk, 10 Bruce st
Brown, John, draper, 37-39 Baker st; house—3
   Allan pk
Brown John, broker, 112-114 Baker st
Brown, John, grocer, 51 Murray pl; house—5
   Newhouse
Brown, John, labourer, 2 George st
Brown, J., bolt mkr., 9½ Weaver row, St. Ninians
Brown, J., furniture dealer, 79-81-83 Baker st
Brown, J., law clerk, St. Leonard's, C'wayhead
Brown, Miss Jane, shopkeeper, 77 Port st
Brown, Lambert, traveller, 5 Park pl
Brown, Miss, 14 Drummond pl
Brown, Miss, teacher, 17 Newhouse
Brown, Mrs Janet, 19 Queen st
Brown, Miss Marion, 23 Queen st
Brown, Miss M., milliner, Manse cr, St. Ninians
Brown, Mrs M., french polisher, 85 Baker st
Brown, Mrs, 30 Broad st
Brown, Mrs, 30 Cowane st
Brown, Rev. Percival, 10 Clarendon pl
Brown, Peter, shoemaker, 8 George st
Brown, P., plumber, 1 Main st, St. Ninians
Brown, R., millwkr., 17 Glasgow rd, St. Ninians
Brown, Richard, miner, 9 Borestone cres
Brown, Robt. A., merchant, 19 Victoria pl
Brown, Mrs Robert, 28 Queen st
Brown, Robert, painter, 33 Friars st
Brown, Robert, miner, 79 Upper Bridge st
Brown, Robt., 3 Calton Cottages
Brown, Thomas, draper, 8 Bruce st

Brown, T., rubber worker, 11 Lower Bridge st
Brown, T. J. Y., solicitor, and Session Clerk for St
    Ninians, 53 Port st; house—31 Randolph rd
Brown, Mrs Thos., 7½ Weaver row, St. Ninians
Brown, W., colliery manager, 49 Glasgow rd, St.
    Ninians
Brown, Mrs William, confectioner, 87 Baker st
Brown, William, weaver, 25 Abbey rd
Brown, William, furniture dealer, 86 Baker st
Brown, William, outfitter, 2 Arcade; house—13
    Coburg av
Brown, Wm., 21 Weaver row, St. Ninians
Brown, Wm., baker, 19 Weaver row, St. Ninians
Brown, Wm., platelayer, 12 Spittal st
Brown, Wm. M., house factor, 10 Princes st
Brown & Murray, solicitors, 10 Barnton st
Brown & Wilson, surgeon dentists, 76 Port st
Bruce, John, agent, 2 Dean cr
Bruce, Wm., timekeeper, 86 St. Mary's wynd
Bruce, H. E., tailor, High st, Cambuskenneth
Brunton, John, lather, 14 Baker st
Brunton, William, miner, 10 Bow st
Brunton, Wm., bootmaker, 15 Well Green
Bryant, Sergt.-Major T., A.O.C., 5 Millar pl
Bryce, James, porter, 8 Douglas st
Bryce, Mrs Janet, 43 Cowane st
Bryce, John, shoemaker, 48 Baker st
Bryce, Wm., cabinetmaker, 33 King st
Bryson, Mrs Helen, 43 Lower craigs
Buchan, Miss Agnes, 24 Snowdon pl
Buchan, David, lathsplitter, 21 Seaforth pl
Buchan, James, lathsplitter, 17 Bruce st
Buchan, Miss Jane, 1 Castle esplanade
Buchan, Robert, clerk, 25 Abbey rd
Buchan, Thomas, baker, 68 Port st
Buchanan, Mrs A., 5 Park lane
Buchanan, Alex., coachman, 28 Park ter
Buchanan, Andw., dairyman, 40 Lower castlehill
Buchanan, Andrew, grocer, 9 Baker st; house
    —17 Abercromby pl
Buchanan, And., fish merchant, 13 Barnton st
Buchanan, Andrew, painter, 14 Baker st
Buchanan, Miss Annie, 10 Albert pl
Buchanan, Mrs Clementina, 76 Spittal st
Buchanan, C., stockbroker, Deroran, Polmaise rd
Buchanan, D., painter, 13 Towers pl, C'wayhead
Buchanan, D., Inland Revenue, 10 Douglas ter
Buchanan, Mrs Ellen, 12 St. Mary's wynd
Buchanan, Mrs Grace, 57 Lower Bridge st
Buchanan, Miss Griffiths, 22 Snowdon pl

Buchanan, Mrs Helen, 2 Forth cr
Buchanan, James, lathsplitter, 63 Baker st
Buchanan, James, joiner, 9 Broad st
Buchanan, Mrs Jane, 32 James st
Buchanan, John, grocer, 7-9 Broad st
Buchanan, J., butcher, 82 Main st, St. Ninians
Buchanan, Private J. L., 25 Married quarters
Buchanan, Miss Kate, 92 Cowane st
Buchanan, Miss, 35 Snowdon pl
Buchanan, Miss, 6 Pitt ter
Buchanan, Mrs, 3 William pl
Buchanan, Robert, baker, 13 Bruce st
Buchanan, William, miner, $38\frac{1}{2}$ Cowane st
Buchanan, W., vanman, 21 Glasgow rd, St. Ninians
Buckingham, S., tailor's manager, 5 James st
Bulloch, George, broker, 96-98 Baker st
Bundy, Edward, fireman, 2 King's stables
Bundy, John, carpenter, 4 Upper Bridge st
Bundy, Joseph, grocer, 10 Bayne st
Buntine, J. R., Hon. Sheriff-Substitute for Stirlingshire, Torbrex House
Burden's Brewery, Irvine pl
Burden, Mrs Janet, The Ridge, 12 Irvine pl
Burgess, Andrew, labourer, 40 Upper castlehill
Burgess, David, cabinetmaker, 25 Newhouse
Burgoyne, Thomas, tailor, 88 St. Mary's wynd
Burke, Mrs Mary, 20 Broad st
Burke, Mich., engine driver, 10 Upper Bridge st
Burmie, William, scavenger, 24 Baker st
Burness, Arthur, upholsterer, 25 Newhouse
Burnett, James, miner, 118 Main st, St. Ninians
Burnett, J., wine merchant, 144-146 Main st, St. Ninians: house—1 Borestone cres
Burnie, William, labourer, 13 Friars st
Burns, Miss Jessie, Lizville, Causewayhead
Burns, John, painter, 3 Middle craigs
Burns, Robt., gardener, Beechwood
Burns, W., coal merchant, Wallace st; house—23 Queen st
Burt, Andrew, 52 Cowane st
Bussell, F. E., photographer, Castle esplanade

C

Caddell, T., waiter, M'Ewen's Buildings C'head
Cairney, David, miner, 41 Bannockburn rd
Cairns, John, traveller, 2 Coburg av

Cairns, Robert, goods guard, 5 Bayne st
Cairns, Robert, accountant, 24 King st
Cairns, William, plumber, 5 Bruce st
Calder, Alex., joiner, 1A Main st
Calder, Mrs M., 25 St John st
Calder, Mrs, 1 Clarendon pl
Caldwell, Thos., labourer, 64 Main st
Callary, Mrs, 6 St. Mary's wynd
Callinan, Peter, labourer, 10 Spittal st
Cambie, Mrs, 12 St. Mary's wynd
Cambridge, Jas., boot salesman, 15 Newhouse
Cameron, Alex., insurance agent, 42 Spittal st
Cameron, Alex., millwright, 8 St. Mary's wynd
Cameron, Alex., tailor, 16 Union st
Cameron, Mrs Christina, 13 Wallace st
Cameron, D., 57 Lower Bridge st
Cameron, Duncan, porter, 29 Spittal st
Cameron, Mrs E., 3 Well Green
Cameron, James, joiner, Cambuskenneth
Cameron, Mrs Jane, 63 Newhouse
Cameron, Mrs Jessie, 10 Upper Craigs
Cameron, John, labourer, 20 Bow st
Cameron, John, guide, 60 Baker st
Cameron, Mrs Mary, 41 Newhouse
Cameron, Miss M., 27 Cowane st
Cameron, Mrs, 19 Victoria sq
Cameron, Peter, joiner, 7 Bruce st
Cameron, Wm., bricklayer, 27 Irvine pl
Cameron, Wm., coachman, 9 Glebe cres
Campbell, Mrs Agnes, 12 Weaver row, St Ninians
Campbell, Alex., plumber, 19 Cowane st
Campbell, Alex. R., joiner, 19 Spittal st
Campbell, Andrew, miner, 29 Queen st
Campbell, Arch., shoemaker, 20 St. John st
Campbell, Charles, miner, 38 St. Mary's wynd
Campbell, Mrs Charlotte, 4 Springfield pl
Campbell, Chas., ostler, 12 Orchard pl
Campbell, Dugald, butcher, 20 Baker st; house
    —7 Abbey rd
Campbell, Duncan, butcher, 61 Wallace st
Campbell, D., iron merchant, 3 Drummond p
Campbell, Mrs Euphemia, 74 Main st
Campbell, Mrs E., 25 Wallace st
Campbell, Miss Grace, 8 Windsor pl
Campbell, Hugh, dyer, 31 Upper Craigs
Campbell, Hugh, labourer, 1 James st
Campbell, Hugh, scavenger, 51 Main st
Campbell, James, butcher, 33 Queen st
Campbell, James, carter, 52 Lower Bridge st
Campbell, James, labourer, 10 Bayne st

Campbell, Jas. H., reader, 53 Lower Bridge st
Campbell, James, bottler, 2 Springfield pl
Campbell, Mrs Jane, 2 Upper Craigs
Campbell, John, 53 Lower Bridge st
Campbell, John, lorryman, 10 Upper Craigs
Campbell, J., tailor, 4 Bank st
Campbell, J., carpet weaver, 35 Upper Craigs
Campbell, Mrs Jessie, 24 Baker st
Campbell, John, coachman, 6 Baker st
Campbell, J. W., Bank of Scotland, and County
  rates office, 10 Friars st
Campbell, Matthew, weaver, 64 Upper Craigs
Campbell, Miss Mary, 18 Abercromby pl
Campbell, Miss, 7 Park ter
Campbell, Mrs, 4 William pl
Campbell, Mrs, 75 King st
Campbell, Mrs, Bridge of Allan rd.,Causewayhead
Campbell, Mrs, 24 Union st
Campbell, Peter, lorryman, 17 Seaforth pl
Campbell, P., Glasgow carrier, 33 King st
Campbell, Robert, mason, 13 Bruce st
Campbell, Robert, tailor, 8 Broad st
Campbell, Thomas, plumber, 2 Bruce st
Campbell, William, moulder, 10 Bow st
Campbell, Wm., miner, 15 Well Green
Campbell & Co., Thomas, plumbers, 8 Spittal st
Cannon, Mrs Ann, 74 St. Mary's wynd
Cannon, James, labourer, 37 King st
Cannon, John, engine driver, 11 Raploch
Cannon, Mrs, 2 Raploch
Cannon, Thomas, labourer, 75 Baker st
Cannon, Thomas, labourer, 18 St. John st
Cargill, George, mason, King's stables
Cargill & Thomson, painters, 16 King st
Carlin, Robert, baker, 5 Upper Craigs
Carmichael, Mrs E., 11 Rosebery pl
Carmichael, James, shoemaker, 44 Baker st
Carmichael, John, woodman, 72 Baker st
Carmichael, John, blacksmith, 13 Well Green
Carmichael, Peter, gardener, 35 Low. craigs
Carmichael, Thos., engineman, 24 Main st
Carnegie, James, traveller, 23 Well Green
Carnegie, Mrs W., dressmaker, 12 Viewfield st
Carnie, Mrs Joan, 4 York pl
Currey, Miss, 72 Port st
Carrick, Miss Elizabeth, 1 Glebe cres
Carruthers, A., laundry manager, 28 Union st
Carruthers, Thomas, gardener, 118 Baker st
Carse, Thomas, signalman, 102 Upper Craigs
Carson, David, painter, 10 Clifford rd

Carson, Mrs, 60 Upper Craigs
Carson & Sons, Wm., painters, 54 Port st
Carter, Miss, 47 Port st
Cartwright, Rev. John, 21 Queen st
Casey & Darragh, contractors, 20 Thistle st
Cassell, John, labourer, 22 Raploch
Cassels, William, merchant, Killorn Villas,
    Park pl
Cassidy, Anthony, shunter, 60 Baker st
Cassidy, Hugh, labourer, 8 St. Mary's wynd
Cassidy, Mrs Martha, 28 St. Mary's wynd
Cassidy, Mrs, 20 Lower Castlehill
Catchel, Mrs Catherine, 3 Ballengeich rd
Cattanach, James, tobacconist, 13-30 Bow st
Cattanach, John, plumber, 24 Broad st
Cottle, Mrs A., Gowanlea, Causewayhead rd
Cavanagh, Patrick, labourer, 54 Spittal st
Cavanagh, Patrick, mason, 72 Baker st
Cave, Horatio, manufacturer, 20 Victoria pl
Chalmers, Dr Alexander, 4 Randolph ter
Chalmers, Mrs Allison, 7 Bruce st
Chalmers, H., french polisher, 9 Newhouse
Chalmers, James, mason, 1 Springfield pl
Chalmers, Miss Janet, 5 St. John st
Chalmers, Mrs Janet, 24 Lower Bridge st
Chalmers, Rev. John, 2 Gladstone pl
Chalmers, Mrs M. A., 39 Upper Craigs
Chapman, Mungo, nurseryman, Torbrex
Chapman, Arthur, Sergt. A.O.C., 7 Albany cres
Chappel, Fred., traveller, 19 Murray pl
Charleston, George, plumber, 6 Allan pk
Charleston, John, labourer, 10 Upper Bridge st
Chelsom, Mrs Barbara, 10 Dumbarton road
Cherry, James, tailor, 12 Spittal st
Cherry, William, smith, 38 Upper Castlehill
Chester, Robert, guide, 15 Lower Bridge st
Chisholm, C. T., upholsterer, 8 Nelson pl
Chisholm, George, 52 Barnton st
Chisholm, James, 28 Union st
Chisholm, John, wire fencer, 2 Springfield pl
Chivers, J. W. S., traveller, 25 Allan pk
Chivers, Q.-M.-Sergeant, 26 Millar pl
Christie, Miss Agnes, grocer, 22 Cowane st
Christie, Alex., joiner, Cambuskenneth
Christie, Andrew, cooper, 107 Lower Bridge st
Christie, Arch., joiner, 32 James st
Christie, Mrs Christina, Cambuskenneth
Christie, David, slater, 31 Lower Craigs
Christie, George, draper, 96 Cowane st; house—
    12 Union st

Christie, George, 25 Newhouse
Christie, James, 19 Bruce st
Christie, James R., coal agent, 20 Forth cres
Christie, James, Coxithill Farm, St Ninians
Christie, Mrs Jane, 55 Lower Bridge st
Christie, Miss Jane, 105 Lower Bridge st
Christie, Miss, 22 Victoria pl
Christie, Lawrence, merchant, 24 Broad st
Christie, Mrs Mary, 100 Upper Craigs
Christie, Mrs, 9 Snowdon pl
Christie, Mrs, 25 Snowdon pl
Christie & M'Donald, grocers, 34 Bow st
Christie, Robert, clerk, 106 Upper Craigs
Christie, Robert, Sun Inn, 55 King st
Christie, William, watchmaker, 2 George st
Christie, Wm., jeweller, 36 Port st
Christie, T., building contractor, 14 Forth cres
Christwood, Geo., insurance agent, 20 Union st
Chrystal, Alex., engine fitter, 32 Port st
Chrystal, David, fitter, 108 Upper Craigs
Chrystal, David, writer, 64 Murray pl; house—
    15 Victoria sq
Chrystal, James, fireman, 12 Spittal st
Chrystal, James, fireman, 110 Upper Craigs
Chrystal, James, 34 James st
Chrystal, John, coachbuilder, 9 St John st
Chrystal, Margaret, outdoor worker, 13 Broad st
Clark, Mrs Agnes, 72 Port st
Clark, Alex., miner, 66 Cowane st
Clark, Hugh, labourer, 44 Baker st
Clark, James, engine driver, 42 Upper Bridge st
Clark, James, joiner, 10 Bayne st
Clark, John, miner, 66 cowane st
Clark, J., butcher, Aitken's bldgs., B'nockburn rd
Clark, J., journalist, Grange House, C'wayhead
Clark, Miss, matron, Combination Fever Hospital
Clark, Robt., gardener, 9 Douglas st
Clark, Wm., miner, 13 St. John st
Clarke, William, painter, 9 Broad st
Clarke, William C., 6 Albany cres
Clarke, W. J., seedsman, 12 Forth cres
Claxton, James, labourer, 41 Broad st
Clay, Asa, accountant, 1 Balmoral pl
Cleghorn, Miss, 7 Douglas ter
Clelland, David, miner, 7 Borestone cres
Clink, William, warehouseman, 71 Cowane st
Coan, Mrs Catherine, 5 Raploch
Coan, Mrs Helen, 38 St. Mary's wynd
Coan, John, labourer, 94 St. Mary's wynd
Cochrane, Alex., smith, 12 Well Green

Cochrane, James, coachbuilder, 10 Glasgow road
Cochrane, Mrs, 10 Lower Bridge st
Cochrane, Wm., draper, Mossbank, Park pl
Coldwell, Alex., miner, 51 Main st
Cole, Honor, dresser, 31 Upper Craigs
Coleman, F., tailor, 42 Queen st
Coleman, Thomas, warder, 30 Bow st
Collier, Ltd., S., bootmakers, 32-34 King st and
    64 Port st
Collins, Major, Novara, 46 Dumbarton road
Collins, Mich., insur. agent, 90 St. Mary's wynd
Collins, Mrs, newsagent, 54 Barnton st
Collis, Mrs Agnes, 74 Cowane st
Colquhoun, Miss E., 8 Royal gardens
Colquhoun, Miss Jane, 13 Cowane st
Colquhoun, Robert, hawker, 1 St. John st
Colston, Mrs Margaret, 18 Main st
Colville, Alexander, 12 Park pl
Common, Robert K., dentist, 9 Pitt ter
Comrie, Daniel, miner, 20 Broad st
Comrie, John, clerk, 10 Union st
Comrie, Mrs Mary, 12 Bayne st
Comrie, Peter, baker, 26 King st and 86 St. Mary's
    wynd; house—43 Arcade
Comrie, Wm., miner, 19 Bruce st
Conaboy, Michael, labourer, 26 Raploch
Condie, Mrs Eliza., 72 Upper Craigs
Condie, Wm., traveller, 75 King st
Condie, William, Sheriff officer, 64 Murray pl
Condroy, John, labourer, 12 Raploch
Conley, Miss Marion, 105 Lower Bridge st
Conn, Thomas, labourer, 4 Bow st
Connal, P., engineman, Aitken's bldgs., B'burn rd
Connall, Miss Margaret, 34 Nelson pl
Connell, Donald, postboy, 68 Port st
Connell, Mrs Janet, Cambuskenneth
Connell, Private John, married quarters, Castle
Connelly, Mrs Nora, 4 Raploch
Connelly, Thomas, labourer, 8 St. Mary's wynd
Connoboy, Michael, plasterer, 53½ Cowane st
Connor, James, weaver, 3 Burghmuir
Conoboy, John, 6-8 St. John st
Constable, M. P., teacher, 20 Barnton st
Convery, Patrick, mason, 36 Broad st
Convery, Thomas, mason, 10 St. John st
Conway, Chas., signalman, 53 Lower Bridge st
Conway, Hugh, labourer, 9 Broad st
Conway, John, labourer, 38 St. Mary's wynd
Conway, Mrs Susan, 44 Broad st
Cook, Joseph, labourer, 8 St. Mary's wynd

Cook, J., railway surfaceman, 18 Bannockburn rd
Cook, Miss, Auchencrieff House, Bellfield rd
Cook, Thomas, labourer, 16 Bannockburn rd
Cook, William, miner, 26 Bannockburn rd
Cook, W. B., editor *Stirling Sentinel*, Blar
    Uallais, Causewayhead
Cook & Wylie, printers and publishers, 9 Barnton
    st. Tel. No. 0169
Cooper & Co., tea merchants, 33-35 Murray pl
Cooper, Francis, guard, 38 Abbey rd
Cooper, James, platelayer, 37 Lower Craigs
Cooper, John, grocer, 43 Upper Craigs
Cooper, John, joiner, 80 Main st
Cooper, John, vanman, 3 Nelson pl
Cooper, Mrs Mary, 1 Bannockburn rd
Copeland, James, miner, 144 Main st
Copley, Richard, fruiterer, 59 Barnton st ; house
    —6 Bank st
Corbett, Donald, labourer, 84 Baker st
Corbett, Miss M., millworker, 28 Newhouse
Cormack, Mrs Ann, broker, 10 St. Mary's wynd
Cormack, Mrs Jane, 88 Cowane st
Corr, James, vanman, 3 Well Green
Corsar, Mrs Jane, 7½ Weaver row, St Ninians
Corser, John, grocer, 33-35 Main st
Corser, Miss Agnes, 23 Weaver row, St Ninians
Coster, H., piano tuner, Rock ter ·
Cotton, Harold, clerk, 7 James st
Cotton, H., rubber worker, 57 Lower Bridge st
Cotton, W., manager, Forthvale cot., Cornton rd
Coull, Mrs J., 3 Middle Craigs
Coulthart, John, gardener, 14 Bruce st
Counter, Mrs Elizabeth, 7 Bow st
Couper, James, merchant, Craigforth
Couper, J., blacksmith, 13 Weaver row, St Ninians
Cousin, Alexander, fireman, 10 Bruce st
Cousin, David, plumber, 59 Cowane st
Coutts, Charles, tailor's cutter, 69 Wallace st
Coutts, Miss J., teacher, 3 Millar pl
Coutts, Miss Mary, 16 Lower Bridge st
Cowan, Archibald, gardener, 14 Baker st
Cowan, A., farmer, 9 Borestone cres
Cowan, D., Sheriff-Clerk depute, 21 Princes st
Cowbrough, Miss Jane, 7 Randolph rd
Cowbrough & Mercer, grocers, 14 Port st, 35
    Wallace st, and 42 Forth cres
Cowbrough, Miss Margaret, 7 Randolph rd
Cowbrough, William, 19 Snowdon pl
Cowie, Mrs, 40 Barnton st
Cowie, Robert, miner, 71 Upper Bridge st

Cowie, Samuel, baker, 6 Lower Craigs
Cowie, Thomas, ostler, 31 Friars st
Cowpar, Mrs Isa, Bellfield, Upper Bridge st
Cox, Don., county road surveyor, 48 Barnton st;
    house—64 Murray pl
Coyle, Mrs Ann, 17 Broad st
Coyle, Francis, miner, 103 Lower Bridge st
Coyne, John, gatekeeper, 15 Raploch
Coyne, Patrick, mason, 2 St John st
Crabb, James, weaver, 3 William pl
Crabtree, Mrs, 52 Baker st
Crae, Mrs, 64 Cowane st
Craig, David, engine cleaner, 26 Abbey rd
Craig, George, foreman porter, 44 Abbey rd
Craig, Hugh, janitor, 11 Glencoe road
Craig, Miss Janet, 2 Stripeside, St Ninians
Craig, John, fruiterer, 3 Murray pl
Craig, James, miner, 38 St. Mary's wynd
Craig's fancy goods warehouse, 15-21 Arcade
Craig, Mrs, Mar Lodge and Palace Tea Rooms,
    Castle wynd
Craig, Robert, machineman, 27 Cowane st
Craigie, J., ret. clergyman,, Viewfield C'wayhead
Cramb, Duncan, fireman, 13 Lower Craigs
Crawford, A., blacksmith, 71 Barnton st
Crawford, Alexander, joiner, 25 Newhouse
Crawford, D., china merchant, 21 Murray pl;
    house—15 Clarendon pl
Crawford, Mrs Euphemia, 32 Glasgow road
Crawford & Fraser, architects, 27 Murray pl
Crawford, Mrs Greig, 110 Main st
Crawford, Hugh, cabinetmaker, 24 Broad st
Crawford, James, joiner, 2 George st
Crawford, James, nailer, 110 Main st
Crawford, James, labourer, 24 Glasgow rd
Crawford James P., clerk, 8 Wallace st
Crawford, Mrs Jane, 25 Well Green
Crawford, Mrs Jane, 69 Main st
Crawford, John, nailer, 1 Bannockburn rd
Crawford, John, law clerk, 7 Bruce st
Crawford, John, nailer, 76 Main st
Crawford, John, joiner, 9 Nelson pl
Crawford, Mrs Mary, 2 Upper Craigs
Crawford, Mrs Mary, 19 Glasgow road
Crawford, Mrs M., 32 Port st
Crawford, Robert, gardener, 7 Borestone cres
Crawford, Robert, tinsmith, 49 King st
Crawford, Thomas, joiner, 95 Lower Bridge st
Crawford, William, foreman, Forthside
Crawford & Co., booksellers, 7 King st

Creagh, J., house furnisher, 35-37 Barnton st
Cree, John, sawyer, 10 Abbey rd pl
Crerar, Mrs Margaret, 59 Cowane st
Crichton, Alex., engine driver, 6 William pl
Crichton, And., perm. way insp., 23 Baker st
Crichton, Mrs Ann, 45 Newhouse
Crichton, Mrs, 25 Randolph ter
Crichton, W. G., glazier, 71 Port st
Croall, Miss A. K., Whinwell Children's Home,
    17 Upper Bridge st
Croall, Miss M., 15 Newhouse
Crockart, D. B., gunsmith, Rock ter
Crockart, D., Woodside, Dumbarton rd
Crockart, G. B., gunsmith, 13 Princes st
Crockart & Son, D., gunmakers, 35 King st
Crocket, Mrs, stationer, 71 King st; house—30
    Queen st
Crocket, Mrs, leather cutter, 22 Spittal st;
    house—37 Wallace st
Crombie, Mrs Ann, 17 Queen st
Crombie, George, plasterer, 7 Abbey rd
Crook, James, fireman, 1 Springfield pl
Cross, Ralph, weaver, 13 Well Green
Crossen, Mrs Margaret, 3 Forth cres
Crowe, Alex., 19 Abercromby pl
Crowe & Rodgers, photographers, 57 Murray pl
Crowe, David, fitter, 19 Burghmuir
Cruickshanks, Alex., butcher, 18 Forth st
Cruickshanks, Mrs Christina, 13 Seaforth pl
Cruickshanks, Mrs Janet, 36 Lower Castlehill
Crystal, J. A., C.R. auditor, 38 Queen st
Cullens, James, flesher, 23 Port st; house—
    4 Drummond pl
Cullens, W. &. J., butchers, 10-12 Baker st
Cullens, William, flesher, 18 Albert pl
Culley, James, mason, 6 Raploch
Culley, William, bricklayer, 7 Raploch
Cully, Thomas, labourer, 60 St. Mary's wynd
Cumming, Andrew, grocer, 38 Baker st; house
    —16 Princes st
Cummings, Miss M., 2 Melville ter
Cunning, George C., clerk, 11 Forth pl
Cunning, David, postman, 5 Bruce st
Cunning, William, clerk, 6 Abbey rd pl
Cunningham, George, miner, 114 Main st
Cunningham, J. & J., merchants, 21 Thistle st
Cunningham, John, cabman 5 Baker, st
Cunningham, William, tailor, 60 Baker st
Cunningham, William, 58 Broad st
Cunninton, Miss Mary, 11 Albert pl

Cunnison, Wm., cashier, Hillside, Causewayhead
Currie, Mrs Agnes, 17 Abbey rd
Currie, Charles, joiner, 1 Well Green
Currie, Mrs Christina, 5 George st
Currie, Daniel, jeweller, 98 Cowane st
Currie, James, joiner, 22 Dumbarton road
Currie, John, miner, 10 Borestone pl
Currie, John, miner, 3 Upper Bridge st
Currie, Robt. M., cab proprietor, 43 Port st
Currie, Thomas, burgh assessor, 16 King st
Currie, William, seedsman, 25 Nelson pl
Currie, William, traveller, 23 Wallace st
Curror, John G., Sheriff Clerk, 5 Gladstone pl
Cussack, Michael, labourer, 45 Broad st
Cuthbert, J., tailor, 60 Baker st
Cuthbert, Wm., 18 Park ter
Cuthbertson, Dr D, 22 Park ter
Cuthill, George, signal fitter, 13 Cowane st
Cuthill, Peter, carter, 14 Baker st

D

Dale, J. T., hairdresser, 30 Port st and 25 Friars st; house—5 Pitt ter
Dalgetty, Alex., joiner, 4 Bruce st
Dalgetty Bros., joiners, 2 Park lane
Dalgetty, H., shoemaker, 95-97 Baker st
Dalgetty, James W., tailor, 95 Baker st
Dalziel, Joseph, glazier, Torbrex
Dalziel, A., headmaster, Causewayhead
Danskin, Miss A., draper, 12 Arcade
Danskin, Miss, dressmaker, 30 Up. Bridge st
Darcy, Pat., labr., 44 Baker st
Darg, W., rubber worker, 31 Low. Bridge st
Darling, T. C., solicitor, 27 Murray pl
Darmody, Mrs C., 23-27 Broad st
Darragh, James, contractor, 68 Port st
Darroch, Capt. D., The Castle
Davidson, A., telegraphist, 11 Low. Bridge st
Davidson, Dun., slater, 10 Borestone pl
Davidson, Geo., architect, 25 Wallace st
Davidson, James, vanman, 9 Borestone cres
Davidson, Miss M. B., Causewayhead rd
Davidson, Misses, dressmakers, 40 Barnton st
Davidson, Robt., miner, 51 Main st
Davidson, Robt., shoemaker, 73 Main st

Davidson, T., gardener, 11 Newhouse
Davidson, Thos., blacksmith, 41 Baker st
Davidson, Wm., clerk, 15 Seaforth pl
Davidson, Wm., signal fitter, 17 Seaforth pl
Davidson & Co., Ltd., bootmakers, 25 Murray pl
Davidson & Stevenson, writers, 27 Murray pl
Davie, Jas., ironfounder, 2 Irvine pl
Davie, John, coachbuilder, 5 Bayne st
Davie, Wm., moulder, 66 Baker st
Davie & Sons, Jas., ironfounders, 26 Orchard pl
Davie, P., cartwright, Cambuskenneth
Davies, H., 30 Married Quarters
Dawber, Ralph, trav., 11 Millar pl
Dawson, James, joiner, 19 Raploch
Dawson, James, ironmonger, 18 Bruce st
Dawson, James, traveller, 2 James st
Dawson, John, engine driver, 23 Baker st
Dawson, Mrs J., 16 Low. Bridge st
Dawson, Miss, 40 Up. Castlehill
Dawson, Mrs, 5 Cowane st
Dawson, Oswald, cabinetmaker, 20 Forth st;
    house—26 James st
Dawson, Robt., teacher, 6 Viewfield pl
Dawson, Wm., 9 Park ter
Day, Chas., labr., 23 Broad st
Deans, A. C., painter, Causewayhead
Deans, T., painter, Causewayhead
Deans, Mrs, 9 Low. craigs
Deans, Mrs, 36 Murray pl
Dempsey, Ed., miner, 70 Up. Craigs
Dempster, John, baker, 14 Bow st
Dempster, John, tobacconist, 6 Port st; house—
    6 Albert pl
Dempster, Miss, 6 Albert pl
Dempster, Wm., cabinetmaker, 48 Broad st
Denham, Thos., messenger, Forthside
Denholm, John, Capt., 6 Victoria pl
Denison, Geo., confectioner, 130 Main st
Dennison, John, musician, 17 George st
Denovan, A., 40 Barnton st
Denovan, Alex., mason, 32 Port st
Denovan, Chas., tailor, 64 Main st
Denovan, James, labr., 9 Bruce st
Denovan, J., bootmaker, Aitken's bldgs., St Nin.
Denovan, John, bootmaker, 112 Main st
Denovan, Mrs Helen, 11 Bruce st
Denovan, Mrs M., 7 Borestone cres
Denovan, Robt., gardener, 84 Baker st
Denovan, Robt., tailor, 27 Weaver row
Denovan, Thos., trav., 25 Port st

Dent, J., labr., Causewayhead
Dermidy, John, labr., 16 Bow st
Derrick, Ed., labr., 18 Low. castlehill
Derrick, Mrs, 4 Bow st
Derrick, O. P., auctioneer, 5½ Drip rd
Derrick, Thos., general dealer, 21 Raploch
Derrick, Wm., gardener, 47 Cowane st
Devine, Chas., labr., 2 St Mary's wynd
Devine, Chas., labr., 38 St Mary's wynd
Devine, John, labr., 38 St Mary's wynd
Devlin, Robt., miner, 14 Well Green
Dewar, A., church officer, 48 Murray pl
Dewar, A., ironmonger, Cambuskenneth
Dewar, A. F., mine inspec., 20 Forth st
Dewar, A., slater, Cambuskenneth
Dewar, And., grain merc., 2 Douglas ter
Dewar, And., farmer, King's Park Farm
Dewar, And., gardener, 37 King st
Dewar, David, farmer, King's Park Farm
Dewar, David, tailor, 3 James st
Dewar, James, ironmonger, 20 Bruce st
Dewar, James, coachman, 18 Park ter
Dewar, J., Alloa Coal Co. agent, 18 Wallace st
Dewar, John, farmer, King's Park Farm
Dewar, John, joiner, 12 Cowane st
Dewar, John, joiner, 15 Newhouse
Dewar, Mrs., art dealer, Arcade
Dewar, Mrs, 98 Cowane st
Dewar, Mrs Isabella, 43 Glasgow rd
Dewar, Mrs J., 37 King st
Dewar, Mrs M., picture dealer, 19 Murray pl
Dewar, P., farmer, King's Park Farm
Dewar, Robt., labr., 28 Newhouse
Dewar, Tom, farmer, King's Park Farm
Dick, Alex., plasterer, 57 Cowane st
Dick, Alex., nailer, 25 Glasgow rd
Dick, And., coachmaker, 5 Forth pl
Dick, David, boilermaker, 15 Douglas st
Dick, David, 2 Forth cres
Dick, Geo., carter, 51 Newhouse
Dick, Geo., clerk, 52 Murray pl
Dick, Mrs Helen, 15 Main st
Dick, Jacob, painter, 1 Main st
Dick, James, blacksmith, 17 Newhouse
Dick, James, miner, 15 Main st
Dick, Mrs Agnes, 27 Glasgow rd
Dick, Misses, dressmakers, 2 Forth cres
Dick, Mrs, 12 George st
Dick, Robt., miner, 15 Glasgow rd
Dick, Robt., miner, 126 Main st

Dick, W., lab., 87 St Mary's wynd
Dick, W., jun., lorryman, 87 St Mary's wynd
Dick, W. G., booking clerk, Springkerse house
Dick, Mrs W., 114 Baker st
Dickie, D., joiner, 18 Union st
Dickson, A. J., Springbank
Dickson, James, bootmaker, 38 Baker st
Dickson, J. L., enginekeeper, 23 George st
Dickson, Lieut., Muirlands cot., Causewayhead
Dickson, Robt., School Board officer, 15 Raploch
Dickson, Sgt., Married Quarters
Dimpsey, T., miner, 39 Low. craigs
Dingwall, C., railwayman, 55 Up. craigs
Dingwall, M., gardener, 14 George st
Dinnet, P., lab., 68 Cowane st
Di Ponio, B., ice-cream shop, 49 Up. craigs
Dixon, Sam., miner, 45 Main st
Dobbie, James, writer, 3 Port st
Dobbie, Miss, 13 Park ter
Dobbie, Mrs, 37 Bannockburn rd
Dobbie, Mrs, 24 Bow st
Dobbie, Robt., engineer, 53 Murray pl
Dobbie, Wm., commission agent, 24 Clarendon pl
Dobbie, Wm., draper, 16 Bruce st
Dobson, Wm. H., organist, 9 Albert pl
Docherty, James, slater, 31 Up. Craigs
Docherty, J., slater, 14 Bow st
Docherty, Pat., shoemaker, 8 Bayne st
Docherty, R., lab., 39 St Mary's wynd
Dodds, Mrs, 34 Newhouse
Doig, Mrs, laundress, 91 Up. craigs
Doig, Peter, policeman, 5 Baker st
Don, And., lorryman, 49 Newhouse
Don, John, lab., 118 Main st
Don, Robt., lorryman, 24 Cowane st
Donachie, John, railwayman, 3 William pl
Donahoe, L., butcher, 38 St Mary's wynd
Donald, Alex., lab., 24 Orchard pl
Donaldson, Alex., mason, 92 Cowane st
Donaldson, C., restr., 46½-48 Baker st
Donaldson, C., dyer, 30 Bow st
Donaldson, Geo., granite cutter, 5 Springfield pl
Donaldson, James, joiner, 17 Abbey rd
Donaldson, Miss Janet, 7 Bruce st
Donaldson, John, bottler, 4 William pl
Donaldson, John, plumber, 10 Up. Bridge st
Donaldson, John, joiner, 17 Nelson pl
Donaldson, Miss, tobacconist, 35 Baker st
Donaldson, Mrs E., 43 Cowane st
Donaldson, Mrs Eliz., 13 Glencoe rd

Donaldson, Mrs, 24 Cowane st
Donaldson, R., clerk, 3 Forth pl
Donaldson, W., carter, Causewayhead
Donaldson, Wm., sculptor, 27 Cowane st
Donaldson, Wm., solicitor, 8 Park ter
Donnachie, Mrs, 2 St Mary's wynd
Donnachie, P., miner, 11 Baker st
Donnachie, Pat., labr., 8 Broad st
Donnelly, Dan., labr., 20 Broad st
Donnelly, Mrs Jessie, 64 Cowane st
Donoghue, T., miner, 44 Low. castlehill
Dormer, Wm. J., 52 Broad st
Dougal, Wm., coachpainter, 35 Cowane st
Dougall, A., grocer, 85 St Mary's wynd
Dougall, Mrs Annie, 21 Newhouse
Dougall, John, coachpainter, 36 Broad st
Douglas, Geo., engine driver, 5 Well Green
Douglas, James, fireman, 23 George st
Douglas, John, lab., 10 St John st
Douglas, P., solicitor, 27 Murray pl
Dow, And., labr., 14 Baker st
Dow, Alex., fisherman, 65 Low. bridge st
Dow, Mrs Elizabeth, 45 Wallace st
Dow, James, engine driver, 37 Low. bridge st
Dow, Jas., hatter, 19 King st; house—14 Mel-
    ville ter
Dow, James, carter, 14 Baker st
Dow, James, fireman, 92 Up. craigs
Dow, John, coal carter, 13 Glencoe rd
Dow, John, smith, 37 Raploch
Dow, John, weaver, 8 George st
Dow, John, coachman, Brentham pk
Dow, Mrs M., 30 Cowane st
Dow, Thomas, ferryman, Cambuskenneth
Dow, Wm., hatter, 11 Newhouse
Dow, Wm., luggage clerk, 7 Douglas st
Dowell, James, clothier, 56 Barnton st; house—
    Crofthead
Dowell, John, organist, Crofthead
Dowell, Mrs Janet, 5 Viewfield st
Dowie, Mrs Jessie, 10 Drummond pl
Dowie, Mrs Minnie L., 15 Borestone pl
Downie, And., baker, 34 James st
Downie, Mrs S. A., 32 Low. castlehill
Doyle, James, miner, 26 Broad st
Drew, John, M.D., 28 Dumbarton rd
Drummond, H. ploughman, 31 Glasgow rd
Drummond, G. T., jeweller. 3 Melville ter
Drummond, Mrs Cath., 13 Newhouse
Drummond, Miss E., 16 Clarendon pl

Drummond, James, seedsman, 69 Newhouse
Drummond, James W., seedsman, Westerlands
Drummond, James, carter, 88 Cowane st
Drummond, Mrs Jane C., Glenelm, Park pl
Drummond, Mrs Janet, 17 Raploch
Drummond, Mrs Jane, 6 Bank st
Drummond, John, hammerman, 7 Mid. craigs
Drummond, John, porter, May Day Yard
Drummond, John T., jeweller, 39 Arcade; house
    —16 Albert pl
Drummond, Misses, 4 Rosebery pl
Drummond, P., seedsman, 27 Albert pl
Drummond, R., lab., 58 Low. Bridge st
Drummond's Tract Depôt, 17 Dumbarton rd
Drummond, Wm., mason, 14 Baker st
Drummond & Sons, R., jewellers, 5 Murray pl
Drummond & Sons, Ltd., W., seed merchants, 13
    Murray pl
Drysdale, Campbell, carter, 10 Forth st
Drysdale, Miss M., 32 James st
Drysdale, Miss, music teacher, 37 Wallace st
Drysdale, Thomas, 46 Up. Bridge st
Dudgeon, James, baker, 41 Up. craigs
Duff, And., engineer, 20 Forth st
Duff, Duncan, brassfinisher, 11 Abbey rd
Duff, James, plumber, 36 Up. craigs
Duff, John, clerk, 69 Wallace st
Duff, John, labr., 31 Cowane st
Duff, John, plumber, 8 Pitt ter (firemaster)
Duff, J. & J., plumbers and sanitary engineers,
    16 and 29 Dumbarton rd
Duff, Mrs J., 103 Baker st
Duff, P., plumber, 11 King st
Duff, Robt., miner, 118 Main st
Duff, Thos., law clerk, 34 James st
Duffin, Mrs J., antique dealer, 17-19 Friars st
Duffy, Ed., rubber worker, 56 Low. bridge st
Duffy, P., labr., 17 Winchel pl
Duffy, P., miner, 44 St Mary's wynd
Duggan, James, hawker, 6 St Mary's wynd
Duguid, James, carter, 4 George st
Duguid, James, 80 Baker st
Dumbreck, Mrs Agnes, 1 Viewfield st
Dunagan, Mrs A., 8 Broad st
Dunagan, P., labr., 2 Barn rd
Duncan, Mrs Ann, 28 St Mary's wynd
Duncan, Arch., printer, 5½ Newhouse
Duncan, Chas., carter, 25 St John st
Duncan, Chas., pensioner, 13 Abbey rd
Duncan, F., miner, 9 Low. craigs

Duncan, Geo., tailor, 33 James st
Duncan, James, fishmonger, 9 Maxwell pl
Duncan, Jas., aerated water maker, 4 Drip rd
Duncan, J. C., electrician, 25 Port st
Duncan, John, professional golfer, 67 Newhouse
Duncan, John, shoemaker, 12 Viewfield st
Duncan, Miss Jessie, 24 Cowane st
Duncan, Mrs, 30 Barnton st
Duncan, Mrs, 74 Cowane st
Duncan, M., surfaceman, 55 Newhouse
Duncan, Pte. R., 8 Married Qrs.
Duncan, Robt., labr., 92 Up. craigs
Duncanson, Chas., 56 Cowane st
Duncanson, James, tailor, 25 Irvine pl
Duncanson, James, chemist, 38 Port st
Duncanson, Mrs Jessie, 15 Abercromby pl
Duncanson, John, plumber, 63 Baker st
Duncanson, Peter, tailor, 4 Middle craigs
Duncanson, Wm., fireman, 11 Bruce st
Duncanson, Wm., tailor, 10 Up. craigs
Dun, Alex., reporter, 37 Murray pl
Dun, John, traveller, 37 Barnton st
Dunk, John, caretaker, Burgh Club, 41 Port st
Dunlop, James, grocer, 15 Irvine pl
Dunlop, Mrs, 59 Wallace st
Dunlop, Miss S., 3 Abbey rd
Dunlop & Co., grocers, 12 Bow st
Dunn Bros., wood merchants, 18 Abbey rd
Dunn, Miss Nora, dressmaker, 72 Port st
Dunn, P., seedsman, 7 Park lane
Dunn, T., painter, 12 Viewfield st
Dunn & Wilson, milliners, 24 Port st
Dunsmore, Michael, 12 Windsor pl
Dunsmore, H., salesman, 36 James st
Dunsmore, Mrs, 12 Windsor pl
Dunsmuir, John, miner, 51 Cowane st
Durie, Hugh, mason, 2 Up. craigs
Durie, Mrs H., 39 Low. craigs
Duthie, Alex., grocer, 60 Up. craigs
Duthie, John, coachbuilder, 24 Broad st
Duthie, Mrs Cath., 43 Cowane st
Duthie, P., hammerman, 5 Mid. craigs
Dyball, Robt., draper, 13 Bruce st

E

Eadie, Hugh, lab., 60 Cowane st
Eadie, James, trav., 3 Viewfield pl
Eadie, John, trav., 18 Forth cres

Eadie, Miss Agnes, 44 Up. bridge st
Eadie, Mrs P., 10 Forth cres
Eadie, P., joiner, 11 Baker st
Eadie, P., vanman, 3 Wallace st
Eadie, Wm., brewer, 10 Irvine pl
Easson, Misses M. and I., 27 Victoria pl
Easson, Wm., grocer, 102 Baker st.; house—
    9 Randolph rd
Easson, Wm., joiner, 1 William pl
Eastmans Limited, butchers, 46 Baker st
Easton, Miss, 4 Clifford rd
Easton, P., weaver, 2 William pl
Easton, Robt., miner, 17 Seaforth pl
Edgar, John, baker, 61 Barnton st
Edmond, P., sup., Nat. Tel. Co., 33 Friars st.;
    house—23 Wallace st
Edmond, P., 51 Wallace st
Edwards, Fred, lab., 24 Low castlehill
Elder, Adam, N.B. goods agent, 9 Forth pl
Elder, J. F., comp., 28 Up. Craigs
Elder, Wm., baker, 21 George st
Elder & Sons, T., bakers, 52 Port st
Ellery, James, stoker, 13 St John st
Elliot, Miss A., 61 Barnton st
Elliot, Miss M., nurse, 61 Barnton st
Elliot, Mrs M., 48 Cowane st
Elrick, Jas., sergeant, 17 Married quarters
Emery, Hally, waggon inspec., 18 Up. craigs
England, H., clerk, 44 Up. Bridge st
Esslemont, Alex., Bridgehaugh
Evans, John, baker, 3B Main st
Evans, Wm., painter, 9 Borestone cres
Ewing, A., draper, Causewayhead
Ewing, A., painter, 73 Newhouse
Ewing, Geo., plumber, 3B Main st and 13
    Bannockburn rd
Ewing, Hugh, nailer, Aitken's bldgs., St Nin.
Ewing, James, engine fitter, 12 Viewfield st
Ewing, J., clothier, 11 King st
Ewing, Miss Agnes, 124 Main st
Ewing, Mrs, caretaker, St. Ninians Parish Halls
Ewing, Mrs Agnes, nurse, 108 Up. craigs
Ewing, Mrs M., 5 Maxwell pl
Ewing, Wm., 1 Glasgow rd

F

Fagen, Mrs Bridget, 46 Low. bridge st
Fairful, Robt., joiner, 17 George st

Fairful, Wilson, & Somers, joiners, 81 Port st
Fairley, James, trav., 13 Low. bridge st
Fairley, James, miner, 30 Broad st
Fairley, Mrs Jessie, 7 Queen st
Fairley, Thos., tele. linesman, 2 St John st
Falconer, John, surfaceman, 13 Low. Craigs
Falconer, Mrs Agnes, 6 Low. craigs
Fallin, P., tobacconist, 100 St Mary's wynd
Fallon, Mrs Eliz., 52 Broad st
Farish, H. J., sergeant, 14 Married quarters
Farish, James, baker, 33 Newhouse
Farish, Mrs M., 6 Low. bridge st
Farman, Thos., janitor, 10 Middle craigs
Farmer, Geo., miner, 111 Baker st
Farmer, Robt., sawyer, 44 Baker st
Farquharson, Joseph, vanman, 12 Low. bridge st
Farquharson, Miss E., 3 Millar pl
Faulds, C., miner, 7 Church wynd
Faulds, Miss Jane, 23 Snowdon pl
Feahrenbach, Miss, 25 Allan park
Fenton, David, grocer, 20 Barnton st
Fenton, James H., watchmaker, 11 Bruce st
Fenton, Miss Janet, 5 Up. craigs
Fenwick, Robt., contractor, 22 Bruce st
Fergie, Mrs Helen, 38½ Cowane st
Ferguson, Adam, gardener, Southfield cres
Ferguson, Alex., blacksmith, 25 Forth cres
Ferguson, Alex., miner, 37 Low. craigs
Ferguson, Alex., joiner, 81 Baker st
Ferguson, And., carpet foreman, 60 Up. craigs
Ferguson, And., joiner, 53 Low. bridge st
Ferguson, And., plumber, 30 Bow st
Ferguson, Arch., grocer, 47 Wallace st.
Ferguson Bros., grocers, 62 Baker st
Ferguson, D., inspec. of works, 4 James st
Ferguson, D., mason, 6 Douglas st
Ferguson, Daniel, banker, 80 Murray pl
Ferguson, David, fireman, 56 Abbey rd
Ferguson, David, lab., 7½ Weaver row
Ferguson, Duncan, draper, 51 Wallace st
Ferguson, Hugh, 67½ Port st
Ferguson, Jas., lorryman, 10 Viewfield st
Ferguson, John, cashier, 5 Millar pl
Ferguson, John, gardener, 24 Newhouse
Ferguson, John, joiner, 7 Newhouse
Ferguson, John, vanman, 6 Bayne st
Ferguson, Miss M., 3 Millar pl
Ferguson, Miss, 24 Queen st
Ferguson, Mrs, 23 Wallace st
Ferguson, Mrs, 101 Low. bridge st

Ferguson, Mrs, 15 Cowane st
Ferguson, Mrs, 5 Middle craigs
Ferguson, Mrs Agnes, 116 Main st
Ferguson, Mrs Jane, 28 Glasgow rd
Ferguson, Mrs Jane, 44 Baker st
Ferguson, Mrs T., Victoria Villa, Causewayhead
Ferguson, P., lab., 55 Lower bridge st
Ferguson, Robt., plastr., 14 Broad st
Ferguson, Robt., ploughman, Cambuskenneth
Ferguson, Robt., photo artist, St Margaret's, Causewayhead
Ferguson, Samuel, tailor, 2 York pl
Ferguson, T., chief-constable, Police Office, 37 Broad st
Ferguson, Thos., joiner, 14 Dumbarton rd; house —14 Princes st
Ferguson, Wm., cabman, 6 Baker st
Ferguson, Wm., hostler, 63 Low. bridge st
Ferguson, Wm., lab., 75 Up. bridge st
Ferguson, Wm., lab., 30 Broad st
Ferguson, Wm., trav., Rowanlea, Linden aven
Ferguson & Sons, H., bootmakers, 2 Port st; house—5 Albert pl
Ferguson & Struthers, drapers, 4 Baker st
Ferrier, David, miner, 19 Weaver row
Ferrier, L., cabinetmaker, 6 Well green
Fields, Samuel, upholstr., 64 Up. craigs
Findlater, James, lab., 10 St John st
Findlay, J., comp., 71 Barnton st
Finlayson, And., brushmaker, 23 Friars st
Finlayson, David, joiner, 2 Springfield pl
Finlayson, James, plumber, 81 Port st
Finlayson, J., engine driver, 10 Up. bridge st
Finlayson, John, shoemaker, 95 Baker st
Finlayson, Miss Bethia, 87 Port st
Finlayson, Miss C., confectioner, 26 Bow st
Finlayson, Misses, dressmakers, 21 Baker st
Finlayson, Miss Ann, 11 Torbrex
Finlayson, Mrs, nurse, 8 Low. bridge st
Finlayson, Mrs, 78 St Mary's wynd
Finlayson, Mrs Janet, 24 Bow st
Finlayson, M., joiner, 14 Nelson pl
Finlayson, Robt., wheelwright, 33 Baker st
Finlayson, T., police inspec., 10 Union st
Finlayson, Thos., engine driver, 57 Low. bridge st
Finlayson, T. L., 28 Union st
Finlayson & Sons, joiners, 4 Springfield pl
Finlayson, W. A., joiner, 8 Wallace st
Finlayson, W., engine driver, 31 Low. Bridge st
Finn, Pvt. George, Castle

Finn, M., lab., 48 Broad st
Fisher, A., draper, 49 Barnton st
Fisher, A., lab., 12 Low. Bridge st
Fisher, Donald, surfaceman, 12 Low. castlehill
Fisher, Geo., 8 Union st
Fisher, John, 12 George st
Fisher, Mrs Eliz., 6 Millar pl
Fisher, Miss E., May Cottage, Cambuskenneth
Fishington, Sam., rubber worker, 80 Cowane st
Fitzpatrick, Mrs Bridget, 95 Baker st
Fitzpatrick, A., miner, 71 Main st
Flannigan, John, lab., 38 St Mary's wynd
Flannigan, Mrs C., 38 St Mary's wynd
Flannigan, Wm., labourer, 18 St John st
Fleming, D., miner, 11 Low. Bridge st
Fleming, Geo., miner, 100 Main st
Fleming, John, fireman, 41 Baker st
Fleming, Matthew, miner, 48 Broad st
Fleming & Buchanan, writers, 26 Port st
Fleming, Reid & Co., Greenock wool shop, 70
    Port st
Fletcher, Alex., plumber, 81 Port st
Flett, Dr Alex., 4 York pl
Flint, Miss Annie, 12 Pitt ter
Flockhart, David, coal agent, Causewayhead
Flockhart, James, fireman, 61 Cowane st
Flockhart, Mrs Jane, 10 Barnton st
Flowers, Wm., pensioner, 6 Low. craigs
Forbes, R. C., shorthand teacher, 15 Newhouse
Forbes, John, traveller, 27 Wallace st
Forbes, Joseph, labourer, 92 Up. craigs
Forbes, Mrs Agnes, 12 Middle craigs
Forbes, Mrs, 36 Broad st
Forbes, Mrs, Riversdale, Causewayhead rd
Forbes, Wm., cabinetmaker, 31 James st
Forbes, W. D, Lyngarth, Causewayhead rd
Ford, Wm., pawnbroker, 31 Friars st
Forfar, P. M., draper, 33 Barnton st
Forgan, David, traveller, 13 Randolph rd
Forgan, D., musicseller, 25 Forth pl
Forgie, H., miner, 39 Bannockburn rd
Forrest, Mrs, 13 St John st
Forrest, R., cabinetmaker, 9 Friars st
Forrester, D., fish mer., 1A Friars st & 41 Broad st
Forrester, John, coachbuilder, 3 James st
Forrester, Miss Catherine, 30 Snowdon pl
Forrester, Mrs, fish merchant, 40-42 Barnton st
Forrester, Wm., plumber, 23 Baker st
Forrester, Wm., sinker, 7 William pl
Forsyth, Geo., cashier, 25 King st

Forsyth, Wm., miner, Calton house
Forsyth, Geo. F., organist, 3 Newhouse
Forsyth, James, bootmaker, 47-49 Main st
Forsyth, James, clothier, 14 Up. Bridge st
Forsyth, John, corkcutter, 15 George st
Forsyth, Matthew B., clerk, 6 Bruce st
Forsyth, Mrs Isabella, 7 Pitt ter
Forsyth, Wm., butcher, 21 Dumbarton rd ; house
    —9 Forth cres
Foster, R., plasterer, The Linden, Linden av
Foster, Mrs Agnes, 7 Glencoe rd
Fotheringham, G., river watcher, 15 Douglas st
Fotheringham, John, builder, 45 Low. Bridge st
Fotheringham, Misses, laundry, 65 B'burn rd
Fotheringham, Mrs Janet, 43 Low. Bridge st
Fotheringham, R., cabinetmaker, 4 Drip rd
Fowler, Alex., stationmaster, Causewayhead
Fowler, And., greenkeeper, Crofthead
Fowler, J., church officer, Guildhall
Fowler, John, Coburg av
Frail, James, miner, 71 Main st
Frame, Geo., surfaceman, 10 Up. craigs
France, A., miner, 7 Borestone cres
France, F. R., refresh. rooms, 11 Broad st
Francis, Mrs Jane, 8 Abbey rd
Francis, John, caretaker, Com. Fever Hospital
Francis, P., cooper, 52 Cowane st
Francis, Walter, cartwright, 20 Bruce st
Francis, Wm., carpet designer, 3 James st
Fraser, A., contractor, 8 Low. Bridge st
Fraser, Alex., gardener, 30 Nelson pl
Fraser, Duncan, postboy, 10 Viewfield st
Fraser, Constable J., Causewayhead
Fraser, John, miner, 60 Baker st
Fraser, John, blacksmith, 5 Baker st
Fraser, Miss G., dressmaker, 10 Wallace st
Fraser, Mrs Elizabeth, 66 Baker st
Fraser, Miss Jessie, Abbey rd dairy
Fraser, Misses Jessie and Jean, 17 Victoria sq
Fraser, Mrs M., 20 Bow st
Fraser, P., miner, 5A Snowdon pl
Fraser, Robt. D., accountant, 4 Snowdon pl
Fraser, Wm. S., grocer, 32 Nelson pl
Fraser, Wm., gardener, 48 Cowane st
Fraser, Robt., miner, 126 Main st
Frater, Robt., plumber, 73 Port st; house—1
    Park ter
Frater, John, carter, Causewayhead
Frater, Miss Jane, 16 Manse cres
Frederick, Arch., mason, 8 Wallace st

Freeland, Mrs M., 23 Broad st
Frew, Mrs Ann, Cambuskenneth
Frew, Rev. Dr, 12 Melville ter
Fuge, Chas., iron merchant, Llewellyn lodge
Fullarton, James, dairyman, 32 Baker st
Fulton, And., storeman, 9 Well green
Fulton, Thomas, lab., 23 Broad st
Fulton, Miss B., 23 Broad st
Furr, Alf. G., Castle
Fyfe, A., barman, 20 Cowane st
Fyfe, J., chemist, 52 Barnton st
Fyfe, John, sanitary inspector, 1 Princes st;
    office—15 Spittal st
Fyfe, John, waggon insp., Cambuskenneth
Fyfe, Thomas, sawyer, 15 Low. Bridge st

G

Gaerty, L., shoemaker, 60 St Mary's wynd
Gair, S., lab., 144 Main st
Galashan, J., hairdresser, 43 Arcade
Galashan, Mrs, 44 Broad st
Galashan, Mrs S., bootmaker, 31 Arcade
Galbraith, Miss A. L. H., 5 Glebe cres
Galbraith, Alex., grocer, Albert pl
Galbraith, Miss E., 5 Glebe cres
Galbraith, Miss J., 11 Laurelhill pl
Gall, Mrs, 4 Randolph rd
Gall, W. R., contr., Orchard pl and Barnsdale pl
Gallacher, Pat., lab., 60 St Mary's wynd
Gallacher, John, surfaceman, 20 Bow st
Gallagher, Pvte., 5 Married Qrs.
Galloway, Geo., plumber, 35 Low. Bridge st
Galloway, James, lab., 38 St Mary's wynd
Galloway, James, brakesman, 23 Abbey rd
Galloway, John O., accountant, 1 Gladstone pl
Galloway, John, soldier, 23 Friars st
Galloway, John, blacksmith, 3 Kirk wynd
Galloway, J. L., draper, 9 Abbey rd
Galloway, Mrs M., 6 Forrest rd
Galloway, Mrs, 111 Low. Bridge st
Galloway, Wm., broker, 41 Baker st
Galloway, Wm., joiner, 8 Broad st
Gardener, D., lab., 45 Broad st
Gardiner, A. Thompson, clerk, 3 Abbey rd
Gardner, Alex., Sheriff-Clerk Depute (Falkirk),
    5 Allan pk

Gardener, Colin, brakesman, 105 Low. Bridge st
Gardner, Miss J., milliner, 63 Barnton st
Gardner, H., coal merc., 41 Murray pl
Gardner, John, mason, 48 Up. castlehill
Gardner, John, joiner, 30 Bannockburn rd
Gardner, Mrs, 5 Allan pk
Gardner, P., mason, 36 Up. Castlehill
Gardner, P., 8 Bannockburn rd
Gardner, Robt., engine driver, 17 Bruce st
Garrett, Miss F., 61 Wallace st
Gartshore, C., seedsman, 3 Queen's rd
Gasser, Mrs, restr., 38 Barnton st
Gavin, Hugh, draper, 6 Glebe cres
Gavin, James, draper, 25 Allan pk
Gavin, James, miner, 1 St John st
Gavin & Son, Hugh, drapers, 1 King st
Geddes, James, miner, 14 George st
Geddes, Mrs L., Easter Livilands
Geegan, John lab., 113 Baker st
Gemmel, John, weaver, 103 Main st
Gemmel, John, miner, 22 Main st
Gemmell, Robt , miner, 20 Main st
Gentleman, E., writer, 9 Abercromby pl
Gentleman, Eben, registrar, collector of rates, 2
    Dumbarton rd
Gentleman, Miss, 17 Albert pl
Gentleman, Miss Alice, 17 Albert pl
Gentles, James, saddler, Bellfield
Gentles, Thomas, saddler, Bellfield
Gentles, Mrs, 10 Barnton st
Gentles & Son, T., saddlers, 50 Barnton st
George, Mrs, 71 Barnton st
Gerrard, David, cabinetmaker, 33 Burghmuir
Giannandrea, A., ice-cream shop, 40, 44, 93
    Baker st
Giannandrea, G., ice-cream shop, 10 Broad st
Gibb, John, carter, 20 Bannockburn rd
Gibb, Mrs, Elderslie, Causewayhead
Gibb, Rich., miner, 3A Main st
Gibb, Wm., auctioneer, 8 Union st
Gibbons, Mrs Mary, 20 Broad st
Gibson, Mrs, 11 Park ter
Gibson, James A., solicitor, 47 Port st
Gibson, James, saltworker, 5 Baker st
Gibson, Thomas, joiner, 36 James st
Gibson, Mrs, 20 Bow st
Gifford, Geo., carter, 33 James st
Gifford, James, painter, 32 James st
Gilchrist, David, mason, 13 Abbey rd
Gilchrist, David, weaver, 2 Springfield pl

Gilchrist, James, plasterer, 24 Broad st
Gilchrist, Miss Jessie, 18 Melville ter
Gilchrist, Mrs Jane, 5 Springfield pl
Gilchrist, P., plasterer, 10 Bayne st
Gilchrist, Robt., weaver, 104 Up. Craigs
Gilfillan, James, plasterer, 99 Main st
Gilfillan, Mrs, 22 Union st
Gilfillan, Robt., wool merchant, 17 Burghmuir
Gilfillan, Wm., spirit merchant, 51 Glasgow rd
Gill, Mrs Edith, confectioner, 45 Cowane st
Gill, John, trav., 47 Cowane st
Gillespie, Mrs Agnes, 104 Main st
Gillespie, Chas., cabinetmaker, 21 Abbey rd
Gillespie, E., tel. linesman, 10 Up. craigs
Gillespie, James, nailworker, 56 Main st
Gillespie, John, grocer, 51 Port st; house—10
     Park av
Gillespie, Miss, spirit merchant, 50 Up. craigs
Gillespie, Miss, 35 Cowane st
Gillespie, Miss M., confect., 77 Main st
Gillespie, Mrs M., 29 Bannockburn rd
Gillespie, P., cooper, 6 Low. craigs
Gillies, James, coachwright, 7 Torbrex
Gillon, T., settmaker, 108 Baker st
Gilmour, D., bootmaker, 57 Barnton st; house—
     32 Queen st
Gilmour, Geo., policeman, 98 St Mary's wynd
Gilmour, John, miner, 13 Low. craigs
Gilmour, Mrs Wm., 24 Bruce st
Gilmour, Wm., gardener, 67½ Port st
Gilvear, Mrs, 22 Low. castlehill
Gilvear, Robt., dairyman, 43 Low. Bridge st
Ging, Austin, lab., 7 Raploch
Ging, Miss Ann, 48 Broad st
Ging, James, lab., 40 Raploch
Ging, M., lab., 14 Baker st
Ging, Thomas, lab., 9 Raploch
Girgan, Pvte. Chas., 16 Married Qrs.
Girvan, Mrs M., 39 Low. castlehill
Girvan, Thomas, bottler, 59 Low. castlehill
Giovanelli, D., ice-cream shop, 45-88 Baker st
Given, John, postman, 3 Broad st
Glancy, Miss M., teacher, 25 Irvine pl
Glancy, Pat., miner, 38 Main st
Glasgow, Wm., miner, 13 Broad st
Glasgow, Wm., lorryman, Crofthead
Glass, Miss E., dressmaker, 33 Baker st
Glass, Mrs T. L., 41 Baker st
Glen, Miss, confectioner, Cambuskenneth
Glen, Mrs Margt., grocer, 44-46 Main st

Glen, Mrs, 73 Newhouse
Glen, Thomas, mason, 17 Newhouse
Glencross, James, miner, 7 Weaver row
Glenday, A., compositor, 11 Abbey rd
Godden, Thomas, coachman, Beechwood
Goldie, D., coach trimmer, 3 Abbey rd pl
Goldie, Miss, 25 Albert pl
Goldie, R., county assis. san. insp., 64 Murray pl
Goldsmith, A., postman, 14 Abbey rd
Good, John R., tailor, 8 Wallace st
Goodall, Robt., cabman, 10 Up. craigs
Goodbrand, Mrs Mary, 1 Springfield pl
Goodfellow, Miss Kate, 15 Up. Bridge st
Goodwillie, R., fish hawker, 7 Low. Bridge st
Goodwillie, Wm., hawker, 9 Albany cres
Gordon, Col.-Sergt., Military Hospital
Gordon, James, surveyor, 1 Douglas st
Gordon, James, teacher of dancing, 24 Bruce st
Gordon, John A., chemist, 12 Barnton st; house
    —23 Millar pl
Gordon, J., salesman, 25 Wallace st
Gordon, Mrs M., 17 Well Green
Gordon, Mrs, ironmonger, 17 Up. craigs
Gordon, Mrs, 24 Bruce st
Gordon, Rich., coachbuilder, 2 Nelson pl
Gordon, Thomas, storeman, 1 Abbey road pl
Gordon, T., fireman, 62 Spittal st
Gordon, Wm., lab., 33 Low. craigs
Gordon, W., saddler, 36 Abbey rd
Gordon, W., newsagent, &c., Sub-Post Office, 120
    Baker st, and 32-38 Forth cres
Gorrie, Miss C., 26 Torbrex
Gotts, Sergt. Wm., Forthside
Goudie, A. H., Master of Works, 1 Rosebery pl
Goudie, Samuel, janitor, 3 Bank st
Goudie, Wm., baker, 36 Baker st
Goudie, Wm., refreshment rooms, 73 King st
Gourlay, Mrs Janet, 16 Glebe cres
Gourlay, John, 32 Abbey rd
Gourlay, Wm., builder, 6 Rosebery pl
Gow, Mrs C., 44 Low. Bridge st
Gow, Miss Ina, 38 St Mary's wynd
Gow, Mrs, 19 Bruce st
Gow, P., tailor, 5 Douglas st
Gow, Thomas, joiner, 2 St John st
Gowans, Miss, tobacconist, 3 Maxwell pl
Graham, T., traveller, 10 Barnton st
Graham, A., teacher, 25 Dumbarton rd
Graham, A., carter, Causewayhead
Graham, Adam, engine keeper, 70 Up. craigs

Graham, Alex. G., merchant, 3 Gladstone pl
Graham, David, trav., 12 Bruce st
Graham, Miss Caroline, 20 Allan pk
Graham, Mrs E., 6 Low, craigs
Graham, Geo., trav., Seaforth pl
Graham, J., molecatcher, 17 Douglas st
Graham, Misses, teachers, 10 Abercromby pl
Graham, Mrs Margt., 10 Abercromby pl
Graham, Mrs, 20 Borestone pl
Graham, Mrs, grocer, Cambuskenneth
Graham, Mrs, 71 Main st
Graham, Mrs, 81 Low. Bridge st
Graham, P., coachman, Deroran lodge
Graham, Robt., 59 Main st
Graham, Thomas, 8 Manse cres
Graham, Wm., N.B. station agent, 1 Forth pl
Graham & Morton, ironmongers, 47-51 King st,
    5-13 Dumbarton rd, and 37 Burghmuir
Grainger, And., draper, 1 Forth cres
Grant, G., police sup., 3 Rosebery pl
Grant, Mrs, 3 Broad st
Gray, Alex., lab., 10 Bayne st
Gray, Alex. P., postman, 34 James st
Gray, And., 11 Newhouse
Gray, Chas., clerk, 25 Port st
Gray, G. C., cashier, 24 Princes st
Gray, Hugh, wool sorter, 4 Low. Bridge st
Gray, James, compositor, 14 George st
Gray, James, joiner, 66 Cowane st
Gray, James, seedsman, 15 Melville ter
Gray, James, tile layer, 15 Maxwell pl
Gray, James, miner, Kirk wynd
Gray, James, lorryman, 36 Newhouse
Gray, James, seedsman, 7 Laurelhill pl
Gray, James, colour mixer, 19 Well Green
Gray, Mrs Jane, 60 St Mary's Wynd
Gray, Mrs Jessie, 4 Gladstone pl
Gray, John, lab., 6 Baker st
Gray, John, seedsman, 1 Main st
Gray, Pvte. John, 7 Married Qrs.
Gray, J. M., weaver, 104 Up. craigs
Gray, Miss, servants' registry, 25 Port st
Gray, Mrs, 59 Cowane st
Gray, Mrs, 7 Douglas st
Gray, P., seedsman, 1 Princes st
Gray, Robt., ironmonger, 44 Queen st
Gray, Thomas, miner, 48 Broad st
Gray & Co., seedsmen, 5-9 Up. craigs
Green, Mrs, 61 Wallace st
Green, Thomas, miner, 1 Up. Bridge st

Greenhill, A., water bailiff, 13 Low. Bridge st
Greenhill, David, policeman, 48 Broad st
Greenhill, Mrs, 32 Forth cres
Greenhorn, A., tailor, 20 Bruce st
Greenhorn, R. & J., fleshers, 16 Up. Bridge st
Gregor, Miss H., 8 Bayne st
Greig, A., carter, 14 Up. craigs
Greig, Alex., tailor, 16 James st
Greig, And. S., spirit merchant, 40-42 Broad st
Greig, Dr. F. J., 16 Melville ter
Greig, Miss, 4 Park av
Greig, P., caretaker, 23 Broad st
Grieve, Mrs Agnes, shopkeeper, 7-9 Murray pl
Grieve, James, tannery, St Ninians
Grieve, James, tanner, 16 Snowdon pl
Griffiths, Daniel, tailor, 10 Bayne st
Griffiths, Wm., blacksmith, 22 Bruce st
Grigor, John, factor, Craigend
Grindlay, R., carriage maker, Causewayhead
Grogan, F., basket maker, 25 Broad st and 15
    King st
Guild, A. M., grocer, 16 Bruce st
Guiliani, R., ice-cream shop, 31 Baker st and 4½
    Cowane st
Gundry, James, trav., 47 Baker st
Gunn, Don., cashier, 41 Wallace st
Gunn, James, guide, 52 Up. castlehill
Gunn, John, miner, Crofthead
Gunn, Mrs, 41 Wallace st
Guthrie, James, compositor, 36 James st
Guthrie, Mrs Sarah, 52 Up. Bridge st
Guthrie, Wm., storekeeper, 17 Cowane st
Gwynne, Mrs C., 44 Baker st

H

Hackney, Miss Jane, 18 Main st
Hadaway, Alex., Randolphfield
Hagemann, Mrs, teacher, 8 Coburg av
Haggart, James, banksman, 60 Baker st
Haggart, Miss Margt., 52 Cowane st
Haggarty, H., confectioner, 3 Glencoe rd
Haggerty, T., motor driver, 7 Bayne st
Hain, David, signalman, 8 Wallace st
Haining, Thos., engine driver, 3 Springfield pl
Hailstone, F., engine keeper, 37 Low. craigs
Haldane, Mrs, Allan park house

Haldane & Co., Forth Cooperage
Halket, Miss Agnes, 17 George st
Hall, Alex , baker, 3 Seaforth pl
Hall, Alex., builder, 19 Glasgow rd
Hall, Alex., fish hawker, 7 Church wynd
Hall, Geo., guard, 13 Bruce st
Hall, Geo., Salvation Army Capt., 1 George st
Hall, James, mason, 14 Park lane
Hall, John, grocer, 10 Abbey rd
Hall, Mrs Mary, 26 Union st
Hall, Mrs, Hunter's bldgs., Causewayhead
Hall, Ralph, lab., 38 St Mary's wynd
Halley, Mrs Eliz., 43 Cowane st
Hamilton, Miss B., confectioner, 40 Arcade
Hamilton, D., 48 Raploch
Hamilton, Mrs Janet C., 23 Wallace st
Hamilton, John, miner, 20 Low. castlehill
Hamilton, John, baker, 6 Ballengeich rd
Hamilton, John, insurance agent, 32 Spittal st
Hamilton, J., gardener, Causewayhead
Hamilton, Mrs, hotelkeeper, 2-3 Castle esplanade
Hamilton, Mrs, 52 Broad st
Hamilton, Wm., miner, 32 Spittal st
Haney, James, lab., 33 King st
Hannah, John, clerk, Forthside
Hannan, Michael, bootmaker, 21 Arcade
Hardie, And., machineman, 66 Baker st
Hardie, David, plumber, 66 Up. craigs
Hardie, Geo., joiner, Polmaise cottages
Hardie, G. K., clerk, 30 Barnton st
Hardie, Miss J., Sub-Post Office, Cowane st
Hardie, Mrs, 5 Mid. craigs
Hardie, Miss Rebecca, 12 Port st
Hardie, Robt., painter, 3 Glasgow rd
Hardie, Sergt.-Major, Military hospital
Hare, M., insurance agent, 78 St Mary's wynd
Hare, Rev. J. B., 38 St Mary's wynd
Harkins, M., lab., 23 Broad st
Harkins, P., storekeeper, 21 Baker st
Harkins, Wm., lab., 7 Barn rd
Harkness, W., clerk, Causewayhead rd
Harley, And., ironmonger, 55 King st
Harley, Cameron, ironmonger, 26-28 Barnton st;
    house—8 Wallace st
Harley, Mrs M., 66 Cowane st
Harley, Hugh, lab., 41 Baker st
Harley, John, painter, 72 Port st
Harley, Thomas, conductor, 16 Cowane st
Harley, Wm., painter, 25 Irvine pl
Harold, Mrs, 16 King st

Harrison, Thos. S., banker, 38 Dumbarton rd
Harris, Mrs, 14 Low. Bridge st
Harris, Mrs, Wallace Arms Inn, Causewayhead
Harris, John, sawyer, 3 Bridge lane
Hart, Miss Isabella, 18 Viewfield st
Hart, Mrs, dressmaker, 37 Murray pl
Hart, John, newsagent, 78 Main st
Harper, Hugh, mechanic, 17 Cowane st
Harper, Thomas, miner, 67 Main st
Harper, Miss, 19 Weaver row
Harper, James, miner, 19 Weaver row
Harrower, D., fireman, 27 Abbey rd
Harvey, Alex., tanner, 64 Main st
Harvey, Alex., tailor, 21 Bannockburn rd
Harvey, Alex., lab., 40 Up. castlehill
Harvey, Mrs C., 26 Park ter
Harvey, Mrs M., 4 Albert pl
Harvey, F., lab., 41 St Mary's wynd
Harvey, John, tailor, 32 James st
Harvey & Harris, tailors, 39 Barnton st
Harvey, P., sexton, Kirk wynd, St Ninians
Harvey, Wm., stone dresser, 2 King's stables
Harvey & Hunter, jewellers, 53 King st
Harvie, Miss, dressmaker, 80 Cowane st
Harvie, Miss Nellie, 17 Up. Bridge st
Haslar, Wm., clerk, 1 Abbey rd
Hastie, Mrs M., 37 Low. Bridge st
Hastings, James H., teacher, 27 Murray pl
Haston, David, soldier, Castle
Hawdon, Chas., engineer, 53 Wallace st
Haxton, Chas., engine driver, 12 Low. Bridge st
Hay, James, joiner, 16 Borestone pl
Hay, Miss Annie, teacher, 5 George st
Hay, Miss, cook, 72 Port st
Hay, Miss E., 19 Randolph ter
Hay, Miss Isa., 8 Millar pl
Hay, Miss L., 15 Randolph ter
Hay, Mrs S. E., newsagent, 6 Dumbarton rd
Hay, Mrs Susan, 77 Port st
Hay, Mrs William, 53 Wallace st
Hay, Wm., piano tuner, 23 Queen st
Headridge, Mrs, Causewayhead rd
Headridge, A., builder, Causewayhead
Headridge, Miss, Craig Wallace View, C'head
Healy, John, surfaceman, 118 Baker st
Heally, Mrs Sarah, 2 St Mary's wynd
Heally, Luke, miner, 75 Main st
Heaps, John, miner, 30 Cowane st
Heatley, Miss, 81 Baker st
Heggie, Alex., shoemaker, 13 St John st

Held, A., hairdresser, 7 Nelson pl
Henderson, A. D., umbrella maker, 38 Murray pl
Henderson, Adam, lab., 18 St Mary's wynd
Henderson, Alex., butcher, 4 Cowane st
Henderson, Arch., compositor, 3 Broad st
Henderson, C., pitsinker, 26 St Mary's wynd
Henderson, David, ironmonger, 1 Abbey rd
Henderson, Geo., vanman, 47 Low. Bridge st
Henderson, Geo., mason, 5 Church wynd
Henderson & Son, G., painters, 20 Viewfield st ;
     house—18 Queen st
Henderson & Bennett, grocers, 110 Baker st
Henderson, Hamilton G., Snowdon house
Henderson, H., slater, 60 Baker st
Henderson, Hector, joiner, 5 Torbrex
Henderson, James, lab., 8 St Mary's wynd
Henderson, James, 18 Snowdon pl
Henderson, Jas., assurance agent, 1 Forth cres
Henderson, John, dairyman, 6-10 Cowane st
Henderson, John, mason, 34 Cowane st
Henderson, John, porter, 116 Up. craigs
Henderson, John, roadman, 45 Low. Bridge st
Henderson, John, plumber, 15 Bruce st
Henderson, J. S., writer, 64 Murray pl
Henderson, J. R., Causewayhead rd
Henderson, Robt., tailor, 10 Up. Bridge st
Henderson, Wm., rub. worker, 31 St Mary's wynd
Henderson, Miss, newsagent, 28 Bow st
Henderson, Miss C., 17 Queen st
Henderson, Miss, 19 Cowane st
Henderson, Miss K. P., 5 Royal gardens
Henderson, Miss Jane, 48 Cowane st
Henderson, Mrs Helen, 1 Springfield pl
Henderson, Mrs, 89 St Mary's wynd
Henderson, Mrs Jeanie, 88 Cowane st
Henderson, Mrs, 2 Victoria pl
Henderson, Mrs, 30 Bow st
Henderson, Mrs, 73 Low. Bridge st
Henderson, P., waiter, 14 Park lane
Henderson, Thomas, joiner, 24 Bruce st
Henderson, Thomas, 19 Albert pl
Henderson, W. T., cabinetmaker, 28 Queen st
Henderson & Son, Thos., joiners, 43 Port st
Henderson, H., stockbroker, 53 Murray pl
Hendry, Geo., brushmaker, 10 Up. Bridge st
Hendry, James, miner, 69 Main st
Hendry, Robt., barman, 52 Up. craigs
Hendry, Mrs M., 24 Queen st
Henley, John, lab., 9 St John st
Hennachen, M., lab., 86 St Mary's wynd

Henny, Robt., 19 St Mary's wynd
Henny, Mrs Jane, 35 Bannockburn rd
Henry, Mrs E., Dunlora, Cambuskenneth
Henry, W., insur. agent, Cambuskenneth
Hensbay, F., tailor, 38 St Mary's wynd
Hepburn, Chas., surfaceman, 25 Irvine pl
Hepburn, Geo., ret. engineer, 9 Royal gardens
Hepting, L., jeweller, 11 Murray pl; house—25
    Princes st
Herron, Adam, 40 Barnton st
Herron, John W., headmaster, Episcopal school
Hetherington, W., grocer, 15 Forth cres
Hetherington, W., grocer, 27 Port st
Hewitt, Mrs E., 38 St Mary's wynd
Higginbotham, Mrs Emily, 13 Gladstone pl
Higgins, Jas., drain tile agent, 17 King st
Highet, Dr. R. C., 5 Park aven
Hill, David, ironmonger, 7 Queen st
Hill, Jas., miner, 51 Main st
Hill, John, machineman, 75 King st
Hill, Mrs Jane, 27 Murray pl
Hill, William, greengrocer, 47 Broad st
Hill & Whyte, solicitors, 4 King st
Hislop, Fred, labr., 97 Low. bridge st
Hislop, Golan, painter, 114 Baker st
Hislop, Mrs Agnes, 37 King st
Hislop, Mrs Cath., 4 Low. craigs
Hislop, Mrs Janet, 15 Douglas st
Hislop, Thos., surfaceman, 20 Bow st
Hislop, Robt., waterman; 6 Bruce st
Hodge, Arch., baker, $14\frac{1}{2}$ St John st
Hodge, Miss G., 72 Port st
Hodge, Miss Mary, 3 York pl
Hodge, Mrs Dan., 64 Murray pl
Hodgson, Mark, china merchant, 27 Spittal st;
    house—3 Albert pl
Hodgson, Mrs H., 36 Broad st
Hogan, Mrs, furniture dealer, 64-66 Baker st;
    house—26 Queen st
Hogg, George, painter, 10 George st
Hogg, J. A., chemist, 79 Port st
Hogg, Misses, 33 Snowdon pl
Hogg, Miss, 4 Melville ter
Hogg, Mrs, 13 Spittal st
Hogg & Co., James, *Journal* office, 9 King st
Hoggan, Robt., miner, 25 St Mary's wynd
Hoggan, Jas., miner, 116 Main st
Holland, Mrs, broker, 109 Baker st
Holmes, Chas., carter, 89 Baker st
Holmes, D., chief warder, Military prison

Holmes, Wm., weaver, 1 Springfield pl
Holdan, Jas., miner, 79 Main st
Honeyman, D., engineer, 21 Main st
Honeyman, R. B., miner, 38 Up. castlehill
Honeyman, Robt., sawmiller, 10 Up. castlehill
Honeyman, Mrs, laundress, 10 Up. bridge st
Honeyman, Mrs, 26 Up. castlehill
Hood, Allan, clerk, 4 Cowane st
Hood, John, baker, 4 Cowane st
Hood, Miss, 81 Port st
Hood, Peter, labr., 14 Cowane st
Hood, Wm., artist, 19 Coburg aven
Hood, Wm., joiner, Bridgehaugh
Horn, John, fitter, 23 Main st
Horn, John, vanman, 43½ Cowane st
Horn, Miss, 81 Cowane st
Horn, Pat., labr., 8 Broad st
Horn, Wm., carter, 8 Union st
Horne, Thos., tanner, 37 Glasgow rd
Horsburgh, Geo., brushmaker, 10 Bayne st
Horsburgh, Geo., confectioner, 19 Murray pl
Horsburgh, Wm., engineer, 10 George st
Houston, Jos., rubber worker, 6 Up. bridge st
Houston, Robt., lathsplitter, 32 Up. bridge st
Houston, T. L., vet. surgeon, 6 Up. craigs; house
   —Allan pk. house
Howat, John, tailor, 17 King st
Howie, John, 5-7 Bank st
Howie, Sam., carter, 3 Abbey rd
Howie, Thos., storeman, 1 Douglas st
Howieson, Mrs C., Causewayhead rd
Howieson, Wm., yardsman, 8 Raploch
Hinves, Mrs Emily, 25 Spittal st
Hughes, Allan, platelayer, 1 Calton Cottages
Hughes, B., miner, 39 Bannockburn rd
Hughes, David, trav., 85 Main st
Hughes, Jas., miner, 6 Raploch
Hughes, Owen, engineman, 7 Borestone cres
Hughes, Robt., fireman, 33 James st
Hughson, Wm., hairdresser, 1 Springfield pl
Hume, John, miner, 39 Low. craigs
Hume, Mrs, dressmaker, 52 Barnton st
Humphries, Jas., butler, 12 George st
Hunslow, W., manager railway refresh. rooms,
   13 Forth pl
Hunt, P., mason, 2 St John st
Hunter, A., spirit merchant, Castle wynd
Hunter, Andrew, lorryman, 12 Bayne st
Hunter, David, wool carder, 15 Seaforth pl
Hunter, David, grocer, 53-57 Baker st

Hunter, Henry, contractor, 1 Abbey rd pl
Hunter, Isaac, timekeeper, 6 William pl
Hunter, Jas., railway guard, 18 Union st
Hunter, John, cabinetmaker, 8 Bruce st
Hunter, John, labr., 15 Maxwell pl
Hunter, John, lorryman, 13 Cowane st
Hunter, John, spirit merchant, 51 Barnton st, and 2 Princes st
Hunter, John, tailor's cutter, 5 James st
Hunter, John, blacksmith, 10 Bayne st
Hunter, L., cabinetmaker, 29 Millar pl
Hunter, Miss J., confect., 1 Broad st
Hunter, Miss. 12 Victoria pl
Hunter, Mrs Ann, 12 Bayne st
Hunter, Mrs C., Cambuskenneth
Hunter, Mrs M., 14 St John st
Hunter, Mrs M., 110 Up. craigs
Hunter, Mrs. 65 Bannockburn rd
Hunter, Wm., miner, 10 Bayne st
Hunter, Mrs. i Randolph ter
Hunter, P., stockbroker, 5 Dean cres
Hunter, Robt., miner, 144 Main st
Hunter, T., lorryman, 13 Cowane st
Hunter, Wm., iron merchant, 12 Victoria pl
Hunter, Wm., Lily cottage, Causewayhead
Hunter, Wm., insur. agent, 25 Wallace st
Hunter, John, overseer, 6 Well green
Hunter, James, wool agent, 8 Globe cres
Hunter, L. & D., cabinetmakers, 17 King st
Hurley, Wm., labourer, 23 Broad st
Hutchinson, T., gardener, Causewayhead rd
Hutchieson, James, Cambuskenneth
Hutchison, James, cooper, 12 Bayne st
Hutchison, James, roadman, 12 Bayne st
Hutchison, Mrs. 34 Abbey rd
Hutchison & Co., dressmakers, 55 King st
Hutton, Eben., storeman, 9 Well green
Hutton, Geo., joiner, Springfield pl
Hutton, James, fireman, 13 Glencoe rd
Hutton, Mrs Agnes, 18 Borestone pl
Hutton & Turnbull, printers, 15 Murray pl
Hutton, James, engine driver, 81 Baker st
Hutton, Wm., lorryman, 4 Low. bridge st
Hynd, Thos., clerk, 1 James st
Hynd, H., tailor, 10 Up. bridge st
Hynd, John, tailor, 4 Bruce st
Hynd, Wm., tailor, 11 King st
Hynde, Geo., miner, 31 Low. craigs

I

Imrie, David, rubber worker, 28 Up. bridge st
Imrie, J., engine driver, 7 Well green
Imrie, Geo., fishing rod maker, 98 Cowane st
Imrie, Murdoch, labourer, 6 Well green
Inglis, Miss, 11 Newhouse
Innes, Alex., goods porter, 38 Abbey rd
Innes, Mrs Ann, 44 Broad st
Ireland, David, lab., 63 Bannockburn rd
Ireland, Mrs, 17 Allan park
Irving, J., vanman, Aitken's bldgs., Ban'burn rd
Irvine, R., bricklayer, 59 Glasgow rd
Isitt, Geo., grocer, 22 Bruce st

J

Jack, Jas., platelayer, 98 St Mary's wynd
Jack, John, cartwright, 1 Snowdon pl
Jack, P., carter, 16 Low. castlehill
Jack, Thos., weaver, 25 Well green
Jackson, Alex., postman, 55 Low. bridge st
Jackson, David, lab., 28 Up. castlehill
Jackson, Hugh, miner, 10 Bayne st
Jackson, John, trav., 23 Abbey rd
Jackson, Jas., trav., 7 Abercromby pl
Jackson, Jas., clerk, 16 Park pl
Jackson, Jas., sawyer, 12 Bayne st
Jackson, Mrs Ann, 3 James st
Jackson, Sergt., Military hospital
Jaffray, Mrs, 9 Newhouse
Jardine, Geo., 9 Melville ter
James, David T., teacher, 5 Coburg avenue
James, Henry, butcher, 24 Union st
James, James, lab., 4 Up. Bridge st
Jamieson, David, wool sorter, 74 Up. craigs
Jamieson, D., Heathfield, Forth st
Jamieson, Geo., glazier, 17 Well Green
Jamieson, H., engine driver, 17 Low. Bridge st
Jamieson, H., mill overseer, 2 William pl
Jamieson, John, headmaster, 5 Allan pk
Jamieson, John, printer, 28-34 Up. craigs
Jamieson, Mrs, 21 Forth cres
Jamieson, Mrs, 1 York pl
Jamieson, Miss, confectioner, 13 Maxwell pl
Jamieson, P., Singer's agent, 2 Dean cres

Jamieson, Thos., surfaceman, 44 Low. castlehill
Jamieson, Wm., waiter, 63 Baker st
Jamieson & Co., J., tailors, 28 King st
Jarvie, Miss M., 12 Viewfield st
Jeffray, P., brakesman, 3 William pl
Jeffrey, Alex., plumber, Causewayhead
Jeffrey, Misses A. and J., 15 Glasgow rd
Jeffrey, E., insurance agent, 7 Nelson pl
Jeffrey, Geo., carriage hirer, 7 Murray pl; stables—Shore rd
Jeffrey, Miss, Holly cot., Causewayhead
Jeffrey, Mrs, 5 Glasgow rd
Jeffrey, P. L., trav, 23 Albert pl
Jeffrey, Robt., night watchman, 22 Thistle st
Jenkins, A., solicitor, Glasgow rd house
Jenkins, A. & J., solicitors, 80 Port st
Jenkins, David, carter, 118 Main st
Jenkins, David, fruiterer, 95-97 Main st
Jenkins, Geo., nailer, 5 Sunnyside
Jenkins, G. R., draper, 43 King st; house—12 Millar pl
Jenkins, John, writer, 11 Clifford rd
Jenkins, M., vanman, 31½ Glasgow rd
Jenkins, P., fisherman, 44 Low. Bridge st
Jenkins, Mrs Robt., 31½ Glasgow rd
Jenkins, Robt., comp., 12 George st
Jenkins, Wm., 23 Forth cres
Jenkins, Sergt. Wm., Military prison
Jenner, Robt., coachman, 59 Newhouse
Jerrat, James, cooper, 17 Abbey Road
Johnstone, And., miner, 1 Church wynd
Johnstone, A., painter, 30-34 Arcade
Johnstone, Miss C., Cambuskenneth
Johnstone, D., platelayer, 1 Springfield pl
Johnstone, James, lab., 1 St John st
Johnstone, Mrs Jane, 59 Cowane st
Johnstone, John, plumber, 3A Main st
Johnstone, John, lorryman, 108 Up. craigs
Johnstone, John, hawker, 44 Baker st
Johnstone, Miss J., dressmaker, 10 Viewfield pl
Johnstone, Mrs M., 23 Broad st
Johnstone, Miss Mary, 37 Wallace st
Johnstone, Wm., painter, 16 Millar pl
Johnstone, Wm., miner, 72 St Mary's wynd
Johnstone, Alex., lab., 21 Well Green
Johnstone, Mrs, 12 Abbey rd
Johnston, Chas. E., trav., 1 Dumbarton rd
Johnston, Chas., headmaster, 6 Douglas ter
Johnston, Duncan, trav., Barnton house
Johnston, James, fitter, 60 Baker st

Johnston, James, wood merchant, Coburg av
Johnston, James, lab, 60 Baker st
Johnston, James, wood merc., 13 Melville ter
Johnston, James, wood yard, 28 Abbey rd
Johnston, James H., 2 Queen's rd
Johnston, John, broker, 31 Main st
Johnston, John, fish merchant, 31 Port st
Johnston, John, fishmonger, 3 Clifford rd
Johnston, John, painter, 114 Baker st
Johnston, John, tailor, 22 Union st
Johnston, Miss, 11 Randolph rd
Johnston, Mrs, fish merchant, 50 Port st
Johnston, Mrs Helen, 41 Baker st
Johnston, Mrs Janet, 31 Queen st
Johnston, Mrs J. C. B., 3 Pitt ter
Johnston, P., lab., Causewayhead
Johnston, T. W. R., editor, *Journal*, Windsor pl
Johnston, W., publican, 1 Barn rd
Johnston, W., spirit mer., 91 St Mary's wynd
Jolley, Sergt. G. H., 10 Dumbarton rd
Jollie, Mrs I., milliner, 36 Arcade
Jones, Miss Kate, 42 Up. Bridge st
Jones, T. J., assis. insp. of poor, 42 Up. Bridge st
Jordan, Staff-Sergt., Military prison
Joyce, John, lab., 16 Raploch
Joyce, Michael, lab., 13 Raploch
Joyce, Mrs, 111 Baker st
Joyce, Mrs, 12 Raploch
Joyce, Thomas, lab., 27 Raploch
Judd, Mrs Janet, 95 Baker st
Jude, Alex., painter, 23 Broad st
Junior, Wm., guard, 2 Springfield pl

K

Kane, Mrs M., 65 Wallace st
Kane, Mrs, 8 St Mary's wynd
Kane, R., shoemaker, 86 St Mary's wynd
Kaney, P., 48 Low castlehill
Kaney, P., lab., 48 Spittal st
Kaney, Thos., slater, 14 Bow st
Kaney, Hugh, lab., 73 Baker st
Kaney, P., lab., 10 Raploch
Kay, Alex., baker, 1 Middle craigs
Kay, James, joiner, 13 Borestone pl
Kay, James, saddler, 61 Up. craigs
Kay, James, tanner, 8 Main st

Kay, John, baker, 64 Up. craigs
Kay, Mrs Jessie, 33 Up. craigs
Kay, Mrs Elizabeth, Bellfield, Up. Bridge st
Kay, Rob., cellarman, 43 Low. craigs
Kay, William, blacksmith, 19 Abbey rd
Keddie, Rob., surfaceman, 19 Abbey rd
Keir, Alex., fruit., 39 King st., 65 and 78 Port st
Keir, Alex., gardener, 11 Manse cres
Keir, John, clerk, 20 Murray pl
Keith, & Ralston, bakers, 10 Port st
Kellie, Thomas, cooper, 34 Abbey rd
Kelly, H., gardener, 21 Low. craigs
Kelly, Michael, stonebreaker, 20 Broad st.
Kelly, Mrs C., 2 St John st
Kelly, Mrs T., 5 St John st
Kelly, John, lab., 48 Baker st
Kelly, Jas., miner. 71 Bannockburn rd
Kelly, P. H., storeman, 57 Low. Bridge st
Kelly, Thos., miner, 13 Low. craigs
Kellock, J., clerk, 8 Wallace st
Kelso, W., miner, 21 St Mary's wynd
Kemp, Mrs, 29 Newhouse
Kemp, And., car. inspec., 68 Cowane st
Kemp, James, platelayer, 23 Burghmuir
Kemp, Jas. D., dairyman, 25 Bannockburn rd
Kemp & Nicholson, engineers, Forth st
Kennedy, Joseph, 38 Abbey rd
Kennedy, A. V., spirit merc., 34 St Mary's wynd
Kennedy & Co. Ltd., manuf. confect., Old bridge
Kennedy, Miss, 27 Bannockburn rd
Kennedy, J. A., 5 James st
Kennedy, John, joiner, 11 King st
Kenny, A., warehouseman, 60 Up. craigs
Kenny, Michael, lab., 46 Low. castlehill
Kenny, Michael, waterman, 4 Bank st
Kenny, Peter, lab., 3 Raploch
Kenny, Thomas, quarryman, 27 Raploch
Kenny, Ed., fireman, 46 Up. castlehill
Kenny, Alf., linotyper, 18 Bruce st
Kenny, Miss, confec., 62 Up. craigs
Kenny, J., printer, 10 Nelson pl
Kerr, Alex., engine driver, 132 Main st
Kerr, Alex., tobacconist, 11 Friars st
Kerr, Hugh, stoker, 29 Glasgow rd
Kerr, James, coachman, 18 Bruce st
Kerr, James, platelayer, 12 St Mary's wynd
Kerr, John, fireman, 41 Baker st
Kerr, Michael, lab., 2 St Mary's wynd
Kerr, Mrs Janet, 15 Broad st
Kerr, Mrs Lilias, 14 Cowane st

Kerr, P., 72 Port st
Kerr, P. wheel inspec., 12 Bayne st
Kerr, Thomas, engine driver, 15 Bow st
Kerr, William, blacksmith, 31 Bannockburn rd
Kerr, Wm., plumber, 44 Broad st
Kerr, J., 2 William pl
Kerr, Miss, 20 Bow st
Ketchen, Wm., blacksmith, 15 Low. Bridge st
Ketchtall, Sergt., 24 Married quarters
Kettle, Jas., grocer, 36 James st
Kettrick, Ed., lab., 3 Bank st
Kettrick, John, mason, 55 Low. Bridge st
Keyden, Theodore, stockbroker, 21 Park ter
Kidd, Bartholomew, tailor, 52 Broad st
Kidston, Misses, 24 Victoria pl
Kidston, R., 12 Clarendon pl
Kidston, Jas. B., 10 Park ter
Kilgannon, James, miner, 34 Broad st
Killingbeck, M., carpet designer, 13 Low. Bdg st
Kilpatrick, Mrs Janet, 1 St John st
Kilpatrick, P., cab driver, 17 Seaforth pl
King, James, guard, 15 Bruce st
King, John, spirit merchant, 55 Port st ; house—
    27 Snowdon pl
King, P., lab., 4 Low. craigs
King, P., tailor, 33 James st
King, Robt., coachman, 9 Snowdon pl
King, Thomas, lab., 23 Raploch
King, W. T., trav., 17 Coburg av
Kinlay, Robt., comp., 34 Cowane st
Kinmonth, John, vanman, 71 Up. Bridge st
Kinnaird, James G., tailor, 4 Port st
Kinnaird, James, joiner, 11 Winchel pl
Kinnaird, Wm., butcher, 1 King's stables
Kinross, David, trav., 5 Windsor pl
Kinross, Geo., coachbuilder, 4 Victoria sq
Kinross, Henry, seedsman, 23 Park ter
Kinross, James, coachbuilder, 11 Allan pk
Kinross, John, Hood farm
Kinross, J., St Leonard's, Causewayhead
Kinross, T., seedsman, Hood farm
Kinross & Sons, coachbuilders, 37 Port st
Kirk, David, engine driver, 35 Cowane st
Kirk, James, plumber, 31 Low. Bridge st
Kirk, Wm., joiner, 13 Low. Bridge st
Kirkpatrick, Thomas, lab., 9 Well green
Kirkwood, Hugh, printer, 6 James st
Kirkwood, John, printer, 13 Princes st
Kirkwood, J., miner, 20 Bow st
Kirkwood & Sons, H. M., printers, 33 King st

Knowles, Geo., cabinetmaker, 1A Friars st
Knowles, H., insur. agent, Cambuskenneth
Knox, H., enginekeeper, Aitken's bdgs, St Ninians
Knox, J., wireman, 10 St John st
Kyle, Misses, 55 Wallace st
Kyle, E. & B., fancy warehouse, 8 Baker st

L

Laidlaw, Mrs, 3 Randolph rd
Laidlaw, Dr. A. B., 13 Randolph ter
Laidlaw, Mrs M., nurse, 16 Friars st
Laing, C., fireman, 24 Raploch
Laing, Mrs, 14 Millar pl
Laing, P., engine driver, 1 Bayne st
Laird, Alex., plumber, 32 Spittal st
Laird, Misses, 2 Glebe cres
Laird, Wm., warehouseman, 7 Park lane
Laird, John, roadman, 70 Main st
Lamb, J., painter, 25 Port st and 27 Dumbarton rd
Lamb, Mrs, 15 Broad st
Lamb, Thos., cycle agent, 23 and 45 Murray pl;
     motor car store—14 Thistle st
Lamb, Thomas, joiner, 4 Allan pk
Lambert, Jas., contractor, 8 Glasgow rd
Lambert, John, joiner, 8 Abbey rd pl
Lamond, A., saddler, 83 Main st; house—26
     Bannockburn rd
Lamont, Neil, insur. agent, Crofthead
Landale, John, 5 Clarendon pl
Lang, Miss Ann H., 2 Royal gardens
Lang, Rev. J. P., 6 Park aven
Langford, Mrs, 2 Ballengeich rd
Langmuir, Mrs Jessie, 15 Nelson pl
Lauder, Alex., guard, Bridgehaugh
Lauder, Mrs, A., 32 Up. Bridge st
Laurie, James, engineman, 4 Sunnyside
Laurie, Robt., jute dresser, 4 George st
Laurie, Thos., Temperance Hotel, 5 King st
Laurie, Mrs, spirit merchant, 66 Baker st
Laverock, G., Scotch whisky blender, 11 Forth
     cres
Lavin, James, lab., 18 St John st
Law, Alex., goods porter, 36 Low. castlehill
Law, Wm., grocer, 100 Cowane st
Lawless, Hugh, gardener, 15 St John st
Lawrie, Mrs, 6 Douglas st

Lawrie, Thos., engine driver, 9 Winchel pl
Lawrie, Wm. lab., 53 Bannockburn rd
Lawrie, John, newsagent, 12 Viewfield pl
Lawrence, Mrs H., 25 Wallace st
Lawrie, Mrs, 1 Bank st
Lawrie, John, cellerman, 8 Winchel pl
Lawrie, Rich., Lily cottage, Causewayhead
Lawson, Mrs, 9 Victoria square
Lawson, John, shoemaker, 48 Low. Bridge st
Lawson, Mrs, 20 Bruce st
Lawson, Robert, Annfield
Lawson, Mrs M., 38 Up. castlehill
Lawson, Mrs, 17 St John st
Lawsons, Ltd, drapers, house furnishers, &c.,
    17-25-34 Baker st
Learmonth, Alex., clerk, 11 Nelson pl
Leary, C., lab., 7 Barn rd
Leathley Bros, fish mercs., 67 Baker st
Leathley, H., fish merchant, Shore rd
Leathley, Jesse, fish hawker, 18 St Mary's wynd
Leathley, John, fish merchant, 44 Low. castlehill
Leathley, Mrs, fish merchant, 4 Bank st
Leckie, Miss Jane, 18 Viewfield st
Leckie, William, lorryman, 27 Irvine pl
Lee, Elizabeth, 76 Cowane st
Lees, Mrs, M., spirit merchant, 94 Baker st
Lees, P., sexton, Castle esplanade
Lees, Thos., assistant sexton, Waterloo house
Legge, Alex., policeman, 90 Main st
Legge, Mrs Anne, 17 St John st
Leighton, Janet, 19 Main st
Leighton, Thomas, tailor, 52 Main st
Leishman, Mrs Agnes Jane, 25 Park ter
Leishman, A., crane inspector, 106 Up. craigs
Leitch, Mrs Marg., 27 King st
Leitch, Mrs M., 24 Princes st
Leitham, Jas., lab., 12 Low. Bridge st
Lennie, Mrs Isabella, 9 Glencoe rd
Lennox, John butcher, 36 Forth cres
Lennox, Adam, cattle dealer, 7 Park lane
Lennox, Colin, grocer, 23 Well green
Lennox, Colin, painter, 17 Bruce st
Lennox, Mrs, Station Hotel, 54-56 Murray pl and
    Station rd
Lennox, Miss Janet, 19 Queen st
Lennox, Mrs Helen, 29 Bannockburn rd
Lenord, Wm., candlemaker, 66 Cowane st
Lenton, Wm., pensioner, 19 Up. castlehill
Leonard, Miss Ann, nurse, 72 Port st
Leslie, G., insurance agent, 10 Bruce st

Leslie, James, engine driver, 33 Up. craigs
Leslie, W., insurance supt., 6 Queen st
Lessels, R., miner, 100 Main st
Lewis, J. painter, Causewayhead
Lewis, Wm., upholsterer, 2 William pl
Lewyllen, John, lab., 30 Broad st
Leyden, M., lab., 38 St Mary's wynd
Leyden, Mrs, 8 Broad st
Leyden, Robt., nailer, 15 Weaver row
Lickrish, John, shoemaker, 84 Baker st
Lickrish, Robt., coachtrimmer, 60 Baker st
Liddel, Robt., grocer, 40 King st; house—4
    Queen's rd
Liddell, Miss, 18 Nelson pl
Liddell, Geo., insurance agent, 17 Douglas st
Liddell, H., insurance agent, 6 Bannockburn rd
Lindsay, Adam, cooper, 2 George st
Lindsay, Adam, mason, 85 Low. Bridge st
Lindsay, Alex., mechanic, 7 Abbey rd
Lindsay, David, editor, 17 Newhouse
Lindsay, Mrs H., 25 Queen st
Lindsay, James, carter, 56 Main st
Lindsay, James, lab., 6 Low. craigs
Lindsay, James, coachman, 18 Newhouse
Lindsay, Mrs Jane, 16 Union st
Lindsay, J., clerk, 14 Bruce st
Lindsay, John, joiner, 53 Port st
Lindsay, P., 22 Nelson pl
Lindsay, R., ret. police sergt., 68 St Mary's wynd
Lindsay, Sergt.-Major, Castle
Lindsay, Thomas, cabman, 72 Port st
Lindsay, Wm., lab., 36 James st
Lindsay, W., Bible reader, 57 Low. Bridge st
Linnell, Capt. A., A. O. Dept., 4 Glebe cres
Linsell, Wm., A.O.C., 28 Union st
Lipton, Ltd., merchants, 47 Barnton st
Lister, James, clerk, 9 Newhouse
Lister, Miss J., 4 Windsor pl
Lister, Mrs M., dressmaker, 41 Millar pl
Liston, Misses, 10 Barnton st
Lithgow, Mrs H., 24 Main st
Lithgow, James, lab., 3 Springfield pl
Littlejohn, John, miner, 63 Baker st
Littlejohn, Mrs, 16 Orchard pl
Littlejohn, Robt., gardener, 69 Low. Bridge st
Livingstone, Donald, shepherd, 21 Well Green
Livingstone, James, carpenter, Causewayhead
Livingstone, James, ret. porter, 2 Wallace st
Livingstone, John, chemist, 58 Baker st; house
    —30 Broad st

Livingstone, John, wood turner, 98 Baker st
Livingstone, John, carter, 35 Glasgow rd
Livingstone, Mrs Agnes, 16-18 Up. craigs
Livingstone, Mrs, 11 Bow st
Livingstone, P., fitter, 102 Up. craigs
Livingstone, Wm., cabinetmaker, 45 King st ;
　　house—2 Wallace st
Loch, Mrs Jane, 45 Newhouse
Lockhart, David, tanner, 10 Glasgow rd
Lockhart, John, coal agent, 44 Cowane st
Lockhart, Mrs, 6 Douglas st
Lockhart, W., grocer, 19 Well Green
Lockhart & M'Nab, electrical engineers and
　　smiths, 36-38 Up. craigs
Logan, David, soldier, 9 Low. craigs
Logan, Misses, 36 Snowdon pl
Logan, Thos., brushmaker, 1 Abbey rd
Logie, Alex., joiner, 8 Union st
Logie, David W., writer, 20 Murray pl ; house—
　　26 Dumbarton rd
Lorimer, Alan, slater, 85 Baker st
Lorimer, J. F., cabinetmaker, 16 Spittal st ;
　　house—61 Cowane st
Lorimer, Mrs, 80 Cowane st
Louden, John, mason, Bridgehaugh
Louden, J. S., seedsman, 1A Main st
Louden, Mrs Jessie, 9 Bruce st
Louden, Miss, Hunter's bldgs., Causewayhead
Louden, Wm., miner, 56 Low. Bridge st
Love, Alex., trav., 21 Forth cres
Low, James, teacher, 3 Douglas ter
Low, Mrs Margt., 26 Newhouse
Low, Miss, 21 Abercromby pl
Low & Co., Wm., grocers, 25 Arcade and 57-59
　　Port st
Lowson, Geo., LL.D., Rector, 14 Park pl
Lowther, Mrs C., hawker, 76 Main st
Lucas, Alex., Craigton, Causewayhead
Lucas, James, Spittal farm, Causewayhead
Lucas, John, Ladysneuk farm, Cambuskenneth
Lucas, Wm., Holehead house, Causewayhead
Lumsden, D., station policeman, 24 Baker st
Lundie, Michael, mason, 15 Broad st
Lundie, Mrs Sylvia, 38 St Mary's wynd
Lupton, A. M., architect, 20 Murray pl
Lupton, Thomas, writer, 16 Abercromby pl
Lyall, John, dentist, Cambuskenneth
Lyle, James, cooper, 1 Bank st
Lyle, Matthew, weaver, 4 Bank st
Lyon, John, cartwright, 45 Murray pl

M

Macandrew, Alex., trav., 2 Queen st
Macaulay, John, porter, 31 Up. craigs
Macdonald, J. L., conf., 10 Windsor pl
Macdonald & Fraser, Ltd., auctrs., 21 Thistle st
Macdonald, John, grocer, 9 Irvine pl
Macdonald, Mrs, 63 Wallace st
Macdougall, Rev. D., 42 Dumbarton rd
Macdowall, A., Abbey Craig Park, C'wayhead
MacEwen Bros., grocers, 16-18 Barnton st
MacEwen, Dan, grocer, 5 Drummond pl
MacEwen, D. & J., grocers, Port st
MacEwen, Mrs J., 2 Viewfield pl
MacEwen, Mrs R., 21 Allan park
MacEwen, Robt., grocer, 2 Albert pl
Macfarlan, Parlan, 28 Forth cres
Macfarlane, John, driver, Causewayhead
Macfarlane, Mrs C., 11 Princes st
Macfarquhar, Miss C., Cressington, C'wayhead
Machan, Wm., barman, Castle esplanade
Machar, John, mason, 14 Bow st
Machar, Thos., bricklayer, 77 Up. Bridge st
Machar, Jas., bricklayer, 6 St Mary's wynd
Macher, John, lab., 26 St Mary's wynd
Macher, Wm., bricklayer, 15 Bow st
Machray, Chas., carriage hirer, 57 Glasgow rd
Macintosh, J. F., bootmaker, and chiropodist. 22
    Viewfield st ; house—Bellfield rd
Mack, Mrs, 82 Spittal st
Mackay, Eneas, bookseller 43 Murray pl
Mackay, John, trav., 24 Princes st
Mackay, Rev. M., retired, 22 Allan park
Mackay, Mrs I., 27 Murray pl
Mackechnie, A., cabinetmaker, 1 Viewfield st
Mackie, D., In. Revenue officer, 21 Coburg av
Mackie, James F., writer, 15 Randolph rd
Mackie, John, bricklayer, 44 Baker st
Mackie, Mrs J., Viewfield, Causewayhead
Mackieson, J., 6 Barnton st and 5 Park lane
Mackin, James, mason, 24 Baker st
Mackintosh, Alex., iron turner, 5 Park lane
Mackintosh, P., tobacconist, 50 Baker st
Mackintosh, Dr W. A., 3 Park ter
Mackintosh & Mackintosh, whisky blenders, 10
    Thistle st
Maclaurin, Robt., Burghmuir
Maclaurin, Robt., 24 Park ter
MacLuckie, Robt., writer, 6 Gladstone pl

MacLuckie, Jas., writer, 6 Royal gardens
MacLagan, J. A. S., 17 Park ter
MacLellan, Miss, Ochilview
MacLuckie, R., banker, 22 King st
Macnaughton, P., tobacconist, 1 Windsor pl
Macnie, Mrs, 15 Victoria pl
Macpherson, Miss A., 60 Baker st
Macpherson, Thos., glazier, 14 Well green
Macpherson, W., Co-op. Soc. sec,, 21 Burghmuir
Macquarrie, Miss C., 33 James st
Macrae, P., insur. agent, 26 Union st
Mailer, Wm., cabinetmaker, 70-72 Baker st
Mailer, Jas, trav., 2 Pitt ter
Mailer & Co., John, farm produce merchants, 49
       55 Up. Craigs, 37 Allan pk (Tel. 5y3)
Mailley, Mrs Bridget, 2 St Mary's wynd
Mailley, Mrs C., 2 George st
Mailley, Peter, lab., 30 Up. castlehill
Mailley, Thomas, tanner, 9 Bannockburn rd
Mains, William, vanman, 34 Cowane st
Mains, Mrs, 64 Up. craigs
Mains, John H., weaver, 23 George st
Mair, John S., boot salesman, 37 King st
Mair, Rev, M., 3 Albert pl
Maitland, James, guard, 17 Abbey rd
Malcolm, Miss, dressmaker, 5 Viewfield st
Malley, John, woodcutter 25 Raploch
Malley, Michael, lab., 68 Cowane st
Malley, John, fireman, 6 Millar pl
Malley, Mrs, 2 Raploch
Maltman, Mrs Mary, 18 Viewfield st
Mann, Alex., brakesman, 2 Gowanbank
Mann, F. G., In. Rev. surveyor, 9 Coburg av
Manning, D., ret. teacher, 8 Low. Bridge st
Manson, Mrs, 16½ Raploch
Marchant, A. W., Mus. Doc., 10 Glebe cres
Marr, George, pointsman, 100 Up. craigs
Marr, Mrs, 4 Bruce st
Marrie, Michael, lab., 50 Low. castlehill
Marriott, John, cabinetmaker, 3 Douglas st
Marriott, Mrs, newsagent, 62 Cowane st
Marry, Michael, lab., 9 Raploch
Marshall, Alex., 53 Wallace st
Marshall, David, dentist, 1 Melville ter.; house
       —31 Snowdon pl
Marshall, D., cardriver, Causewayhead
Marshall, Duncan, weaver, 108 Up. craigs
Marshall, Geo., postman, 2 George st
Marshall, Geo., tailor, 88 Cowane st
Marshall, H., miner, 9 Glencoe rd

Marshall, J., Dunard, Causewayhead rd
Marshall, James, cardriver, Causewayhead
Marshall, James, candlemaker, 48 Cowane st
Marshall, James, tailor, 10 Low. Bridge st
Marshall, Miss Helen, 1 Millar pl
Marshall, Miss I., dairy, 39 Forth cres
Marshall, Miss, 32 Up. Bridge st
Marshall, Mrs Annie, 22 Glasgow rd
Marshall, Mrs Eliza, 92 Cowane st
Marshall, Mrs Jane, 13 Bruce st
Marshall, Mrs, 7 Bruce st
Marshall, Mrs, 28 St Mary's wynd
Marshall, Mrs M., 4 Bow st
Marshall, P., settmaker, 21 Abbey rd
Marshall, P., quarry contractor, 49 Wallace st
Marshall, Rev. A. Miller, Cowie
Marshall, Robt., lab., 14 Bow st
Marshall, Robt., Woodbank, Burghmuir
Marshall, Robt., 26 Glasgow rd
Marshall, R., saddler, Cambuskenneth
Marshall, Thos., confectioner, 14 Arcade
Marshall, Wm., lab., 118 Baker st
Marshall, Thos., smith, 14 George st
Marshall, T., engineer, 5 Ballengeich rd
Marshall, W., lab., 53½ Cowane st
Marshall, W. & T., engineers, 16 Dumbarton rd
Martin, Alex., nailmaker, Barnsdale pl
Martin, Donald, miner, 74 Main st
Martin, John, smith, 22 Orchard pl
Martin, Mrs Cath., 46 Up. Bridge st
Martin, James, joiner, 26 Union st
Martin, Mrs Jane, 89 Main st
Martin, John, 32 Up. Bridge st
Martin, Miss, 24 Orchard pl
Martin, P., lathsplitter, 24 Bow st
Martin, Rich., carter, 5 Bruce st
Martin, Rich., miner, 37 Main st
Martin, Robt., joiner, 31 Up. craigs
Martin, Wm., postman, 8 Douglas st
Martin, Wm., nailer, 152 Main st
Martin, Wm., nailer, 132 Main st
Martin, Wm., canteen steward, Castle
Mason, Frank, miner, 79 Main st
Masson, Mrs, 8 Douglas ter
Mathers, James, guard, 43½ Cowane st
Mathie, H. G., 4 Barnton st and 10 Bruce st
Mathie, MacLuckie & Lupton, sois., 22 King st
Mathieson Bros., engravers, 25 Port st
Mathieson, C., patternmaker, Cambuskenneth
Mathieson, Mrs, dressmaker, 60 Low. Bridge st

Mathieson, Mrs J., 76 Cowane st
Matthews, Col.-Sergt., Castle
Mavor, R., tailor, Causewayhead
Maxton, Mrs, 8 Bruce st
Maxwell, T., slater, Douglas st and Queensbaugh
Maxwell, Wm., merchant, 6 Clifford rd
Maypole Dairy Co., Ltd., 15½ Murray pl
Meffen, Thomas, lorryman, 46 Low. Bridge st
Meigle, Geo., surfaceman, 5 St John st
Meiklejohn, Alex., ironmonger, 3 Snowdon pl
Meiklejohn, David, lab., 26 Bannockburn rd
Meiklejohn, Ed., trav., 8 Dean cres
Meiklejohn, John, baker, 2 Spittal st
Meiklejohn, Mrs Margt., 55 Wallace st
Meiklejohn, P., dairyman, 51-53 Cowane st
Meiklejohn, Robt., engineer, 23 Abbey rd
Meiklejohn, Wm., 9 Clifford rd
Meikle, Mrs E., 26 Port st
Meldrum, Thomas, lab., 7 Borestone cres
Meldrum, Wm., groom, 52 Low. castlehill
Melrose, James, maltman, 5 Up. Bridge st
Melville, Miss Agnes, 17 Cowane st
Melville, W. D., hawker, 41 St Mary's wynd
Melville, Wm., plumber, 13 Spittal st
Menteith, John, lab., 5 Wallace st
Menteith, Robt., hawker, 8 Broad st
Menzies, Arch., teacher, 5 Millar pl
Menzies, James, miner, 142 Main st
Menzies, J., engine driver, 3 Bruce st
Menzies, Mrs Eliz., 20 Nelson pl
Menzies, Mrs, Rosemount, Causewayhead
Menzies, Mrs, 53 Low. Bridge st
Menzies, P., grocer, 20 Up. craigs; house—25 Dumbarton rd
Menzies, Robt., grocer, 7 Viewfield pl
Menzies, Robt., miner, 142 Main st
Menzies, Thomas, draper, 4 Abercromby pl
Menzies, W. J. Milne, Ashfield, Park pl
Menzies & Co., Robt., grocers, 22 Bow st
Menzies & Co., Thomas, drapers, 36 King st
Menzies, James, comp., 35 Low. craigs
Merrilees, J., plumber, 14 Friars st and 16 King st
Merrilees, James, comp., 35 Low. craigs
Meston, Fred, Staff-Sergt., 2 Mar pl
Meston, James, gardener, Springbank
Middleton, Miss, 40 Queen st
Middleton, W., Wallace Monument
Milgrew, James, slater, 25 St John st
Millar, Alex., 14 Torbrex
Millar, Alex., coal merchant, 19 Forth pl

Millar, A. D., H.M. Insp. of Schools, 1 Victoria sq
Millar, David, plasterer, 23 Cowane st
Millar, David, sexton, 72 Up. craigs
Millar, Eben., fancy goods shop, 74 Baker st
Millar, Eben., vanman, 16 Low. Bridge st
Millar, James, mason, 9 St John st
Millar, J., miner, 11 Low. Bridge st
Millar, John, plasterer, 15 Cowane st
Millar, John, plumber, 7 Well Green
Millar, John, 5 Abercromby pl
Millar, Miss A., milliner, 15 Friars st
Millar, Miss M., 1 Princes street
Millar, Mrs Susan, 69 Baker st
Millar, Mrs, 21 Low. craigs
Millar, Mrs, 4 Cowane st
Millar, Robt., lab., 31 Low. Bridge st
Millar, R., miner, 17 Abbey rd
Millar, R., baker, 27 Up. craigs
Millar, Sam. F., baker, 6 Abercromby pl
Millar, Thomas, lab., 52 Murray pl
Millar, W., dairyman, Shiphaugh
Millar, Wm., blacksmith, 64 Up. craigs
Millar, Wm., coachbuilder, 2 King's stables
Millar & Sons, Jas., bakers, 17 Murray pl and 47
    Up. craigs
Miller, Alex., cooper, 10 Abbey rd
Miller, G., lab., Causewayhead
Miller, Geo., carter, Causewayhead
Miller, James C., brewer, Burghmuir
Miller, James, carter, Causewayhead
Miller, J., lab., Causewayhead
Miller, J. & J., brewers, 25-29 Burghmuir
Miller, Miss, 10 Queen st
Miller, Mrs M., 28 Newhouse
Miller, P., Causewayhead
Miller, Wm., blacksmith, 37 Wallace st
Miller, Wm., painter, 9 Broad st
Miller, Wm., blacksmith, Causewayhead
Miller, W. painter, Causewayhead
Miller, Wm., blacksmith, 4 Park lane
Millie, David, trav., 12 Bruce st
Mills, Alex., fireman, 39 Up. craigs
Mills, Alex., gardener, 3a Main st
Mills, David, cashier, 25 King st
Mills, John, lab., 18 Low. castlehill
Mills, Miss M., 4 Coburg av
Mills, P., confectioner, 12 Barn rd
Milne, A., guard, Tweedbank, Causewayhead
Milne, Alex., saddler, 13 Viewfield pl
Milne, Geo., Abbey Inn, Cambuskenneth

Milne, Geo., lab., 17 Up. castlehill
Milne, J., clerk, 72 Port st
Milne, James, salesman, 21 Well green
Milne, Mrs J., 12 Friars st
Milne & Co., Wm., slaters, 5 Up. craigs
Milner, Miss K., dressmaker, 10 Cowane st
Milroy, Mrs, 40 Raploch
Milton, D., tailor, 29 Queen st
Minty, James, clothier, 48 King st; house—
    Castle esplanade
Mirk, Mrs, 3 Nelson pl
Miskell, John, glazier, 41 Low. craigs
Mitchell, Arch., cabinetmaker, 63 Cowane st
Mitchell, David, lab., 19 St Mary's wynd
Mitchell, James, cellarman, 21 Forth pl
Mitchell, James, lab., 23 Broad st
Mitchell, James, 4 Windsor pl
Mitchell, John, kilnman, 90 Up. craigs
Mitchell, John, overseer, Craigforth
Mitchell, John, spirit merchant, 14-16 Baker st
Mitchell, Miss A., matron, Girls' Indus. School,
    Spittal st
Mitchell, Misses, 32 Forth cres
Mitchell, Miss, 12 Glebe cres
Mitchell, Miss, 8 Abercromby pl
Mitchell, Mrs Jane, 21 Wallace st
Mitchell, Mrs Jessie, Rose Cot., Springfield pl
Mitchell, Mrs, 7 Forth pl
Mitchell, Mrs, Hillside, Causewayhead
Mitchell, Wm., baker, 3-5 Bannockburn rd
Mitchell, Wm., spinner, 5 Low. craigs
Moffat, James, vanman, 9 Well green
Moir, Edward, steeplejack, 80 Main st
Moir, Geo., mason, 72 Cowane st
Moir, John, engine driver, 31 Low. bridge st
Moir, Miss, 1A Friars st
Moir, Thos., cooper, 25 Up. craigs
Monachan, Mrs, 48 Baker st
Monaghan, Geo., 76 Cowane st
Monaghan, John, lab., 24 Broad st
Moncrieff, Mrs M., 20 Cowane st
Moncrieff, Chas., shoemaker, 41 Up. castlehill
Monnachan, Michael, hawker, 7 Church wynd
Monteath, Eben., lab., 30 Lower castlehill
Monteath, John, surfaceman, 38 Raploch
Monteath, Mrs Janet, 19 Cowane st
Monteath, Mrs Jane, 6 Main st
Monteath, Mrs, 32 Newhouse
Monteith, Duncan, engine driver, 20 Forth st
Monteith, Jas., 18 Manse cres

Monteith, Geo., engineman, 112 Up. craigs
Monteith, Wm., lorryman, 36 Abbey rd
Montgomery, Thos., 2 Up. craigs
Moodie, A., mechanic, 12 Viewfield st
Moody, Daniel, lab., 31 Raploch
Moore, Geo., guard, 55 Low. Bridge st
Moore, Sergeant J., 9 Married Qrs.
Moore, T. chemist, 25 Allan park
Moore, Thos., coachwright, 35 Port st
Moore. Wm. J., chemist, 30 Dumbarton rd
Moore & Son, Wm. J., chemists, 21 Murray pl
Moore, John, miner, 54 Low. castlehill
Moores, David, trav., 4 Bruce st
Moorhouse, Dr James, 6 Melville ter
More, George, tailor, 25 Cowane st
Moreland, W., coachman, Causewayhead
Moran, John, lab., 36 Broad st
Moran, John, lab., 23 Broad st
Moran, Walter, brakesman, 17 Seaforth pl
Morgan, George, draper, 67 Port st
Morgan, Jas., lorryman, 12 Newhouse
Morgan, Mrs, Douglas hotel, 2½-4 Arcade
Morgan, Robert, miner, 85 Main st
Morgan, Thomas, candlemaker, 9 Weaver row
Morgan, Mrs I., 7 Bow st
Morris, David B., Town Clerk, 15 Gladstone pl
Morris, John, lab., 10 Viewfield st
Morris, Mrs Alison, 2 Laurelhill pi
Morris, F., miner, 13 Broad st
Morris, Wm., butcher, 12 Viewfield st
Morrison, Eben., writer, 13 Allan pk
Morrison, James, saddler, 16 Friars st
Morrison, D., Smith and cycle agent, 37 Raploch
Morrison, Geo., sailor, 14 Mid. craigs
Morrison, Miss Christian, 27 Park ter
Morrison, C., miner, 16 Low. castlehill
Morrison, James, carter, 8 Broad st
Morrison, James, weaver, 41 Low. craigs
Morrison, James, surfaceman, 92 Cowane st
Morrison, J., miner, 37 Low craigs
Morrison, Miss, dairy, &c., 11 Viewfield pl
Morrison, P., carter, 13 St Mary's wynd
Morrison, P., lab., 88 Main st
Morrison, Robt., engine driver, 2 Springfield pl
Morrison, Robt., tailor, Elmbank, Burghmuir
Morrison, T., miner, 51 Main st
Morrison, Walter, mason, 23 Broad st
Morrison, Wm., joiner, 2 Abercromby pl
Morrison, Wm., tailor, 69 Baker st
Morrison, Wm., miner, 12 Low. castlehill

Morrison, W. S., 8 Victoria sq
Morrison & Taylor, solicitors, 46 Barnton st
Mortimer, James, trav., 3 Well Green
Morton, David, ironmonger, 1 Pitt ter
Morton, James, baker, 11 Low. Bridge st
Morton, Robt., clerk, 28 Up. craigs
Morton, Robt., ironmonger, 17 Victoria pl
Morton, T. M., ironmonger, 12 Abercromby pl
Moulton-Barrett, H. P., Adjt., Castle
Mowat, C., butcher, 91 Baker st and 76 Spittal st
Mowat, Thomas, flesher, 37 Low. craigs
Mowat & Sons, Thomas, butchers, 77 Baker st
Mowatt, Mrs, 28 Newhouse
Mowbray, A. G. H., 7 Glebe cres
Moyes, Alex., headmaster, 11 Douglas ter
Moyes, A. C., insur. agent, 49 Wallace st
Moyes, Chas., goods guard, 8 Maxwell pl
Moyes, Thomas, insur. agent, 49 Wallace st
Muir, David, lab., 8 St Mary's wynd
Muir, David, tobacconist, 31 Up. castlehill
Muir, Geo., lab., 63 Newhouse
Muir, James, wood manager, 2 Forth cres
Muir, John, lab., 38 St Mary's wynd
Muir, John, miner, 20 Main st
Muir, R., gardener, Williamfield
Muir, Robt., lab., 38 St Mary's wynd
Muir, Mrs Sarah, 13 Clarendon pl
Muir, Thomas, spirit merchant, 47 Murray pl;
    house—1 Randolph rd
Muir, Wm., head porter, Station rd
Muir, Wm., lab., 28 St Mary's wynd
Muir, Son & Patton, Ltd., Thos., coal merchants,
    5 Thistle st
Muirhead, Alex., bricklayer., Torbrex
Muirhead, Alex., shepherd, 2 Bruce st
Muirhead, Geo., shepherd, 14 Wallace st
Muirhead, James, painter, 38 Main st
Muirhead, Mrs Ann, 66 Main st
Muirhead, Mrs C., 23 Princes st
Muirhead, Mrs Helen, 150 Main st
Muirhead, Mrs Wm., 11 Newhouse
Muirhead, T. & J., solicitors, 4 Port st; house,
    23 Princes st
Mulhearn, Jas., lab., 1 St John st
Mulherron, Mrs., 14½ St John st
Mulherron, Mrs., 31 St Mary's wynd
Mulherron, Thos., carter, 14½ St John st
Mullan, A. J., pawnbroker, 6-8 Baker st
Mullan, H., lab., 80 St Mary's wynd
Mullen, Thos., lab., 61 St Mary's wynd

Mundell, David, joiner, 18 Queen st
Mungall, Jas., lab., 30 St Mary's wynd
Munnoch, Wm., tailor, 25 Cowane st
Munro, Alex., uphol., 40 Broad st
Munro, And., warper, 11 Well green
Munro, Chas., trav., 27 Millar pl
Munro, E., gardener, Causewayhead
Munro, Hugh, boiler washer, 89 Baker st
Munro, John J., printer, 4 Douglas ter
Munro, Laurence, lab., 23 Broad st
Munro, Robt., porter, 8 Douglas st
Munro, Robt., porter, 35 Low. craigs
Munro, Thos., lab., 47 Baker st
Munro, Wm., gardener, 20 Cowane st
Murdoch, A., spirit mer., 55 Baker st
Murdoch, Allan, cartwright, 32 Cowane st
Murdoch, Geo., stockbroker, Cliffside
Murdoch, John, lab., 9 Weaver row
Murdoch, John, trav., 7 Abbey rd
Murdoch, Miss A., Stripeside
Murdoch, Miss Frances, 87 Port st
Murdoch, Wm., storeman, 73 Newhouse
Murnin, Hugh, miners' agent, 7 Park lane
Murphy, Joseph, lab., 28 St Mary's wynd
Murphy, Matthew D., 26 Up. Bridge st
Murphy, Michael, lab., 37 Up. Castlehill
Murphy, N. M'L., insur. agent, 26 Up. Bridge st
Murphy, A., miner, 38 Up. Bridge st
Murphy, Jas., miner, 31 Low. Bridge st
Murphy, Jas., miner, 142 Main st
Murphy, Pat., lab., 39 Raploch
Murray, Adam, carter, 75 Baker st
Murray, Alex., railway insp., 18 Bruce st
Murray, Dr J. H., 19 Glebe av
Murray, Geo., miner, 15 Weaver row
Murray, Hugh, miner, 22 Raploch
Murray, James, proprietor, Polmaise Castle
Murray, John, blind maker, 32 Baker st
Murray, John G., writer, 19 Clarendon pl
Murray, John, joiner, 5 Park lane
Murray, John, wood carter, 118 Baker st
Murray, M., surfaceman, 37 King st
Murray, Miss, 12 Snowdon pl
Murray, Mrs Christina, 9 Abbey rd pl
Murray, Mrs Janet, 13 Low. bridge st
Murray, Mrs, 3 Seaforth pl
Murray, Mrs, 6 Irvine pl
Murray, P., coal merchant, 7 Clifford rd
Murray, P., 1 Glebe av
Murray, Thos., mason, 6 Low. bridge st

Murray, Wm., cooper, 62 Spittal st
Murrie, And., engine driver, 6 Well green
Murrie, Miss, 34 Snowdon pl
Murrie, Stewart, banker, 34 Snowdon pl
Myles, Thos., miner, 10 Bayne st
Myles, R., miner, 21 Well green

Mᶜ

M'Adam, Hugh, butcher, 26 Low. bridge st
M'Adam, Mrs Hugh, 86 Up. craigs
M'Adam, Sam., fisherman, 15 Winchel pl
M'Adam, Sam., lab., 8 Broad st
M'Allister, A., rubber worker, 26 Low. bridge st
M'Allister, M., lab., Causewayhead
M'Allister, Ninian, coachbuilder, 43 Newhouse
M'Alpine, Duncan, grocer, 4-6 Borestone pl
M'Alpine, John, saltman, 36 Broad st
M'Alpine, Mrs Jessie, 7 Snowdon pl
M'Alpine, P., Waverley Hotel, 2-4 Murray pl
M'Anany, Jas., blacksmith, Cambuskenneth
M'Andrew, W., carter, 2 Broad st
M'Aree Bros., drapers, 57-59 King st
M'Aree, David, draper, 23-25 Up. bridge st
M'Aree, James, dairyman, 1 Glencoe rd
M'Ardle, Mrs, 8 St Mary's wynd
M'Aree, John, draper, 2 Balmoral pl
M'Aree, Robert, draper, 24 James st
M'Aree, Mrs, 3 Douglas st
M'Arthur, Alex., fireman, 35 Port st
M'Arthur, Arch., painter, 43½ Cowane st
M'Arthur, J., contractor, 59 Bannockburn rd
M'Arthur, Miss, 15 Newhouse
M'Arthur, Miss, 18 Cowane st
M'Arthur, Mrs Jane, 14 Bow st
M'Arthur, Wm., plumber, 3 Nelson pl
M'Arthur, Mrs, 61 Bannockburn rd
M'Arthur, Mrs, 17 Broad st
M'Arthur, Miss J., baby-linen shop, 74 Port st
M'Arthur, Wm., hairdresser, 33 Up. craigs
M'Arthur, Jas., seedsman, 24 Princes st
M'Arthur, P., 5 Viewfield st
M'Aulay, Jas., 6 Clarendon pl
M'Aulay, Mrs Eliz., 25 St John st
M'Avoy, James, porter, 24 Up. castlehill
M'Bain, Miss C., tobacconist, 28 Arcade
M'Beath, H. Singer's salesman, 18 Union st
M'Bean, M., Lily cottage, Causewayhead
M'Beth, James, lab., 15 George st

M'Beth, Mrs Isabella, 13 Low. craigs
M'Beth, W. engine driver, 116 Up. craigs
M'Bride, Hugh, painter, 41 Newhouse
M'Caffer, Neil, dairyman, 7 Crofthead
M'Call, George, gardener, Langgarth
M'Callum, And., blacksmith, 14 Spittal st ; house
    15 Cowane st
M'Callum, David, farmer, Broadleys
M'Callum, David, tailor, 35 Newhouse
M'Callum, John, lab., 8 St Mary's wynd
M'Callum, Malcolm, miner, 9 Borestone cres
M'Callum, Mrs Agnes, 17 Cowane st
M'Callum, Wm., dairyman, 19 Broad st
M'Callum, Wm., tailor, 10 St John st
M'Callum, Wm., tailor, 52 Cowane st
M'Callum, Arch., postboy, 43 Port st
M'Callum, Alex., miner, 26 Main st
M'Callum, Geo., miner, 103 Main st
M'Callum, Jas., singalman, 102 Up. craigs
M'Callum, Jas., clerk, 33 James st
M'Callum, Mrs, 26 Nelson pl
M'Callum, Wm., lab., 18 St Mary's wynd
M'Callum, Wm., hawker, 18 St Mary's wynd
M'Cann, Mrs, J., 8 Borestone pl
M'Cartney, Mrs, 56 Cowane st
M'Caully, Miss, Causewayhead
M'Coll, Jas., miner, 47 St Mary's wynd
M'Coll, B., lab., 19 St Mary's wynd
M'Coll, Jas , miner, 48 Baker st
M'Combie, Miss, 3 Queen st
M'Connachie, Mrs C., 36 Broad st
M'Connachie, H., trav., 27 Cowane st
M'Connachie, Miss E., 3 Forth cres
M'Cormack, John, mason, 14 Cowane st
M'Cormack, John, postal clerk, 25 Abbey rd
M'Cormack, Mrs Jane, 44 Baker st
M'Cormack, Mrs Janet, 25 Abbey rd
M'Cormack, Mrs, pawnbroker, 5 Bow st
M'Creadie, Ed., gardener, 48 Broad st
M'Cue, Jas., labourer, 2 Barn rd
M'Culloch, Col.-Sergt., Military Hospital
M'Culloch, H., miner, 75 Baker st
M'Culloch, James, slater, 66 Spittal st
M'Culloch, John, Col.-Sergt., Mar pl
M'Culloch, Miss, refreshment rooms, 42 Baker
    st ; house—9 Bruce st
M'Culloch, Pte., 22B Married Qrs
M'Culloch, Robt., draper, 10 Allan pk
M'Culloch & Young, drapers, 79 King st and
    1 Baker st

M'Dermont, A. J., cashier, 9 Laurelhill pl
M'Dermont, Mrs Jane, 31 Low. Bridge st
M'Diarmid, Dan, postboy, 47 Port st
M'Diarmid, D. B., grocer, 9 Low. Bridge st
M'Diarmid, H., baker, 55 Newhouse
M'Diarmid, J., candlemaker, 7 Newhouse
M'Diarmid, Miss, 20 Melville ter
M'Diarmid & Sons, D., candlemakers, 59 Upper
　　craigs and 85 Main st
M'Donald, A., coachbuilder, 13 St John st
M'Donald, A., engine driver, 104 Up. craigs
M'Donald, A., lab., 44 Up. Castlehill
M'Donald, Alex., wine mer., 16 Main st
M'Donald, And., nailmaker, 15 Main st
M'Donald, C., watchmaker, 3 Cowane st
M'Donald, D., porter, 116 Up. craigs
M'Donald, D., rubber worker, 4 Bank st
M'Donald, Duncan, saddler, 15 King st; house
　　2 Windsor pl
M'Donald, Duncan, tailor, 3 Bruce st
M'Donald, Ed., smith, 53½ Cowane st
M'Donald, H., Singer's salesman, 20 Union st
M'Donald, Hugh, carter, 22 Orchard pl
M'Donald, James, lab., 56 Low. Bridge st
M'Donald, James, rubber worker, 51 Cowane st
M'Donald, J., inspector of weights and measures,
　　13 Viewfield pl; office—County Buildings
M'Donald, John C., mason, 54 Abbey rd
M'Donald, John, carter, 98 Baker st
M'Donald, John, engine driver, 1 William pl
M'Donald, John, gardener, the Shieling, Park pl
M'Donald, Dugald, grocer, 71 Baker st
M'Donald, L., gamekeeper, 23 Baker st
M'Donald, Miss Helen, 3 Park av
M'Donald, Miss S., 36 Queen st
M'Donald, Miss, 53 Wallace st
M'Donald, Mrs Anne, 23 Clarendon pl
M'Donald, Mrs Annie, 7 Park av
M'Donald, Mrs C., 37 Low. castlehill
M'Donald, Mrs C., 15 Cowane st
M'Donald, Mrs Helen, 72 Murray pl
M'Donald, Mrs Jane, 3 Wallace st
M'Donald, Mrs Janet, 3 Cowane st
M'Donald, Mrs, 20 Bannockburn rd
M'Donald, Mrs, 17 Broad st
M'Donald, Mrs, 28 Up. castlehill
M'Donald, Mrs, 55 Low. bridge st
M'Donald, Mrs, 11 St Mary's wynd
M'Donald, P., miner, 38 St Mary's wynd
M'Donald, P., auctioneer, 14 James st

M'Donald, Mrs C., 32 Up. castlehill
M'Donald, R., butcher, 67½ Port st
M'Donald, R., gardener, 28 Park ter
M'Donald, Robt., brakesman, 27 Cowane st
M'Donald, Thos., carter, 17 Seaforth pl
M'Donald, W., rubber worker, 24 Bow st
M'Donald, Wm., auctioneer, 21 Thistle st
M'Dougall, Dan., cooper, 14 Middle craigs
M'Dougall, Hugh, bricklayer, 66 Baker st
M'Dougall, John, hairdresser, 61, 92 Baker st
M'Dougall, John, cashier, 2 Forrest rd
M'Dougall, John, baker, 7 Park lane
M'Dougall, John, Woodville
M'Dougall, Miss, 16 Friars st
M'Dougall, Pat., 21 Albert pl
M'Dougall, Wm., joiner, 8 George st
M'Dougall, Wm., draper, 20 Bruce st
M'Dougall, Wm., mason, Causewayhead
M'Dougall & Sons, Wm., joiners, 11-13 George st
M'Dowall, Alex., 32 Forth cres
M'Elfrish, J. R., trav., 1 Millar pl
M'Elfrish, Miss, music teacher, 4 Queen st
M'Ewan, A., baker, 35 Cowane st
M'Ewan, A., blacksmith, 13 St John st
M'Ewan, Alex., smith, 24 Low. bridge st
M'Ewan, And., stockbroker, 38 Allan pk
M'Ewan, A., painter, Aitken's bldgs., St Ninians
M'Ewan, A., spirit mer., 27-29 King st; house
     —9 Windsor pl
M'Ewan, Chas., lab., 10 St John st
M'Ewan, Duncan, grocer, 36 Barnton st
M'Ewan, Duncan, grocer, 9 Millar pl
M'Ewan, Geo., grocer, 10 Dean cres
M'Ewan, James, miner, 8 Barn rd
M'Ewan, John, stonebreaker, 28 St Mary's wynd
M'Ewan, J. B., clerk, 87 Port st
M'Ewan, Rev. John, 12 Clifford rd
M'Ewan, Miss, 48 Port st
M'Ewan, Miss, 54 Port st
M'Ewan, Mrs, 76 Up. craigs
M'Ewan, Mrs P., 60 Baker st
M'Ewan, P., brassfinisher, 25 Abbey rd
M'Ewan, T., lab., 64 St Mary's wynd
M'Ewan, Wm., joiner, 15 Bruce st
M'Ewan, Wm., lab., 14 Bow st
M'Ewen, Miss A., 15 Albert pl
M'Ewen, Miss H., 3 Park lane
M'Ewen, Jas., iron merchant, 23 Dumbarton rd;
     house—8 Allan pk
M'Ewen, Jas., coachpainter, 75 Low. Bridge st

11

M'Ewen, John, grocer, South Lodge
M'Ewen, John, electrician, Bridgehaugh
M'Ewen, Misses, South Lodge
M'Ewen, Wm., ironmonger, 3 Park lane
M'Ewen & Co., perambulator works, 48 Abbey rd
M'Fadyen, Dr D., 1 Park av
M'Fadyen, Geo., fireman, 29 Spittal st
M'Fadyen, John, lorryman, 5 Abbey rd
M'Fadyen, J., blacksmith, Causewayhead
M'Fadyen, Dr P., 1 Park av
M'Farlane, Dr P. F., 11 Pitt ter
M'Farlane, Alex., cabinetmaker, 44 Baker st
M'Farlane, Alex., lab., 92 Cowane st
M'Farlane, Miss E., confectioner, 10 Main st
M'Farlane, Mrs E., 7 Queen's rd
M'Farlane, James, baker, 84 Baker st
M'Farlane, James, tailor, 5 Well green
M'Farlane, James, 47 Bannockburn rd
M'Farlane, Jas., quarryman, 9 Bannockburn rd
M'Farlane, Jas., foreman printer, 9 Abbey rd
M'Farlane, John, lorryman, 35 Low. Bridge st
M'Farlane, John, polisher, 84 Baker st
M'Farlane, John, 7 Newhouse
M'Farlane, John, miner, 47 St Mary's wynd
M'Farlane, John, shoemaker, 5 Low. Bridge st
M'Farlane, Miss K., baby linen, 33 Arcade
M'Farlane, Matt., lab., 44 Baker st
M'Farlane, Miss, 59 Glasgow rd
M'Farlane, Miss, Burnbank. Burghmuir
M'Farlane, Miss Susan, 19 Princes st
M'Farlane, Mrs, 1 Dean cres
M'Farlane, Mrs, 33 Glasgow rd
M'Farlane, Mrs, 58 Cowane st
M'Farlane, Mrs, 27 Victoria pl
M'Farlane, P., miner, 12 Low. craigs
M'Farlane, P., lab., 23 Broad st
M'Farlane, Sergt. John, County buildings
M'Farlane, T., Braehead farm
M'Farlane, Wm., cooper, 33 James st
M'Farlane, Wm., lab., 3 Springfield pl
M'Farlane, Wm., lab., 28 Bannockburn rd
M'Farlane, Wm., trav., 9 Allan pk
M'Farlane, Wm., mason, 19 Bannockburn rd
M'Figgins, John, painter, 14 Bow st
M'Figgins, Wm., painter, 55 Low. Bridge st
M'Garry, James, 8 Broad st
M'Geoch, Pat., miner, 13 Low. craigs
M'Gibbon, A., baker, 7 Newhouse
M'Gibbon, D., postman, 13 Well green
M'Gibbon, James, baker, 35 Low. craigs

M'Gibbon, Miss Janet, 5 Abbey rd
M'Gibbon, Miss, dairykeeper, 72 Up. craigs
M'Gibbon, M., lab., 43 Up. castlehill
M'Gibbon, P., ropespinner, 36 Newhouse
M'Gill, D., surfaceman, 72 Port st
M Gill, D. B., traveller, 72 Port st
M'Gill, T., miner, 19 Weaver row
M'Ginlay, F., keeper, Casual sick house
M'Ginnigal, Mrs Isabella, 63 Wallace st
M'Glennan, P., miner, 12 Broad st
M'Gloan, Mrs, 40 Up. castlehill
M'Gloin, Pat., mason, 25 Forth cres
M'Gonville, Mrs, broker, 84 Baker st
M'Gowan, A., cartwright, Causewayhead
M'Gowan, Isaac, miner, 56 Abbey rd
M'Gowan, Misses, 10 Royal gardens
M'Gowan, Mrs, 52 Barnton st
M'Gowan, Mrs, refresh. rooms, 114 Main st
M'Graw, Alex., groom, 24 Newhouse
M'Graw, Mrs Ann, 38 St Mary's wynd
M'Gregor, Alex., cooper, 11 Well green
M'Gregor, Daniel, lab., 10 Bayne st
M'Gregor, David, lorryman, 33 King st
M'Gregor, Hugh, miner, 42 Up. castlehill
M'Gregor, James, baker, 7 Bannockburn rd
M'Gregor, James, fireman, 4 Springfield pl
M'Gregor, John, publican, 2 Cowane st ; house--
    8 Viewfield pl
M'Gregor, John, carter, 4 Springfield pl
M'Gregor, John, smith, 49 King st
M'Gregor, J., manufacturer, 7 Gladstone pl
M'Gregor, Miss, dressmaker, 59 Cowane st
M'Gregor, Miss, 4 Balmoral pl
M'Gregor, Miss Janet, 15 Bannockburn rd
M'Gregor, Mrs, Butterflats
M'Gregor, P., engine driver, 16 Low. castlehill
M'Gregor, P., guide, 33 Low. castlehill
M'Gregor, Robt., 2 Springfield pl
M'Gregor, Thomas, lorryman, 66 Baker st
M'Gregor, & Co., D., slaters, 4 George st
M'Gregor, Jos., goods guard, 58 Cowane st
M'Gregor, Wm., forester, Polmaise cottages
M'Gregor, Mrs M., 27 Queen st
M'Gregor, Mrs Agnes, 24 Orchard pl
M'Gregor, P., moulder, 53 Low. Bridge st
M'Gregor & Geddes, Devonshire Creamery
    agents, 34 Forth cres
M'Grigor, Alex., writer, Beechwood
M'Gribben, Thos, miner, 5 Barn rd
M'Grouther, Miss Isabella, 5 Randolph ter

M'Guire, James, miner, 44 Baker st
M'Guire, Mrs James, 76 Baker st
M'Guire, H., miner, 8 St Mary's wynd
M'Guire, Jas., lab., 26 Forth cres
M'Guire, Mrs E., 114 Baker st
M'Ilreid, John, lab., 97 Low. Bridge st
M'Ilvean, Mrs C., grocer, 52-56 St Mary's wynd
M'Ilroy, Jas., cabman, 76 Spittal st
M'Indoe, James, 46 King st
M'Innes, David, baker, 105 Low. Bridge st
M'Innes, Donald, baker, 13 Low. Bridge st
M'Innes, George, cartwright, 6 Bayne st
M'Innes, John, lab., 38 Low. castlehill
M'Innes, John, porter, 23 Friars st
M'Innes, John, sawyer, 19 Cowane st
M'Innes, Mrs C., 6 Middle craigs
M'Innes, Robt., joiner, 19 Bruce st
M'Innes, Wm., weaver, 24 Up. craigs
M'Innes, Wm., weaver, 23 Up. craigs
M'Innes, And., baker, 5 Bruce st
M'Innes, Duncan, seedsman, 64 Up. craigs
M'Innes, Jas., vanman, 1 King's stables
M'Intosh, Alex., engineer, 1 Douglas ter
M'Intosh, David, trav., 23 Wallace st
M'Intosh, Geo., hairdresser, 53 Newhouse
M'Intosh, Geo., lab., 61 Cowane st
M'Intosh, John., lab., 61 Cowane st
M'Intosh, John, lab., 20 Low. castlehill
M'Intosh, A., police constable, 10 Up. Bridge st
M'Intosh, A., blacksmith, 24 Baker st
M'Intosh, J. Y., compositor, 52 Barnton st
M'Intosh, Mrs Helen, 14 Up. Bridge st
M'Intosh, Mrs H., 61 Cowane st
M'Intosh, Mrs, 1 King's Stables
M'Intosh, Mrs Janet, 25 Well green
M'Intosh, T. B., baker, 25 Cowane st
M'Intosh, Mrs W., 21 Bruce st
M'Intyre, Dan, cartwright, 45 Bannockburn rd
M'Intyre, J., gardener, Causewayhead
M'Intyre, Mrs, 13 Viewfield pl
M'Intyre, Misses, 20 Barnton st
M'Intyre, Neil, gardener, Vineburgh cottage
M'Intyre, Robert, printer, 43 Wallace st
M'Isaac, D., gardener, Annfield
M'Ivor, Joseph, miner, 20 Main st
M'Jannet, John D., Woodlands
M'Kay, A., S.P.C.A. inspector, 27 Queen st
M'Kay, Don., broker, 108 Baker st
M'Kay, Geo., mason, 15 Bruce st
M'Kay, J., engine driver, 111 Low. Bridge st

M'Kay, James, compositor, 27 Queen st
M'Kay, John, clothier, 49 Port st; house—57
    Wallace st
M'Kay, John, traveller, 3 Millar pl
M'Kay, John, factor, 1 Coburg av
M'Kay, John, lab., 38 St Mary's Wynd
M'Kay, Miss, dressmaker, 9 Viewfield pl
M'Kay, Mrs H., 77 Up. Bridge st
M'Kay, Miss Janet., 56 Cowane st
M'Kay, Mrs C., refresh. rooms, 21 Up. Craigs
M'Kay, Mrs, 20 Bow st
M'Kay, P., broker, 101 Baker st
M'Kay, Thomas, shipowner, 13 Clifford rd
M'Kay, Wm., miner, 103 Low. Bridge st
M'Kay, Wm., baker, 35 Cowane st
M'Kay, Wm., lab., 24 Up. castlehill
M'Kean, Mrs H., 2 Rosebery pl
M'Kean, Mrs Jane, 5 Millar pl
M'Kean, W. A., organist, 5 Millar pl
M'Kechnie, Geo., tailor, 15 Bruce st
M'Kee, Jas., miner, 5 Weaver row
M'Keen, Wm., lab., 33 Low. Bridge st
M'Kellar, John, miner, 24 Broad st
M'Kelvie, P., lab., 36 James st
M'Kendrick, Mrs, 12 Raploch
M'Kendrick, Wm., miner, 74 Main st
M'Kenstrie, Ed., engineman, 103 Main st
M'Kenna, John, miner, 2 St Mary's wynd
M'Kenzie, A., rubber worker, 111 Low. Bridge st
M'Kenzie, A., assist. postmaster, 5 Rosebery pl
M'Kenzie, Major A. F., Queensgate
M'Kenzie, Alex., pensioner, 37 Low. craigs
M'Kenzie, Alex., waiter, 11 Bruce st
M'Kenzie, Donald, traveller, 13 Viewfield pl
M'Kenzie, D. R., dancing master, 6 Maxwell pl
M'Kenzie, James, clothier, 50 Cowane st
M'Kenzie, J., trav. sec., Y.M.C.A., 71 Barnton st
M'Kenzie, James, porter, 24 Up. craigs
M'Kenzie, James, tailor, 13 Glencoe rd
M'Kenzie, James, weaver, 11 Abbey rd
M'Kenzie, John, lorryman, 15 Low. bridge st
M'Kenzie, John, M.A., teacher, 3 Victoria pl
M'Kenzie, John, postman, 50 Spittal st
M'Kenzie, John, lorryman, 1 St John st
M'Kenzie, John, tanner, 25 St. John st
M'Kenzie, Mrs, 1 St John st
M'Kenzie, Mrs, 5 St John st
M'Kenzie, Mrs Ann, 4 George st
M'Kenzie, Mrs Isabella, 21 Wallace st
M'Kenzie, Mrs M., 48 Low. castlehill

M'Kenzie, Mrs M., 23 Broad st
M'Kenzie, Mrs L., 47 St Mary's wynd
M'Kenzie, Rev. Colin, 2 Randolph ter
M'Kenzie, Robt., boot salesman, 25 Queen st
M'Kenzie, Robt., insur. agent, 11 Broad st
M'Kenzie, Wm., jeweller, 7 Baker st
M'Kerchar, Donald, trav., 16 Allan pk
M'Kerchar, Mrs Annie, 18 Viewfield st
M'Kerracher, Alex., dairyman, Raploch farm
M'Kerracher, Daniel, Raploch farm
M'Kerracher, D., 1 Bridge lane
M'Kerracher & Son, D., coal merchants and
    contractors, 7 Thistle st
M'Kerracher, Mrs John, Causewayhead
M'Kerron, J., lab., 20 Bow st
M'Killop, D., County Temp. Hotel, 28 Murray pl
M'Killop, Mrs Helen, 7 Low. craigs
M'Kinlay, A., lorryman, Corn exchange rd
M'Kinlay, B., goods guard, 39½ Low. bridge st
M'Kinlay, Matt., saddler, 5 and 7 Friars st
M'Kinlay, John, clerk, 45 Murray pl
M'Kinlay, W., grocer, 18 Bruce st
M'Kinlay & Son, J., tailors, 59-63 Murray pl
M'Kinnon, Chas., joiner, 47 Cowane st
M'Kinnon, Don, engineman, 17 Spittal st
M'Kinnon, D., joiner, 7 Well green
M'Kinnon, Mrs, 3 Broad st
M'Kutcheon, W., miner, 44 Baker st
M'Knight, Robt., miner. 38 Broad st
M'Lachlan, Arch., 4 Irvine pl
M'Lachlan, C., joiner, 35-37 St Mary's wynd
M'Lachlan, Colin, carter, 8 St Mary's wynd
M'Lachlan, Duncan, mason, 33 King st
M'Lachlan, James, pensioner, 3 Dean cres
M'Lachlan, John, miner, 92 Main st
M'Lachlan, John, draper, 25 Victoria pl
M'Lachlan, Miss Jessie, 19 Well green
M'Lachlan, Mrs, 24 Up. castlehill
M'Lachlan, Rev. Jas., M.A., 13 Millar pl
M'Lachlan, Wm., miner, 20 Main st
M'Lachlan, Son & Co., A., cement merchants, 10
    Viewfield st and 18 Park lane
M'Lachlan & Brown, milliners, 8-12 Murray pl
M'Lachlan, Mrs J., 40½ Bannockburn rd
M'Laren, A., enginekeeper, 14 George st
M'Laren, Alex., engine driver, 1 William pl
M'Laren, Alex., gardener, 15 Well green
M'Laren, Dan., baker, 25 Irvine pl
M'Laren, Don., drover, 31 Low. Bridge st
M'Laren, James, guard, 17 Abbey rd

M'Laren, James, plumber, 37 King st
M'Laren, James, porter, May Day yard
M'Laren, John, joiner, 69 Wallace st
M'Laren, John, surfaceman, 50 Spittal st
M'Laren, J. T., factor, Bearside
M'Laren, Miss, Causewayhead
M'Laren, Miss C., 4 Low. Bridge st
M'Laren, Miss J., dressmaker, 30 Bow st
M'Laren, Miss, 14½ St John st
M'Laren, Miss, 59 Main st
M'Laren, Miss, 1 Drip rd
M'Laren, Mrs, Causewayhead
M'Laren, Mrs Jessie, nurse, 24 Newhouse
M'Laren, Mrs M., 101 Low. Bridge st
M'Laren, Mrs, 12 Nelson pl
M'Laren, Mrs, 15 Burghmuir
M'Laren, Mrs C., 15 Forth pl
M'Laren, Nicol, carter, 5 Nelson pl
M'Laren, Robt., bellhanger, 22 Union st
M'Laren, P., warehouseman, 35 Burghmuir
M'Laren, Wm., carter, 24 Thistle st
M'Laren, Wm., engine driver, 11 Bruce st
M'Laren, Wm., painter, 4 Maxwell pl
M'Laren, Wm., tailor's cutter, 7 James st
M'Lauchlan, H., baler, 72 Baker st
M'Lauchlan, James, lab., 44 St Mary's wynd
M'Lauchlan, John, butcher, 35 Cowane st
M'Lauchlan, Pte. James, 19 Married qrs
M'Lauchlan, Pte. R., 26 Married qrs
M'Lauchlan, Mrs, 8 Abercromby pl
M'Lay, John, stair railer, 21 Abbey rd
M'Lay, Wm., warehouseman, 4 Crofthead
M'Lean, A., postboy, 10 Viewfield st
M'Lean, Capt. Chas., A. & S.H., Kildean
M'Lean, Colin, lorryman, 48 Cowane st
M'Lean, Colin, printer, 4 Douglas st
M'Lean, Colin, stableman, 9 Maxwell pl
M'Lean, Col.-Sergt. D., Castle
M'Lean, Dan., carter, 68 Cowane st
M'Lean, Geo., corkcutter, 19 Murray pl
M'Lean, James, tailor, 93 Low. Bridge st
M'Lean, John, Bridge Custom
M'Lean, John, Killorn villas, Park pl
M'Lean, Lieut., Castle
M'Lean, Matthew, tailor, 4 George st
M'Lean, Janet, millworker, 60 Baker st
M'Lean, Mrs Elizabeth, 3 Clarendon pl
M'Lean, Mrs Grace, 17 George st
M'Lean, Mrs M., 11 Low. Bridge st
M'Lean, Mrs, Causewayhead

M'Lean, R., plasterer, 93 Low. Bridge st
M'Lean, W., lorryman, 48 Baker st
M'Lean, Robt., china mer., 48 Main st
M'Lean, Stewart, miner, 38 St Mary's wynd
M'Lean, Thomas, tailor, 10 Up. bridge st
M'Lean & Henderson, st'ckbrok'rs, 53 Murray pl
M'Lees, Rev. D. P., 11 Abercromby pl
M'Leish, William, joiner, 26 Port st
M'Lellan, H. D., solicitor, 48 Barnton st; house
    —20 Millar pl
M'Lellan, Angus, lab., 11½ St John st
M'Lellan, Mrs Ann, 3 Douglas st
M'Lellan, Rev. Wm., 15 Manse cres
M'Lellan, Thos., lab., 38 St Mary's wynd
M'Lennan, Alex., gardener, Laurelhill
M'Leod, Miss Margt., 2 Dumbarton rd
M'Leod, Jas., rubber worker, 81 Low. bridge st
M'Leod, Misses, dressmakers, 2 Dumbarton rd
M'Leod, Mrs Jane, 2 Barn rd
M'Leod, Miss L, dressmaker, 53 Port st
M'Leod, S., hosiery manufacturer, 9 Park aven
M'Leod, Wm., carter, 23 Cowane st
M'Luckie, Mrs Jessie, 11 Queen st
M'Luckie, John, joiner, 3 Middle craigs
M'Luckie, Maxwell, plumber, 2 George st
M'Luckie, Mrs, 33 Low. castlehill
M'Luckie & Walker, architects, 15 Dumbarton rd
M'Mahon, Miss Cath., 53 Low. bridge st
M'Mannes, Michael, lab., 98 St Mary's wynd
M'Martin, Finlay, lab., 17 Seaforth pl
M'Master, Hugh, foreman carter, 3 Park lane
M'Menemy, Ed., lab., 25 Up. craigs
M'Menemy, John, miner, 13 Low. craigs
M'Menemy, Mrs F., 13 Low. craigs
M'Millan, A., miner, 30 Broad st
M'Millan, Don.,governor,Combination Poorhouse
M'Millan, Miss, laundrymaid, Causewayhead
M'Millan, Miss Jane, 7 William pl
M'Millan, J., foreman cooper, 26 James st
M'Millan, Neil, fish salesman, 32 Spittal st
M'Millan, Rob., baker, 3 Bruce st
M'Millan, Jas., gardener, 15 Cowane st
M'Murdo, Thos., miner, 3A Main st
M'Murtrie, Mrs A., 13 Glencoe rd
M'Nab, C., miner, 10 Low. bridge st
M'Nab, Dan., lorryman, 21 Bow st
M'Nab, Alex., carter, 21 Bow st
M'Nab, James, clerk, 45 King st
M'Nab, James, lab., 4 Low. bridge st
M'Nab, Mrs M., 60 Baker st

M'Nab, Mrs, 24 Bow st
M'Nab, Mrs, 22 Thistle st
M'Nab, P., engineer, 13 Nelson pl
M'Nab, P., smith, 36 Up. Craigs
M'Nab, Thomas, joiner, 18 Friars st; house—
  6 Queen's rd
M'Nair, John, clerk, 22 Borestone pl
M'Nair, Mrs Agnes, 22 Victoria pl
M'Nally, John, gardener, Clifford Park
M'Naughtan, Miss, dressmaker, 59 Wallace st
M'Naughtan, Wm., engineer, Forth st; house
  —59 Wallace st
M'Naughton, And., nailer, 7 Bannockburn rd
M'Naughton, D., ironmonger, 3 James st
M'Naughton, Geo., carter, 7 Glasgow rd
M'Naughton, Miss, 7 Murray pl
M'Naughton, Mrs Jane, 11 Baker st
M'Naughton, W., engine driver, 69 Main st
M'Naughton, W., millworker, 12 Bannockburn rd
M'Naughton, Wm., keeper, Guild Hall
M'Nee, David, hairdresser, 33 James st
M'Nee, Mrs, 25 St John st
M'Neil, James, cleaner, 114 Up. craigs
M'Neil, Miss H., outdoor worker, 23 Broad st
M'Neil, Miss, 30 Bow st
M'Neil, P., draper, 29 Low. Bridge st
M'Neil, Robt., finisher, 19 Cowane st
M'Neil, Wm., miner, 71 Up. Bridge st
M'Neil, Wm., miner, 9 Glasgow rd
M'Nicol, Mrs, 10 Pitt ter
M'Nicol, James, clerk, 52 Broad st
M'Nulty, John, carter, 8 St Mary's wynd
M'Phee, James, lab., 37 Up. castlehill
M'Phee, Wm., hawker, 8 St Mary's wynd
M'Pherson, James, reporter, 21 Wallace st
M'Pherson, John, soldier, 30 Broad st
M'Pherson, Miss, 2 James st
M'Pherson, Mrs, 64 Cowane st
M'Pherson, Mrs A., 10 Low. Bridge st
M'Pherson, Mrs M., 73 Up. Bridge st
M'Pherson, Rev. John (ret.), 17 Glebe av
M'Pherson, Thos., glazier, 16 Dumbarton rd
M'Pherson, Wm., boilermaker, 5 Springfield pl
M'Pherson, Wm., caretaker, County Buildings
M'Pherson, Wm., joiner, 20 Forth st; house—
  Dean cres
M'Que, Mrs, 14 Low. castlehill
M'Que, Mrs, 40 Barnton st
M'Que, Rich., miner, 44 Baker st
M'Queen, Geo., clerk, 94 St Mary's wynd

M'Queen, John, cabinetmaker, King's Park cot
M'Queen, John, Cambuskenneth
M'Queen, Mrs, 19 Newhouse
M'Queen, Wm., vanman, 1 Bayne st
M'Quiggan, David, smith, 92 Cowane st
M'Quillan, Jas., engine driver, 8 St Mary's wynd
M'Rae, J., supt., Forth fisheries, 18 Union st
M'Rae, Jas., writer, 19 Allan pk
M'Rae, Miss, 5 Viewfield st
M'Robbie, Mrs Jessie, 37 Murray pl
M'Robbie, Robt., cooper, 36 Abbey rd
M'Robbie, Wm., lathsplitter, 47 Cowane st
M'Ronald, P., upholsterer, 46 King st
M'Rorie, Jas., porter, 53½ Cowane st
M'Rorie, Misses, laundresses, 44 Up. bridge st
M'Rorie, Mrs, 19 Murray pl
M'Rorie, Thos., gardener, 44 Up. bridge st
M'Shean, Wm., clerk, 61 Wallace st
M'Vey, Jas., lab., 8 St Mary's wynd
M'Vey, John, lab., 20 Bow st
M'Vey, Pat., lab., 43 Broad st
M'Vey, Pat., lab., 45 Broad st

N

Nairn, P. D., photographer, Allan pk
Nairn, Wm., trav., 25 Allan pk
Naismyth, David, miner, 7 William pl
Naismyth, R., miner, 8 William pl
Napier, James, lab., 15 Seaforth pl
Napier, Jas., plasterer, 15 Main st
Napier, Wm., joiner, 15 Main st
Nash, Mrs A., grocer, 81 Main st
Nealus, Miss C., 59 Baker st
Neil, James, baker, 7 Friars st
Neil, James, baker, 15 Baker st and 15 Broad st
Neil, James, butcher, 3 Bow st; house—Drip rd
Neil, James, butcher, 16 Bruce st
Neil, James, caretaker, C'wayhead Mission hall
Neil, Robt., mill manager, 78 Up. craigs
Neil, R., joiner, Causewayhead
Neilson, James, lab., 8 St Mary's wynd
Neilson, J. R., quarrymaster, 10 Manse cres
Neilson, Mrs, 66 Spittal st
Neilson, P., lab., 37 Up. castlehill
Neilson, R. T., writer, 28 Snowdon pl
Neilson, Wm., gardener, 25 Cowane st
Neish, Thomas, engineer, 4 Gowanbank

Nelson, Mrs Christina, 26 Forth cres
Nelson, Thomas, loco. foreman, Bridge cottage
Newlands, Hugh, lab., 41 St Mary's wynd
Newport, Henry, Col.-Sergt., Married Qrs.
Newton, Wm., hawker, 26 St John st
Newsome, John, lab., 17 Winchel pl
Nichol, Thomas, valet, 24 Main st
Nicholson, Mrs Jane, Cambuskenneth
Nicholson, Mrs, 2 Victoria sq
Nicol, D. B., stationer, 11 Randolph ter
Nicol, James, joiner, 27 Queen st
Nicol, James, clerk, 31 Up. craigs
Nicol, James, clothier, 69 King st
Nicol, Miss C., 36 Up. Bridge st
Nicol, Miss Maggie, 15 Glencoe rd
Nicol, Miss, 16 Bow st
Nicol, Mrs M., 45 Wallace st
Nicol, Mrs, 11 Albert pl
Nicol, Mrs, 17 Well green
Nicol, Mrs, 1 Main st
Nicol, Wm. J., postal clerk, 59 Wallace st
Nicol, Wm. C., postal clerk, 59 Wallace st
Nicolson, Mrs G., 4 Forth cres
Nimmo, Mrs A., Cambuskenneth
Nimmo, James, coal merchant, 12 Victoria sq
Nisbet, A., teacher, 35 Forth cres
Nisbet, Chas., lab., 70 St Mary's wynd
Nisbet, H. C., dairyman, 8-10 Barnton st
Nisbet, John, upholsterer, 31 Burghmuir
Nisbet, Rich., lorryman, 7 Douglas st
Nisbet, Mrs Susan, 14 Glebe cres
Nish, Alex., grain porter, 54 Abbey rd
Niven, John, miner, 18 St Mary's wynd
Noble, Mrs Sarah, grocer, 39 Low. Bridge st
Noble, Thomas, wood carver, Bridgehaugh
Nokes, James, grocer, 54-58 Main st
Norris, Alex., restaurateur, 53-55 Murray pl
Norwell, Miss Helen, 11 Albany cres
Norwell & Sons, bootmakers, 77 King st

O

O'Brien, Francis, tanner, 14 Glasgow rd
O'Brien, Michael, mason, 3B Main st
O'Brien, Michael, 12 Glasgow rd
O'Brien, Thomas, shoemaker, 1 Bow st
O'Connor, M., miner, 52 Low. Bridge st
O'Connor, Mrs Mary, 83 Low. Bridge st

O'Donnel, M., miner, 16 Low. castlehill
O'Donnell, John, miner, 18 Broad st
Ogilvie, Miss Helen, 59 Cowane st
Ogilvie, John, upholsterer, 7 William pl
Ogilvie, Wm., caretaker, 27 Arcade
O'Hare, F., miner, 36 Broad st
O'Hare, James, miner, 30 Broad st
Oliphant, A., biscuit agent, 14 Bayne st; house
   —Causewayhead rd
Oliphant, Jas., confectioner, 6 Forth st; house-
   —26 James st
Oliver, A., car conductor, Causewayhead
Oliver, Sergt. A., Married Qrs.
Oliver, James, porter, 23 George st
Oliver, James, spirit merchant, 11 Main st
Oliver, J. H., Ordnance foreman, 11 Abbey rd pl
Oliver, Major, R.A., 18 Victoria pl
Oliver, Robt., carter, 98 Baker st
Oliver, Wm., lab., 10 St Mary's wynd
O'Neil, M., car driver, 11 Winchel pl
O'Neil, Martin, lab., 97 Low. Bridge st
O'Neil, Miss Maggie, 82 St Mary's wynd
Oram, Chas., dealer, 24 St Mary's wynd
Orne, James, hairdresser, 72 Port st
Ormiston, James, tailor, 33 Baker st
Ormiston, J., musical inst. dealer, 18 James st
Ormond, Rev. D. D., 17 Princes st
Orr, Mrs, 55 King st
Orr, T. Paterson, draper, 21 King st; house—21
   Randolph rd
Orr, Wm., fireman, 23 Broad st
Orr, Wm., miner, 18 Up. Craigs
Osborne, Mrs Joanna, 12 Murray pl
Oswald, John, stationer, 23 Randolph ter
Oswald, Miss Agnes, 17 Manse cres
Oswald, Miss A., tea rooms, 42-44 Arcade
Oswald, Miss Isabella, 40 Spittal st
Oswald, Mrs Jane, 71 Barnton st
Oswald, Robt., slater, 82 Spittal st
Owen, Geo., motor agent, 54, 69, 81 Port st
Owen, Geo., retired smith, 55 Wallace st

P

Pagan, James, miner, 35 Low. craigs
Page, J., Star Bar, 2 Baker st; house—1A Friars st
Page, John, shoemaker, 2 King's Stables

Palmer, W. S., umbrella maker, 44-46 Port st,
    and 41 Barnton st ; house—17 Randolph ter
Palombo, F., ice cream shop, 37 Main st
Panton, Chas. E., 4 Abercromby pl
Park, Alex., brush manufacturer, 31 Millar pl
Park Bros., brushmakers, 4 Forth st
Park, James, brush manufacturer, 24 Millar pl
Parker, James, patternmaker, 72 Baker st
Parker, John, carpet dresser, 72 Baker st
Parnie, John, Conservative agent, 20 Barnton st
Parshall, Mrs, St Leonard's, Causewayhead
Partridge, W., rubber worker, 111 Low. Bridge st
Pate, David, shoemaker, 1 Nelson pl
Pate, Miss Maggie, 3 Nelson pl
Paterson, A., tailor, 3 Park Lane
Paterson, Alex., lab., 80 Main st
Paterson, Alex., solicitor, 62 Port st
Paterson, And., warder, 28 Cowane st
Paterson, Arch., 113 Baker st
Paterson, Daniel, joiner, 39 Newhouse
Paterson, James, fireman, Crofthead
Paterson, R., tailor, 28 Cowane st
Paterson, Miss A., stationer, 29 Up. craigs
Paterson, Mrs A., 2 Borestone pl
Paterson, Mrs Ann, 5 Mid. craigs
Paterson, Miss Christina, 1 Princes st
Paterson, Mrs E., 21 Wallace st
Paterson, Geo., cashier, 5 Manse cres
Paterson, Mrs H., 13 Wallace st
Paterson, Mrs Hugh, 21 Nelson pl
Paterson, James, carter, 70 Up. craigs
Paterson, James, draper, 9 Bellfield rd
Paterson, James W., trav., 6 Forth cres
Paterson, James, draper, 42-44 King st
Paterson, James, lab., 7 Borestone cres
Paterson, Mrs Janet, 16 Victoria pl
Paterson, John, inspector of poor, 1 Victoria pl ;
    office—Parish Council Office, Broad st
Paterson, John, slater, 113 Baker st
Paterson, John, tailor, 47 Cowane st
Paterson, John A., trav., 5 Drip rd
Paterson, Miss M., dressmaker, 39 Up. craigs
Paterson, M. H., The Shieling, Park pl
Paterson, Mrs, 48 Broad st
Paterson, Mrs, 39 Bannockburn rd
Paterson, Robt., iron turner, 5 George st
Paterson, R., dairyman, 39-41 Cowane st
Paterson, Wm., lab., 57 Main st
Paterson, Wm., miner, 35 Low. craigs
Paton, Miss A., Rockdale lodge

Paton, Mrs Agnes, 10 Bannockburn rd
Paton, D. (St'gshire Rubber Co.), 1-3 Arcade ;
    house—Craigfoot, Causewayhead
Paton, Mrs E., 64 Main st
Paton, Mrs Elizabeth, 18 Torbrex
Paton, Geo., miner, 8 Bannockburn rd
Paton, Geo. R., wood carver, 17 Low. craigs and
    37 Newhouse
Paton, Private H., Married Qrs.
Paton, James, nailer, 33 Bannockburn rd
Paton, James, trav., 65 Newhouse
Paton, John, tanner, 12 Glasgow rd
Paton, J., smith, Aitken's bldgs., St Ninians
Paton, Matthew, gardener, 12 Main st
Paton, Miss M., 23 Wallace st
Paton, Mrs M., 47 Glasgow rd
Paton, Mrs, 4 Victoria pl
Paton, Thomas D., auctioneer, 10 Victoria sq
Paton, Wm., nailer, 134 Main st
Paton, Wm., stonebreaker, 16 Torbrex
Paton, Wm., comp., 26 Main st
Pattie, David, baker, 25 Cowane st
Pattie, John, engine driver, 76 Cowane st
Pattison, — electrician, 10 Barnton st
Paul, A. T., general draper, 5-7 Arcade ; house
    —Bellfield rd
Paul, H., soldier, 70 Main st
Paul, Wm., seedsman, 1 Low. Bridge st
Peacock, Mrs, 17 Broad st
Pearson, David, reporter, 5 Abbey rd
Pearson, F. L., warehouseman, 10 Wallace st
Pearson, Geo., gardener, Viewforth
Pearson, H., fruiterer, &c., 12 Up. Bridge st and
    5 Queen st
Pearson, Wm., keeper, Public Hall
Peddar, Mrs M., 23 Broad st
Peddie, Henry, carter, 6 Low. Bridge st
Peebles, M., lab., 46 St Mary's wynd
Peebles, James, furniture dealer, 16-18 Bow st
Peebles, James, hawker, 8 Broad st
Peebles, Miss J., matron, Royal Infirmary
Peebles, Thos., water bailiff, Crofthead
Pegler, David, electrician, 25 Newhouse
Pender, Robt., coachtrimmer, 60 Baker st
Penman, Alex., miner, 16 Orchard pl
Penman, And., wine merchant, 61 Port st
Peter, Miss E., dressmaker, 15 Queen st
Petrie, C., vanman, Causewayhead
Petrie, David, 3 Park lane
Petrie, Geo., gardener, 27 Park ter

Petrie, Joseph, viceman, 73 Newhouse
Petrie, Mrs A., Causewayhead
Petrie, Robt., cellarman, 36 James st
Peyton, Mrs, 105 Low. Bridge st
Phee, Hugh, miner, 68 Cowane st
Phibbs, Wm., miner, 104 Up. craigs
Phibbs, J., weaver, 31 Up. craigs
Philip, R. B., headmaster, 23 Newhouse
Philip, John, joiner, 103 Low. Bridge st
Philips, B., surfaceman, 33 James st
Phillips, Corporal, Married Quarters
Phillips, James, music teacher, 2 James st
Philliban, Ed., platelayer, 34 St Mary's wynd
Philliban, John, lab., 30 Raploch
Philliban, Patrick, miner, 5 St John st
Philp, Jas. S., insurance agent, 5 Well green
Philp, Mrs Elizabeth, 23 Victoria pl
Philp & Dobbie, solicitors, 3 Port st
Pinkerton, John, miner, 46 Low. Bridge st
Pirrie, Alex., carter, 12 Low. castlehill
Pitblado, Miss M., 68 Port st
Platt, Leon J., 21 Victoria pl
Platt & Common, surg. dentists, 74 Murray pl
Plenderleith, Geo., smith, 6 Up. craigs ; house
    —1 Allan pk
Pollock, A., miner, 12 Bruce st
Pollock, David, miner, 74 Main st
Pollock, Miss I., 57 Wallace st
Pollock, James, signalman, 10 Up. craigs
Porteous, Geo., Ardenlea, Causewayhead
Porteous, Geo., lorryman, 71 Up. Bridge st
Porter, A. spirit merchant, 2 Low. Bridge st
Porter, John, plumber, 52 Up. castlehill
Porter, Wm., baker, 12 Bayne st
Porter, W., spirit mer., 63 Port st and 1 Newhouse
Pow, John, fitter, 12 Middle craigs
Pow, Miss M., nurse, 52 Cowane st
Power, Thos., 10 Winchel pl
Powrie, David, sawyer, 88 Cowane st
Powrie, Geo., coachbuilder, 148 Main st
Preston, F., lab., 98 Baker st
Preston, Wm., engine driver, 60 St Mary's wynd
Pride, John H., insur. agent, 25 Queen st
Pride, Mrs, Cambuskenneth
Primrose, Alex., gardener, 6 Up. Bridge st
Primrose, Alex., gardener, 32 Up. Bridge st
Proudfoot, James, guard, 30 Cowane st
Prowe, Arthur, miner, 41 Baker st
Prowett, J. F., 6 Dean cres
Prowett, J. C., artist, Castle esplanade

Pryde, Thos, sawyer, 97 Low. Bridge st
Pullar, James, porter, 74 Cowane st
Pullar & Sons, J., dyers, 91 Port st
Purves, Rev. James, 3 Victoria sq
Pye, Mrs Janet, 15 Millar pl
Pye, Wm., tailor, 36 Abbey rd

Q

Queen, John, miner, 44 Baker st
Quigley, Pat., lab., 78 St Mary's wynd
Quigley, Thomas, bricklayer, 6 Raploch
Quin, Mrs B., 32 Up. castlehill
Quin, David, miner, 79 Main st
Quin, Thomas, lab., 2 St Mary's wynd
Quinn, Wm., lab., 36 Broad st

R

Rabbit, Mrs, 8 St Mary's wynd
Raffan, John, chemist, 16 Port st; house—34
    Dumbarton rd
Rae, F., grocer, 72 Port st
Rae, H., signalman, 53½ Cowane st
Rae, Jas. G., insur. agent, 22 Bruce st
Rae, Mrs Elizabeth, 5 Clifford rd
Rae, Mrs M., 9 Randolph ter
Rae, Sergeant, Married Quarters
Rae, Wm., baker, 3A Main st
Raeoch, J., carter, Causewayhead
Rafferty, P., miner, 40 Bannockburn rd
Raines, R., Penroseville
Raines, Ld., threshing mill proprs., Bridgehaugh
Ralston, John S., confectioner, 1 Albert pl
Ralston, Wm., rubber worker, Causewayhead
Ramage, Alex., miner, 76 Main st
Ramsay, David, weaver, 19 Abbey rd
Ramsay, Geo., painter, 5 William pl
Ramsay, James, engine driver, 1 Bruce st
Ramsay, James, tinsmith, 21 Low. craigs
Ramsay, John, clerk, 14 Bruce st
Ramsay, Mrs M., 23 Well green
Ramsay, Robt., fireman, 8 Douglas st
Ramsay, Wm., weaver, 106 Up. craigs

Ranger, Staff-Sergt. Wm., 35 Forth cres
Rankine, Geo., miner, 111 Low. Bridge st
Rankine, Geo., miner, 69 Baker st
Rankine, Mrs T., 14 Baker st
Raphael, David, lab., Castle esplanade
Rawding, James, plumber, 2 George st
Rawding, Thomas, engineer, 53½ Cowane st
Reekie, Walter, tailor, 4 Bayne st
Reid, Alex., carter, 76 Cowane st
Reid, Alex., lab., 41 St Mary's wynd
Reid, Miss E., 23 Forth pl
Reid, Geo., miner, 30 Broad st
Reid, James, Williamfield
Reid, James, joiner, 6 Low. craigs
Reid, Miss L., laundress, 22 Queen st
Reid, Mrs L., 24 Baker st
Reid, Mrs M., 25 Dumbarton rd
Reid, Miss, 1 Dumbarton rd
Reid, Miss, 22 Newhouse
Reid, Misses, baby linen warehouse, 32 Murray pl
Reid, Mrs, 12 Low. Bridge st
Reid, Mrs, 5 Park lane
Reid, Mrs, 63 Newhouse
Reid, Mrs, 18 St Mary's wynd
Reid, Nicol, waiter, 62 Spittal st
Reid, P., lorryman, 1 Burghmuir
Reid, P., dairyman, 22 Up. craigs
Reid, R., postmaster, 5 Queen's rd
Reid, R., lab., 2 Torbrex
Reid, S., inspector of poor, 4 Main st; house—
     3 Randolph ter
Reid, S., 44 Low. Bridge st
Reid, Private S., Married Quarters
Reid, Thos., banker, 5 Douglas ter
Reid, Thos., brewer, 27 Irvine pl
Reid, W., hatter, 21 Friars st; house—11 Baker st
Reid, Wm., electrician, 3 Balmoral pl
Reid, Wm., hawker, 38 St Mary's wynd
Reid, Wm., lorryman, 31 Up. craigs
Reid, Wm., plumber, Newhouse
Reilly, Patrick, poulterer, 3 Barn rd
Renfrew, Mrs, 34 Abbey rd
Rennie, James, cooper, 39 Up. castlehill
Rennie, John, engine driver, 10 Bayne st
Renwick, Wm., Langgarth
Reyburn, W., banker, Corn Exchange rd
Reynolds, Bernard, builder, 27 Randolph ter
Reynolds, F., mason, 3 Bank st
Reynolds, M., miner, 100 Main st
Reynolds, Mrs, dealer, 16 St Mary's wynd

Reynolds, P., bricklayer, 67 Low. Bridge st
Rhind, James, 67 Low. Bridge st
Riach, Alex., 1 St Mary's wynd
Richards, Henry M., labourer, 53½ Cowane st
Richardson, — miner, 4 Bruce st
Richardson, David, law clerk, 9 Forth cres
Richardson, D., surfaceman, 1 Well green
Richardson, James, millworker, 30 Newhouse
Richardson, James, engine driver, 7 Nelson pl
Richardson, James, jun., clerk, 1 William pl
Riddle, Geo., tobacconist, 60 and 62 Port st
Riddle, John, coachman, 61 Cowane st
Rintoul, James, spinner, 53 Baker st
Risk, John, distiller, 15 Snowdon pl
Risk, Miss, 14 Clarendon pl
Ritchie, D., lab., 10 Low. Bridge st
Ritchie, James, ploughman, King's pk farm
Ritchie, Mrs, 11 Gladstone pl
Ritchie, Mrs Jane, 66 Cowane st
Ritchie, Mrs Margaret, 76 Cowane st
Ritchie, Mrs, 70 Up. craigs
Ritchie, Mrs, 7 Abbey Road pl
Ritchie, Miss Cath., 9 Queen st
Ritchie, Mrs Frances, 10 Gladstone pl
Ritchie, Mrs M., 27 Murray pl
Ritchie, Mrs Mary, 66 Cowane st
Ritchie, Mrs Mary, 15 Bruce st
Ritchie, Robt., tailor, 9 Abbey rd
Ritchie, Wm., organist, 27 Murray pl
Ritchie, Wm., lab., 14 Broad st
Robb, Chas., painter, 72 Port st
Robb, H., carter, 58 St Mary's wynd
Robb, Henry, writer, 3 Abercromby pl
Robb, James, plumber, 23 Baker st
Robb, Hugh, shunter, 9 Irvine pl
Robb, Miss M., 10 Wallace st
Robb, Mrs Isabella, 30 Bow st
Robb, Wm., grocer, 5 George st
Robb, Wm., porter, 43½ Cowane st
Roberton, Miss S., 17 Forth cres
Roberts, Alex., publican, 27-29 Baker st
Roberts, Jonathan, lab., 48 Baker st
Roberts, J. T., spirit mer., 8 Newhouse
Roberts, J. W., Sunnyside, Park pl
Roberts, Mrs, 2 George st
Roberts, Richd., porter, 23 Well green
Roberts, Robt., flesher, King's pk rd
Roberts, Wm., gardener, 7 James st
Robertson, A. H., postal clerk, 16 Bruce st

Robertson, Alex., carter, 13 Well green
Robertson, Alex., lab., 5 St John st
Robertson, Alex., lab., 36 Baker st
Robertson, And., painter, 72 Port st
Robertson, Arch., waiter, 45 Murray pl
Robertson, A., postman, 16 Bruce st
Robertson, Chas., Cambuskenneth rope works
Robertson, Chas., tailor, 4 Douglas st
Robertson, Chas., engine driver, 3 Bruce st
Robertson, Corpl., Married Quarters
Robertson, D., barman, 25 Irvine pl
Robertson, David, 9 Bruce st
Robertson, E., lab , 8 Low. Bridge st
Robertson, E., gasworker, 57 Newhouse
Robertson, G., lab., Causewayhead
Robertson, Geo., plasterer, 24 Cowane st
Robertson, H., miner, 26 Main st
Robertson, James, wood mer., 37 Murray pl
Robertson, James, cabinetmaker, 29 Cowane st
Robertson, James, coachbuilder, 98 Up. craigs
Robertson, James, lab., 10 Bannockburn rd
Robertson, John C., watchmaker, 5 William pl
Robertson, John, vanman, 23 Queen st
Robertson, John, lorryman, 3 Drip rd
Robertson, J., 63 Up. craigs
Robertson, John, gardener, 5 Viewfield pl
Robertson, John, lab., 48 Broad st
Robertson, John, postman, 10 Up. craigs
Robertson, John, vanman, 12 Orchard pl
Robertson, Joseph, miner, 12 Newhouse
Robertson, Louis, clothier, 25 Wallace st
Robertson, Mrs, 44 Baker st
Robertson, Mrs, Spittalfield Cot., Causewayhead
Robertson, Miss M. C., Dunvegan, Causewayhead
Robertson, Miss Annie, 8 Queen st
Robertson, Miss, dressmaker, 13 Friars st
Robertson, Miss Isabella, 10 Wallace st
Robertson, Miss Maggie, 47 Port st
Robertson, Miss M., 40 Dumbarton rd
Robertson, Miss, 5 Victoria sq
Robertson, Mrs J. C., 14 Viewfield st
Robertson, Mrs E., 19 Seaforth pl
Robertson, Mrs C., china mer., 17 Barnton st
Robertson, Mrs C., 97 Low. Bridge st
Robertson, Mrs M., 39 Up. castlehill
Robertson, Mrs Margaret, 20 Low. castlehill
Robertson, Mrs, 19 Up. craigs
Robertson, Mrs E., 31 Up. craigs
Robertson, Mrs Janet, 95 Low. Bridge st
Robertson, Miss Janet, 26 Torbrex

Robertson, Mrs Jessie, 7 Maxwell pl
Robertson, Mrs Margaret, 8 Up. Bridge st
Robertson, Mrs Margaret, 17 Bruce st
Robertson, Misses, Roseville, Park pl
Robertson, Mrs E., 21 Princes st
Robertson, Mrs, 25 Wallace st
Robertson, Mrs, 112 Up. craigs
Robertson, Peter, clothier, 57 Low. Bridge st
Robertson, Rev. John M., D.D., The Manse, St Ninians
Robertson, R., candlemaker, 85 Main st
Robertson, Robt., cellarman, 6 Baker st
Robertson, Robt., engine driver, 91 Up. craigs
Robertson, Robt., plasterer, 32 Up. castlehill
Robertson, Robt., clothier, 27 Wallace st
Robertson, Sergt. F., Forthside
Robertson, Thos., cooper, 20 Low. castlehill
Robertson, Thos., coal agent, 12 Orchard pl
Robertson, Wm., bus hirer, 57 Up. craigs
Robertson, Wm., lab., Clay Toll
Robertson, Wm., tailor, 3 James st
Robertson, Wm., miner, 39 Low. craigs
Robertson, Wm., tanner, 5 Queen st
Robertson & Macfarlane, grocers, 42 Port st
Robertson & Sons, James, tailors, 16 Murray pl
Robinson, Wm., vanman, 98 Up. craigs
Robson, H. S., banker, Murray pl
Robson, Miss M., 19 Melville ter
Rodger, Jas., police constable, County Buildings
Rodger, Mrs Wm., 11 King st
Rodger, Alex., gas collector, 12 Bayne st
Rodgers, Wm., photographer, 13 Victoria sq
Rodwell, Corpl. G. T., Married Quarters
Rogers, Wm., gardener, 13 Albany cres
Rogers, Wm., joiner, 23 Friars st
Rolland, Alex., Cambuskenneth
Rollo, Francis, clerk, 35 Cowane st
Rollo, James, gardener, 21 Baker st
Ronald, J. & W., builders, 20 James st
Ronald, Thomas, 2 Park pl
Rose, Alex., engine driver, 100 Up. craigs
Ross, Geo., 19 Glencoe rd
Ross, Geo., tailor, 3 Park lane
Ross, James, plasterer, 35 Cowane st
Ross, Miss Minnie, 33 Friars st
Ross, Chas., lab., 5 St John st
Ross, Mrs F., confectioner, 92 St Mary's wynd
Ross, Thomas, carter, 31 Low. craigs
Ross, Thomas, sculptor, Station rd; house—3 Bruce st

Ross, Walter, vanman, 17 Seaforth pl
Ross, Wm., hawker, 20 Broad st
Rough, Thomas, carter, 63 Main st
Rouney, James, miner, 19 Abbey rd
Roxburgh, Alex., carpet manager, 33 Millar pl
Roxburgh, Miss J., confectioner, 7 Barnton st
Roy, And., miner, 2 St Mary's wynd
Roy, And., grocer, 55 Low. Bridge st
Roy, John, lorryman, 23 Cowane st
Roy, Miss, dressmaker, Craigroyston, C'wayhead
Roy, Wm., engine driver, 31 Low. Bridge st
Ruddock, T. L., Ellerslea, Drip rd
Russell, David, baker, 72 Port st
Russell, Miss E., 3 Low. Bridge st
Russell, Mrs Elizabeth, 4 Royal gardens
Russell, Mrs M., 17 Forth pl
Russell, James, coachtrimmer, 36 James st
Russell, Mrs Maggie, 13 Cowane st
Russell, Robt., nailer, 55 Glasgow rd
Rutherford, A., postal clerk, Rock ter
Rutherford, Mrs Helen, 39 Wallace st
Rutherford, James, gardener, 15 George st
Rutherford, Miss, milliner, 46 Arcade
Rutherford, Mrs, Jessamine cot., Causewayhead
Rutherford, Walter, fireman, 60 Baker st
Ryan, Mrs C., broker, 11A St Mary's wynd
Ryan, Thomas, broker, 6 and 15 Bow st

S

Salmond, R. W., hatter, 53 Barnton st
Salter, Sergt.-Major B., R.E., 41 Wallace st
Salton, Mrs Ann, 4 Barn rd
Samson, Robt., engineman, 11 Well green
Samson, Wm., fitter, 14 Well green
Samson, Wm., engineer, 5 Park lane
Samuel, James, stationmaster, 12 Princes st
Sandeman, Mrs, 10 Winchel pl
Sandeman, Ridley, laundryman, 22 Forth cres
Sanderson, Wm., yardsman, 27 Nelson pl
Sands, Alex., joiner, 46-47 Raploch
Sands, Chas., joiner, 53 Low. Bridge st
Sandes, Lieut.-Col. Chas., A.P.C., 26 Snowdon pl
Sangster, Mrs A., china merchant, 81 Spittal st
Sangster, A., technical instr., Spittal st
Saunders, L., In. Revenue officer, 3 Manse cres
Saunders, P., guard, 34 James st
Sceales, Lieut., Castle
Schofield, Michael, painter, 94 St Mary's wynd

Schoffield, Pat., lab., 96 St Mary's wynd
Schoffield, P., ret. postman, 2 Wallace st
Scobie, And., mason, 4 Winchel pl
Scobbie, James, miner, 17 Weaver row
Scorgie, Geo., 13 Seaforth pl
Scotland, Mrs Cecilia, nurse, 3 Burghmuir
Scotland, Mrs H., 7 Low. craigs
Scotland, Thomas, painter, 76 Baker st
Scotland, Wm., smith, 35 Low. craigs
Scott, A., carter, Causewayhead
Scott, Alex., engine driver, 22 Union st
Scott, Alex., janitor, High School
Scott, And., clerk, 9 Dean cres
Scott, David, reporter, 10 Union st
Scott, Donald, mason, 24 Main st
Scott, Donald, shepherd, 24 Broad st
Scott, James, railwayman, 45 Broad st
Scott, John, contractor, 27 Wallace st
Scott, John, lorryman, 24 Orchard pl
Scott, John, joiner, 17 Torbrex
Scott, J., plumber and electrician, 128 Main st
Scott, J., tram. foreman, Causewayhead
Scott, Mrs Jessie, 82 Spittal st
Scott, Robt., engine driver, 28 Nelson pl
Scott, Rev. Walter, 15 Princes st
Scoular, John, Crook
Scullion, John, miner, 10½ Raploch
Scully, Mrs, 38 Up. castlehill
Scully, H., cabman, 11 Baker st
Seardison, James, lab., 6 Baker st
Seaton, Mrs, St Leonard's, Causewayhead
Sellars, James, draper, 16 Bruce st
Sempill, J. D., chief constable, 1 Drummond pl
Sewell, Geo., porter, 16 Orchard pl
Shakespeare, Ed., cycle agent, Alexandra pl
Shakespeare & Chalmers, 32 Baruton st
Shand, Miss H. E., 8 Drummond pl
Shand & Co., James, oil works, Causewayhead
Sharp, Chas., packer, 6 Douglas st
Sharp, David, barman, 5 Well green
Sharp, James, linotyper, 5 William pl
Sharp, Miss Janet, 1 St John st
Sharp, Miss K., 44 Cowane st
Sharp, Mrs, 3 Port st
Sharp, Peter, lab., 7 Winchel pl
Sharp, Mrs R., 3 Low. Bridge st
Shaw, James, printer, 12 Viewfield st
Shaw, John, bootmaker, 37 Cowane st
Shaw, Mrs J., 8 Low. craigs
Shaw, Mrs, 40 Broad st

Shaw, Robt., lab., 25 Up. craigs
Shaw, William C., traveller, 12 Bruce st
Shaw, Wm Carstairs, 7 Allan pk
Shaw, Jas., miner, 3 Sunnyside, St Ninians
Shearer, And., gardener, Deroran lodge
Shearer, G., nurseryman, Rockdale cot, Park pl
Shearer, John E., bookseller, 1 Queen's rd
Shearer, Misses L. E. and C., 1 Queen's rd
Shearer & Son, R. S., booksellers, 6 King st
Shennan, B. D., bootmaker, 45 Port st; house—
    51 Wallace st
Shennan, J. W., bootmaker, 49½ Cowane st;
    house—3 Douglas st
Shepherd, Adam, lab., 7 Mid. craigs
Shepherd, Thos., cooper, 36 James st
Sheridan, John, lab., 50 St Mary's wynd
Shirra, Chas., postman, 3 Bruce st
Shirra, Patrick, waste merchant, 23 Broad st
Shirra, Walter, postman, 6 Winchel pl
Shirra, William, bookseller, 83 Port st;—house 8
    Albert pl
Short, Mrs A., 39 Up. craigs
Sim, John, bank teller, 21 Millar pl
Simpson, Andrew, auctioneer, 44 Barnton st;
    house—13 Abercromby pl
Simpson, And., miner, 62 Main st
Simpson, James, brushmaker, 25 St John st
Simpson, E. W., solicitor, 1 Princes st; house—2
    Randolph ter
Simpson, E., archt., 16 King st; house—14 Aber-
    cromby pl
Simpson, J. & Co., motor car engineers, Whins of
    Milton
Simpson, J. D., butcher, 120 Main st
Simpson, J., foreman yardsman, 43½ Cowane st
Simpson, James, clerk, 11 Bruce st
Simpson, James, porter, May Day yard
Simpson, James, telegraph super., 7 Dean cres
Simpson, John, tailor, 92 Cowane st
Simpson, John, moulder, 4 Barn rd
Simpson, John, painter, 72 Port st
Simpson, John, signalman, 7 Park lane
Simpson, Miss Jane, 2 St Mary's wynd
Simpson, Wm., auctioneer, 27 Princes st
Simpson, Wm., pawnbroker, 32 Bow st; house
    —11 Irvine pl
Sinclair, Alex., mason, 17 Bannockburn rd
Sinclair, David, barman, 5 Baker st
Sinclair, Daniel, joiner, 1 James st; workshop
    12 Thistle st

Sinclair, Daniel, sawyer, 49 Newhouse
Sinclair, James, trav., 18 Millar pl
Sinclair, James, confectioner, 15 Murray pl;
    house—8 James st
Sinclair, John, compositor, 49 King st
Sinclair, Peter, gardener, 80 Cowane st
Sinclair, Peter, lorryman, 60 Baker st
Sinclair, R., rubber worker, 69 Low. Bridge st
Singer's Sewing Machine Co., 22 Barnton st
Sives, James, linesman, 8 George st
Skeoch, Rev. Thomas, 17 Millar pl
Sloan, John, cigar mer., 66 Murray pl
Sloan, John, steward, County Club, Murray pl
Skinner, Dr Graham, Allan park house
Skinner, John, miner, Crofthead
Skinner, John, chemist, 24 Princes st
Skinner, P., cutter, Burghmuir
Smart, James, engine driver, 27 Irvine pl
Small, John, watchmaker, 8 Mid. craigs
Smeaton, A., baker, 76 St Mary's wynd
Smeaton, John, gardener, 23 Broad st
Smeaton, John, carter, 10 Low. Bridge st
Smeaton, John, lab., 23 Broad st
Smellie, Wm., photographer, 5 Viewfield pl
Smith, A. P., carter, 56 Cowane st
Smith, Chas, dairyman, 1 Raploch
Smith, Chas., 2 Ballengeich rd
Smith, Dan., gardener, Randolphfield
Smith, David, porter, 17 Seaforth pl
Smith, F., lab., 74 St Mary's wynd
Smith, Geo., joiner, 10 Up. Bridge st
Smith, James, gardener, Rockdale cot
Smith, James Kemp, engineer, 13 Windsor pl
Smith, James, miner, 13 Weaver row
Smith, James, painter, Cambuskenneth
Smith, James, porter, 3 Springfield pl
Smith, James, tobacconist, 39 Murray pl
Smith, James, D., gas manager, 2 Randolph rd
Smith, J. B., Clifford pk
Smith, J. D., engineer, 27 Wallace st
Smith, J. D., painter, 46 Up. Bridge st
Smith, John, gardener, Easter Livilands
Smith, Miss, 3 Glebe av
Smith, Mrs Agnes, nurse, 102 Up. craigs
Smith, Mrs C., 6 Coburg av
Smith, Mrs E., 5 Low. craigs
Smith, Mrs E., 1 Friars st
Smith, Mrs G., 37 King st
Smith, Mrs Jane, 4 Forth cres
Smith, Mrs, 6 Bruce st

Smith, Mrs, 73 Baker st
Smith, Pipe-Major, Married Quarters
Smith, Rev. David, 5 Laurelhill pl
Smith, Rev. Gabriel, 21 Randolph ter
Smith, R., joiner, 11 Barnton st and 53 Murray pl
Smith, R., blacksmith, 15 Main st
Smith, R. Tennent, produce merc., Thistlecroft,
    Linden av
Smith, Robt. Alex., 20 Snowdon pl
Smith, Robt., vanman, 9 Maxwell pl
Smith, Robt., painter, 14 Bow st
Smith, Robt., slater, 66 Spittal st
Smith, Thomas, cabinetmaker, 6 Barn rd
Smith, Very Rev. Monseigneur, 17 Irvine pl
Smith, Wm., engine driver, 60 Up. craigs
Smith, Wm., trav., 18 Bruce st
Smith, Wm., carter, 14 Up. craigs
Smith, Wm., tel. linesman, 47 Baker st
Smith, Wm., cabinetmaker, 10 Up. Bridge st
Smith, Wm., lab., 17 Broad st
Smith & Co., R. W., coal merchants, Wallace st
Sneddon, James, tailor, 2 King's stables
Sneddon, James, weaver, 4 Low. craigs
Sneddon, Mrs Annie, 74 Main st
Sneddon, Mrs Wm., 4 Low. craigs
Snyder, Mrs, 16 Glebe av
Soddin, Chas., baker, 44 Baker st
Somers, R., ret. schoolmaster, 14 Glebe cres
Somers, Wm., joiner, 10 Dumbarton rd
Somerville, D., ironmonger, 13 King st and 16
    Dumbarton rd
Somerville, James, tailor, 15½ Burghmuir
Somerville, James, nailmaker, 75 Newhouse
Somerville, James, scavenger, 11 Low. Bridge st
Somerville, J., manufacturer, 34 Main st
Somerville, John, nailmaker, 7 Randolph ter
Somerville, John & Wm., nailmakers, 36 Main st
Somerville, Robt., baker, 79 Main st
Somerville, Wm., dentist, 4 Viewfield pl
Somerville, Wm., newsagent, 2 Barnton st;
    house—19 Forth cres
Somerville, Wm., iron mer., 11 Melville ter
Somerville & Valentine, ironmongers, 1-5 Port st
Sorton, Chas. W., postal clerk, 17 Queen st
Sorton, Joseph, storeman, 2 George st
Soutar, A., ostler, 32 Spittal st
Soutar, C., bricklayer, 4 George st
Soutar, Geo., waiter, 23 George st
Soutar, David, cabman, 72 Port st
Soutar, David, clothier, 67 Wallace st

Soutar, Duncan, warehouseman, 72 Port st
Soutar, James, mason, 4 George st
Soutar, Peter, engine driver, 5 Mid. craigs
Soutar & Co., clothiers, 53 Murray pl
Soutar, James, lab., 18 St Mary's wynd
Sowdan & Forgan, musicsellers, 6 Murray pl
Spalding, C. C., engine driver, 103 Low. Bridge st
Spalding, Jas, plasterer, 97½ Low. Bridge st
Speed, Arch., ironmonger, 3 and 5 Broad st
Speedie Bros., Ltd., auctioneers, 14 Wallace st
Speirs, James, grocer, 49 Cowane st ; house—27
    Wallace st
Speirs, Miss A. E., Laurelhill
Speirs, Mrs Mary, 16 Park ter
Spite & Co., F., Ltd., chemists, 56 Port st
Spittal, Sergt. E., Military prison
Spowart, James, engineer, 2 Abbey rd pl
Sproat, Miss, 45 Up. craigs
Squair, D., postman, 25 Cowane st
Squair, Mrs Janet, 25 Cowane st
Stalker, Mrs C., 50 Low. Bridge st
Stalker, Mrs M., 47 Cowane st
Stanborough, Geo., brakesman, 34 James st
Stanborough, Mrs, 15 Murray pl
Stanley, David, lab., 21 Low craigs
Starkey, Geo., grocer, 58 Port st
Steel, Chas., brassfounder, 37 Murray pl
Steel, John, plumber, 22 Murray pl ; house—
    Wellwood, Albert pl
Steel, John Dickson, C.A., 7 Royal Gardens
Steel, J. & C., Stirling Brass Works, Forth st
Steel, Wm., miner, 126 Main st
Steele, John, engine driver, 53½ Cowane st
Stenhouse, Alex., forester, Polmaise cots.
Stephen. W. S., bootshop manager, 62 Port st
Steven, John, hawker, 1 St John st
Steven, Mrs Agnes, 7 Victoria sq
Stevens, H. law clerk, 25 Newhouse
Stevens, Jas., hairdresser, 34 Barnton st ; house
    —39 Millar pl
Stevens, Peter, Crown Hotel, 11 Arcade
Stevens, Geo., draper, 20 Bruce st
Stevens, H., rubber worker, 34 Abbey rd
Stevenson, A., clerk, 15 Glencoe rd
Stevenson, A., hotelkeeper, 45 King st
Stevenson, Alex. D., 6 Windsor pl
Stevenson, Bros., Golden Lion Hotel
Stevenson, Chas., P., musicseller, 23 Arcade ;
    house—13 Park pl
Stevenson, Hugh, engine keeper, 1 Forth cres

Stevenson, James, weaver, 4 William pl
Stevenson, Jas., cabinetmaker, 12 Bayne st
Stevenson, John, cabman, 60 Baker st
Stevenson, Mrs J., 13 Low. craigs
Stevenson, Miss J., dressmaker, 37 Murray pl
Stevenson, Mrs Janet, 25 Port st
Stevenson, Miss M., 12 Main st
Stevenson, Mrs, 8 St Mary's wynd
Stevenson, R., fancy goods mer., 75-77 Port st
Stevenson, Robt., weaver, 5 Middle craigs
Stevenson, Thomas, vanman, 3B Main st
Stevenson, Thomas, vanman, 13 Glencoe rd
Stevenson, Wm., J. manufacturer, 7 Melville ter
Stevenson, W., live stock agent, 11 Park aven
Stevenson, Wm., miner, 9 Torbrex
Stevenson, Wm., potato merchant, 10 Barnton st
Stevenson, Alex., miner, 43 Bannockburn rd
Stevenson, Alex., miner, 72 Port st
Stevenson, Bros., potato mer., 10 Maxwell pl
Stevenson, John, potato merchant, 7 Coburg av
Stevenson, Miss, confectioner, 26 Arcade
Stevenson, J., tailor, 19 Spittal st
Stevenson, T., stationer, 13 Baker st
Stevenson, T., newsagent, 1 Church wynd
Stewart, Alex., lorryman, 3 Park lane
Stewart, Alex., railwayman, 68 Cowane st
Stewart, And., rubber worker, 66 Baker st
Stewart, Arch., plumber, 42 Cowane st
Stewart, C., lab., 8 Bruce st
Stewart, A., plumber, 60 Up. craigs
Stewart, A. W., seedsman, 62 Port st
Stewart, A., lab., 3 Douglas st
Stewart, And., carrier, Causewayhead
Stewart, Daniel, jeweller, 24 Dumbarton rd
Stewart, D. & J., jewellers, 22 Port st
Stewart, D., jeweller, 3 Coburg av
Stewart, E. M., fireclay goods manufacturer, 29
    Randolph rd
Stewart, H., lab., 12 Bayne st
Stewart, Hamilton, 10 Melville ter
Stewart, Hugh, clockmaker, 12 Bayne st
Stewart, James, gardener, 6 Millar pl
Stewart, James, millwright, Low. craigs
Stewart, James, millwright, 7 Friars st
Stewart, James, signalman, 3 Winchel pl
Stewart, James, comp., 35 Low craigs
Stewart, James, clerk, 49 King st
Stewart, James, postboy, 10 Dumbarton rd
Stewart, James, pitsinker, 11 Well green
Stewart, John, blacksmith, 13 Friars st

Stewart, John, bootmaker, 40 Barnton st
Stewart, John, mason, 16 Union st
Stewart, John, shoemaker, 15 Up. craigs
Stewart, John, tinsmith, 16 Orchard pl
Stewart, J. M., vet. surgeon, 49-72 Murray pl
Stewart, J., Tower orchard, Cambuskenneth
Stewart, Major, Forthside
Stewart, Michael, engine driver, 6 Bruce st
Stewart, Miss Elizabeth, 10 Melville ter
Stewart, Miss M., 18 Glebe av
Stewart, Miss M., Barnsdale pl
Stewart, Miss M., confectioner, Causewayhead
Stewart, Miss, Bellfield rd
Stewart, Miss, 63 Cowane st
Stewart, Misses C., J. and J., 3 Windsor pl
Stewart, Mrs Ann, 46 Up. castlehill
Stewart, Mrs Elizabeth, 22 Torbrex
Stewart, Mrs Helen, 19 Torbrex
Stewart, Mrs Jane, 26 Port st
Stewart, Mrs M., 19 Bruce st
Stewart, Mrs M., 51 Main st
Stewart, Mrs, 84 Cowane st
Stewart, Mrs, 78 St Mary's wynd
Stewart, Mrs, 92 Cowane st
Stewart, Mrs, 21 Raploch
Stewart, P., gardener, 35 Dumbarton rd
Stewart, P., grocer, 9 Abbey rd
Stewart, Private, Married Quarters
Stewart, Sam., tailor, 35 Low. craigs
Stewart, Thos., brushmaker, 94 St Mary's wynd
Stewart, Walter, smith, 41 Low. craigs
Stewart, Wm., brakesman, 3 Douglas st
Stewart, Wm., pedlar, 20 Low. castlehill
Stirling, Duncan, vanman, 7 Up. Bridge st
Stirling, James, clerk, 1 James st
Stirling, James, farmer, 25 Dumbarton rd
Stirling, John, joiner, 61 Cowane st
Stirling, Miss R., confectioner, 2 Spittal st
Stirling, Mrs Janet, 77 Up. Bridge st
Stirling, Peter, dairyman, Drip rd
Stirling, P., pointsman, 8 William pl
Stirling, Thos., corkcutter, 32 Up. Bridge st
Stirling Nurs. Asso.—Nurses' home, 53 Murray pl
Stirling, Wm., draper, Beechwood, Causewayhead
Stocksley, James, shoemaker, 16 Friars st
Stocksley, James, tailor, 21 Spittal st
Stocksley, Wm., carter, 63 Main st
Stocksley, Wm., shoemaker, 45 Broad st
Stoddart, Miss L., bootmaker, 12 Port st
Storrier, Miss Ann., 12 Manse cres

Stoddart, M. &. J., bootmakers, 8 Dumbarton rd
    and 60 Murray pl
Strachan, Jas., cabinetmaker, 32 James st
Strachan, Miss Johann, 86 Cowane st
Strachan, H. D., rubber worker, 17 Bruce st
Strang, James, tailor, 11 Douglas st
Strang, Joseph, coachman, 6 Well green
Strang, Robt., traveller, 8 Bruce st
Strang, William, draper, 5 Princes st
Strang & Co., W., drapers, 67 Barnton st
Strang, John, joiner, 4 George st
Strang, J., coal agent, Causewayhead
Stronach, Miss J., 13 Pitt ter
Struthers, Miss, 17 Snowdon pl
Struthers, James, cartwright, 26 James st
Struthers, John, nailer, 55 Bannockburn rd
Struthers, Matthew, draper, 57 Wallace st
Struthers, Mrs Margaret, 61 Cowane st
Stuart, Miss Janet, 13 Princes st
Sugget, R., 62 Port st
Sullivan, Thos, lab., 4 Bayne st
Summers, Wm., vanman, 34 Cowane st
Sussams, Mrs., 10 Barn rd
Sutherland, James, signal fitter, 33 Cowane st
Sutherland, John, telegraphist, 22 Bruce st
Sutherland, Q.-M.-Sergt. J., Castle
Sutherland, J., Glasgow carrier, 27 King st
Sutherland, Misses C. and M., 87 Port st
Sutherland, Mrs Janet, 53 Port st
Sutherland, Wm., fireman, 36 Abbey rd
Sutherland, Mrs A., Cambuskenneth
Sutherland, A., mason, Causewayhead
Sutherland, John, mason, Causewayhead
Suttie, Miss Alice, 76 Cowane st
Swan, Alex., bricklayer, Low. craigs
Swan, Andrew, jeweller, 7 Clarendon pl
Swan, A. & R., jewellers, 8 Port st
Swan, David, jeweller, 31 Friars st
Swan, Geo., tanner, 10 Glasgow rd
Swanston, Jas., fireman, 71 Up. Bridge st
Swanston, Miss Jessie, 51 Cowane st
Swanston, Mrs C., 84 Cowane st
Swift, Sergt. Geo., Forthside
Sword, James, curator, Smith Institute
Syme, John, smith, 29 Abbey rd
Syme, Mrs Elizabeth, 105 Low. Bridge st
Syme, Robt., gardener, Torbrex House
Symon, Misses, 12 Albert pl
Symon, John, blacksmith, 53 Low Bridge st
Symons, Mrs Agnes, 25 Well green

T

Tabor, Wm., engine driver, 7 Borestone cres
Tainsh, James, coach painter, 10 Up. Bridge st
Tainsh, Miss E., 12 James st
Tait, Geo., painter, 80 Cowane st
Tait, R., confectioner, 1 Sunnyside, St Nin.
Tait, Wm. J., tailor's cutter, 7 James st
Tasker, Capt., 22 Clarendon pl
Taylor, Alex., guard, 19 Abbey rd
Taylor, Alex., carter, 11 Bannockburn rd
Taylor, David, contractor, 26 Bannockburn rd
Taylor, David, insur. agent, 24 Main st
Taylor, Duncan, tailor, 47 Wallace st
Taylor, F., painter, Cambuskenneth
Taylor, Henry, bootcloser, 53½ Cowane st
Taylor, James, tailor, 43 Cowane st
Taylor, James, 3 Well green
Taylor, John B., Sub-Post Office, St Nin.
Taylor, John, coachbuilder, 17 St John st
Taylor, John, hawker, 51 Bannockburn rd
Taylor, John, nurseryman, 1 Raploch
Taylor, Joseph, clerk, 12 Bruce st
Taylor, Miss Agnes B., 46 King st
Taylor, Miss Janet, 35 Cowane st
Taylor, Miss Helen, 8 Maxwell pl
Taylor, Miss, 36 Queen st
Taylor, Mrs A., 46 King st
Taylor, Mrs Ann, Cambuskenneth
Taylor, Mrs Catherine, 14 Up. Bridge st
Taylor, Mrs C., 7 Douglas st
Taylor, Mrs, 37 Barnton st
Taylor, Mrs, spirit merc., 73-75 St Mary's wynd
Taylor, Mrs, spirit merc., 7 St John st
Taylor, P., wright, 1 Springfield pl
Taylor, Robt., carter, 65 Main st
Taylor, Robt., plumber, 32 Spittal st
Taylor, Robt., writer, 19 Park ter
Taylor, Sergt.-Major J. G., Bellfield
Taylor, Thomas, clerk, 54 Port st
Taylor, Thomas, contractor, 16 Bannockburn rd
Taylor, Wm., lab., 60 Baker st
Telfer, James, lab., 12 Winchel pl
Telford, Wm., shoemaker, 21 Bow st
Templeton, Mrs, restaur., 68 Murray pl
Templeton, Wm., tobacconist, 85 Port st; house 5 Snowdon pl
Tennant, R. B., ironfounder, Benarty House
Tetstall, James, cooper, 63 Cowane st

Tetstall, Mrs, 63 Cowane st
Third, A. S., science master, 4 Manse cres
Thompson, James, trav., 32 Queen st
Thompson, John, mechanic, 10 Up. craigs
Thompson, Mrs C., grocer, 55 Main st
Thompson, Mrs Jane, 24 Princes st
Thompson, Wm., 63 Wallace st
Thomson, A., corkcutter, 23 George st
Thomson, Alex., tanner, 41 Baker st
Thomson, Alex., tanner, 25 Weaver row
Thomson, Alex., nailer, 26 Main st
Thomson, Alex., blacksmith, 60 Baker st
Thomson, Alex., miner, 9 Borestone cres
Thomson, And., gas collector, 71 Newhouse
Thomson, And., carter, 12 Abbey rd pl
Thomson, Arch., law clerk, 14 Manse cres
Thomson, Chas., ret. coachpainter, 10 Bruce st
Thomson, D., ironmonger, 14 Bruce st
Thomson, David, 26 Torbrex
Thomson, David, trav., 16 Nelson pl
Thomson, David, miner, 93 Main st
Thomson, Duncan, butcher, 35 Friars st and 11
    Up. craigs; house—12 Bruce st
Thomson, D., cabinetmaker, 56 Low. Bridge st
Thomson, Wm., clerk, 16 Nelson pl
Thomson, Geo., coachbuilder, 30-32 Orchard pl
Thomson, George, billposter, 11 baker st
Thomson, George, joiner, 14 Bruce st
Thomson, James, coachbuilder, 2 Drummond pl
Thomson, James, slater, 26 Torbrex
Thomson, James, carter, 22 Raploch
Thomson, Jas., gardener, 30 Glasgow rd
Thomson, John, lorryman, 33 Broad st
Thomson, J., ret. watchmaker, 43 Wallace st
Thomson, Miss C., bookseller, 55, 74 Cowane st
Thomson, Misses, milliners, 9-11 Arcade
Thomson, M. O., jeweller, 18 Murray pl
Thomson, Mrs Annie, laundress, 27 Abbey rd
Thomson, Mrs Annie, 4 Springfield pl
Thomson, Mrs M., 3 Douglas st
Thomson, Mrs, 20 Cowane st
Thomson, Mrs William, 18 Dumbarton rd
Thomson, Peter, gardener, Butterflats cot
Thomson, Robt., butcher, 29 Port st; house—
    Queenshaugh
Thomson, Robt., storekeeper, 19 Bruce st
Thomson, Thos., lathsplitter, 73 Bannockburn rd
Thomson, Walter, weaver, 1 Well green
Thomson, Wm., retired draper, 8 Forth cres
Thomson, Wm., 1 Main st

Thomson, John, watchmaker, 16 Viewfield st
Thomson, H., miner, 50 Low. castlehill
Thomson, James, 65 Bannockburn rd
Thomson, James, plumber, 17 Bruce st
Thomson, Mrs G. P., 17 Gladstone pl
Thomson, Mrs M. A., 13 Rosebery pl
Thomson, Mrs J. J., Ravenswood, C'wayhead rd
Thomson, Mrs., Lyngarth, Causewayhead rd
Thomson, R., Grange house, Causewayhead
Thomson, T., saddler, 6 William pl
Thomson, Private R., married quarters
Thomson, Wm., saddler, 20 Barnton st
Thorburn, Robert, carter, 150 Main st
Thorley, Adam, 2 Drip rd
Thorley, Mrs., 111 Low. Bridge st
Thornton, Anthony, lab., 16 Bow st
Thornton, Mrs Mary, 18 Raploch
Thornton, M., lab., Causewayhead
Thornton, A., lab., 61 Cowane st
Thornton, Robt., brakesman, 34 Abbey rd
Threlfall, Chas., trav., 28 Millar pl
Thurman & Co., J. E., Forth Bridge mills
Tod, Frederick, banker, 10 Victoria pl
Todd, James, driver, 32 James st
Todd, Miss, 33 James st
Todd, P., lorryman, 108 Up craigs
Todd, Thomas, 20 Park ter
Todd, Wm., engine driver, 92 Up. craigs
Todd, Wm., railwayman, 6 Douglas st
Todd, Alex., lab., 14½ St John st
Todd, David, miner, 23 Baker st
Togneri, Pietro, ice-cream shop, 81 Baker st
Togneri Bros., ice-cream vendors, Causewayhead
Torrance, Mrs, 24 Union st
Tortolano, A., ice-cream vendor, 87 Main st
Towers, John, porter, 108 Up. craigs
Towers, W., electrician, Burghmuir
Townsend, Mrs Elizabeth, 23 Abbey rd
Traynor, W. J., spirit merchant, 4 St Mary's w'd ;
    house—33 Friars st
Tracey, J., mason, 86 St Mary's wynd
Trench, F., gardener, Causewayhead
Tritton, Mrs E., grocer, 21 Broad st
Troup, Alex., coachtrimmer, 85 Port st
Troup, David, postal clerk, 6 Glasgow rd
Turnbull, Adam, printer, 3 Queen st
Turnbull, Miss Elizabeth, 21 Wallace st
Turner, John, lab., 3 Church wynd
Turner, John, lab., 36 Broad st
Turner, Miss Anita, 1 Laurelhill pl

Turner, Miss H., dressmaker, 52 Broad st
Turner, Peter, lab., 20 Bow st
Turpie, And., plumber, 8 Bruce st
Tully, Mrs, C., 19 St Mary's wynd
Tyler, H. P., bootmaker, 28 Port st

U

Ure, Alex., lab., 39 Main st
Ure, John R., ironfounder, Snowdon pl
Upfold, J., Epis. Church officer, 10 Bow st
Urquhart, James, brakesman, 59 Cowane st

V

Valentine, Henry D., 11 Princes st
Valentine, Jas. D., ironmonger, 24 Nelson pl
Vance, John, tailor, 34 Up. castlehill
Venters, J., In. Revenue officer, 15 Allan pk
Virtue & Co., ironmongers, cabinetmakers, and
    furnishers, 14, 26-30 Murray pl

W

Waddell, R. D., sausage mer., 29 Murray pl
Wadsley, Mrs M., 12 Bayne st
Walbanks, H., miner, $14\frac{1}{2}$ St John st
Walker, Fred, lorryman, 17 Abbey rd
Walker, James, joiner, 34 Cowane st
Walker, James, painter, Causewayhead
Walker, James, miner, 118 Baker st
Walker, John, baker, Corn Exchange rd
Walker, John, chemist, 15 Coburg av
Walker, John, peram. maker, 52 Barnton st
Walker, Miss, Garscube, Causewayhead
Walker, Mrs Agnes, 5 Victoria pl
Walker, Mrs Agnes, 11 Queen st
Walker, Mrs I., 60 Main st
Walker, Mrs M., 1 Well green
Walker, Robt., engineman, 14 Borestone pl
Walker, Robt., sawyer, 3 Broad st
Walker, Ronald, architect, 12 Allan pk

Walker, R., miner, 40 Up. Bridge st
Walker, T., Spittal Villa, Causewayhead
Walker & Paton, peram. makers, 17 Low. craigs
Walker & Skinner, chemists, 67 King st
Wallace, David, lab., 98 Cowane st
Wallace, Geo., baker, 142 Main st
Wallace, John, postman, 9 Bruce st
Wallace, John, watchmaker, 44 Broad st
Wallace, John, engine driver, 3 Abbey rd
Wallace, Mat., laundryman, 53, 76 Up. craigs
Wallace, P., policeman, 2 Bruce st
Wallace, Robt., draper, 89 Port st ; house—1
    Queen st
Wallace, Robt. B., upholsterer, 77-81 Port st
Wallace, Wm., engineer, 18 Forth st
Wallace, W., signalman, Causewayhead
Wallace, W., coachman, Clifford Park
Walls, Alex., plasterer, 28 Thistle st ; house—11
    Allan pk
Walls, Alex., plasterer, 9 Manse cres
Walls, Arch., glazier, 1 Dumbarton rd
Walls, James, blacksmith, 1A Main st
Walls, John, ret. painter, 16 Forth cres
Walls, Robt., miller, 66 Port st
Walls, Thos., horseshoer, 9-11 Bannockburn rd
Walls, T., blacksmith, Aitken's bldgs., St Nin.
Walton, Walter, waiter, 8 Union st
Wann & Condie, 37 Murray pl
Wardrop, John, lab., 13 Glencoe rd
Wares, Miss, 13 Manse cres
Watchman, W., mining surv., 4 Ballengeich rd
Watson, Alan, blacksmith, 34 James st
Watson, A., gardener, Cambuskenneth
Watson, Daniel, grocer, 1 Dumbarton rd
Watson, Geo., slater, 15 Well green
Watson, Geo., lab., 98 Baker st
Watson, H., gardener, 76 Spittal st
Watson, James, lorryman, 8 Douglas st
Watson, John, tanner, 24 Torbrex
Watson, John, warehouseman, 15 Low. Bridge st
Watson, John, miner, 3B Main st
Watson, Mrs A., 43½ Cowane st
Watson, Mrs Janet, 3 Forth cres
Watson, Mrs Janet, 1 Drip rd
Watson, Mrs, 20 Bow st
Watson, Mrs, 21 Albert pl
Watson, Mrs, Craigview, Causewayhead
Watson, Robt., nailer, 23 Glasgow rd
Watson, Sergt., 6 Married Quarters
Watson, T., cartwright, Cambuskenneth

Watson, Wm., bootmaker, 15 Barnton st; house
  —Drip road
Watson, Wm., tailor, 44 Up. castlehill
Watson, Wm., tinsmith, 68 Cowane st
Watt, A., pitheadman, 144 Main st
Watt, H. P., auctioneer, 22-32 Baker st; house—
  Causewayhead rd
Watt, John, guide, 10 Borestone pl
Watt, John, seedsman, 11 Princes st
Watt, John, lab., 12 Low. craigs
Watt, John, baker, 10 Barn rd
Watt, Misses J. C. and I., 8 Gladstone pl
Watt, Mrs C., 57 Low. Bridge st
Watt, Mrs, 61 Murray pl
Watt, Peter, grocer, 1 Princes st
Watt, Peter, grocer, 6 Broad st
Watt, Robt., contractor, 29 Spittal st
Watt, Robt., ironmonger, 63 Wallace st
Watters, A., lab., 30 Forth cres
Watters, Alex., spirit merchant, 65 Baker st:
  house—25 King st
Watters, Sgt.-Major L. G., Drill Hall, Princes st
Waugh, Robt., law clerk, 7 Albert pl
Waugh, W. C., librarian, Corn Exchange rd
Webb, Q.-M.-Sergt. W. E., 40 Forth cres
Webster, Alex., guard, 12 Bayne st
Webster, H., assist. registrar, 9 Rosebery pl
Webster, James, insur. agent, 5 Wallace st
Webster, John, vanman, 29 Queen st
Wedderspoon, Miss, dressmaker, 16 King st
Weir, Alex., 50 Up. Bridge st
Weir, Gavin, miner, 5 William pl
Weir, John, draper, 26 Union st
Weir, John, trav., 2 Forth cres
Weir, Miss Cath., 3 Forth cres
Weir, Mrs J., 50 Up. Bridge st
Weir, Thomas B., trav., 6 Bruce st
Weir, Thomas, trav., Parkgate, Victoria pl
Weir, Wm. A., trav., 5 Forth cres
Wells, Mrs S , 118 Baker st
Welsh, Alex., boltmaker, 104 Main st
Welsh, Ed., general-dealer, 14-16 Broad st
Welsh, James, Borestone cottage
Welsh, James, lab., 42 Low. castlehill
Welsh, James, lab., 6 Raploch
Welsh, John, lab., 12 Low. castlehill
Welsh, John, lab., 3 Low. Bridge st
Welsh, John, carter, Cambuskenneth
Welsh, John, miner, 33 Raploch
Welsh, Michael, lab., 76 Baker st

Welsh, Mrs M., 6 Main st
Welsh, Patrick, writer, Springwood
Welsh, Mrs Ann, 16 Spittal st
Welsh, Wm., blacksmith, 16 Low Bridge st
Welsh, J. P., postman, 61 Barnton st
Wentworth, A., store worker, 69 Low Bridge st
Westwater, Miss E., 12 Bayne st
Westcott, Mrs J., Cambuskenneth
Whammond, David, grocer, 13 Forth cres
Whiteford, P., hawker, 8 Broad st
Whitehead, Miss M., 12 Gladstone pl
Whitehead, Thomas, guard, 19 Abbey rd
White, D. G., town clerk depute, 7 Forth cres
White, James, baker, 60 Baker st
White, James, lab., 11 Baker st
White, John, mason, 16 Orchard pl
White, John, Borestone, pl
White, Miss Fanny, 15 Up. Bridge st
White, Miss Janet, 61 Cowane st
White, Thomas, pensioner, 1 Ballengeich rd
White, Wm., rubber worker, 75 Upper Bridge st
White, N., miner, 21 Raploch
White, Wm., clerk, 7 Newhouse
White, Wm., draper, 59 Cowane st
Whyte, Mrs Janet, 19 Nelson pl
Whyte, John, miner, 7 Bayne st
Whyte, Miss L., baby linen, 22 Arcade
Whyte, Robt., solicitor, Maygate, Victoria pl
Whyte, Wm., lab., 40 Raploch
Whytock, Jas., lab., 14 Main st
Whytt, Dr. A., 20 Clarendon pl
Wiggan, Mrs., 38 Up. Bridge st
Wilkie, James, sawyer, 11 Abbey rd
Wilkie, Jas., railway inspector, 5 Springfield pl
Wilkinson, Miss, 11 Cowane st
Wilkinson, T., lab., 40 Broad st
Wilkins, Richmond, storeman, 99 Low. Bridge st
Williams, David, engine driver, 39 Wallace st
Williams, G., chauffeur, 7 Friars st
Williamson, Alex., lorryman, 75 King st
Williamson, Geo. F., moulder, 31 St Mary's wynd
Williamson, James, baker, 51 Broad st
Williamson, Mrs M., 1 Low. craigs
Williamson, Walter, 10 Up. Bridge st
Williamson, W., gardener, 18 Viewfield st
Williamson, W. S., Burgh officer, 23 Baker st
Williamson, Joseph, dairyman, 17 Glencoe rd
Willis, Robt., iron merchant, 5 Melville ter
Wilson, And., grocer, 106 Up. craigs
Wilson, And., public analyst, Whins of Milton

Wilson, And., barman, 23 George st
Wilson, A., mason, 10 George st
Wilson, A., miner, 71 Up. Bridge st
Wilson, Charles, 15 Park ter
Wilson, Dr, 1 Viewfield pl
Wilson, Geo., coachman, 75 King st
Wilson, James Irvine, dentist, 3 Millar pl
Wilson, James, lab., 63 Cowane st
Wilson, J., inspector of schools, 7 Windsor pl
Wilson, John, miner, Calton cot
Wilson, Miss, Helen, 24 Union st
Wilson, Miss Janet, 25 Millar pl
Wilson, Mrs Margaret, 25 St John st
Wilson, Robt., plumber, 12 George st
Wilson, Robt., tailor, 13 Cowane st
Wilson, Samuel, lab., 18 St Mary's wynd
Wilson, Wm. B., joiner, 8 Irvine pl
Wilson, Wm., goods agent, 9 Dean cres
Wilson, Wm., miner, 15 Low. Bridge st
Wilson, R., sailor, 15 Cowane st
Wilson, Wm., tweed manuf., 10 Drummond pl
Wilson, Jas., miner, 22 Raploch,
Wilson, John, tailor, 2 Bruce st
Wilson, Joseph, miner, 76 Spittal st
Wilson, Mrs J., 40 Forth st
Wilson, Mrs L., 17 Cowane st
Wilson, Miss J., 51 Wallace st
Wilson, — coachbuilder, 24 Union st
Wilson, Thomas, 1 Viewfield pl
Wingate, James, roadman, 37 Bannockburn rd
Wingate, John, compositor, 5 Bruce st
Wingate, Peter, engine driver, 114 Up. craigs
Wingate, Thos., weaver, 98 Up. craigs
Wingate, & Curror, writers, 2 Dumbarton rd
Wing, M. T., trav., 2 Clifford rd
Winks, Mrs, 15 Seaforth pl
Winter, John, miner, 33 Broad st
Wishart, David, lorryman, 62 Spittal st
Wood, Chas., grocer, 15 Newhouse
Wood, R. B. Victoria villa, Causewayhead
Wood, John, miner, 32 Up. Castlehill
Woodburne, Mrs, 18 Clarendon pl
Wordie, James, lab., 47 St Mary's wynd
Wordie, Mrs, cooperage, 75 King st
Wordie, Mrs Agnes, 33 King st
Wordie & Co., carting contract., 3 Thistle st
Wotherspoon, Alex., lab., 98 Baker st
Wotherspoon, John, lab., 28 St Mary's wynd
Wotherspoon, David, lab., 17 St John st
Wotherspoon, Mrs C., 3 James st

Wright, Alex., plumber, 17 Cowane st
Wright, James, blacksmith, 6 Douglas st
Wright, James, engine driver, 17 St John st
Wright, John, draper, 40 Cowane st; house—69
　　Wallace st
Wright, John, grocer, 37 Friars st, 14 Viewfield
　　pl; house—7 Manse cres
Wright, John, plumber, 10 Maxwell pl; house—3
　　Queen st
Wright, John, tailor, 4 Torbrex
Wright, M., confectioner, 17 Main st
Wright, Miss, Allandale, Causewayhead rd
Wright, Misses Isa, M., and Jane, 26 Victoria pl
Wright, Mrs Janet, 54 Up. Bridge st
Wright, Rev. Thos., 10 Gladstone pl
Wright, Walter, guard, 24 Forth st
Wright, William, lab., 41 Broad st
Wright, P., coachpainter, 9 Borestone cres
Wright, Wm , miner, 150 Main st
Wright, Thos., fireman, 6 Millar pl
Wyatt, Ben, machineman, 5 Middle craigs
Wylie, Daniel, printer, 5 Glebe aven
Wylie, David, engine driver, 74 St Mary's wynd
Wylie, James, foreman cleaner, 100 Up. craigs
Wylie, John, carter, 8 Broad st
Wylie, Mrs Helen, tea rooms, 1 Seaforth place
Wylie, Thomas, draper, 13 Low. Bridge st
Wylie, William, carter, 15 Bow st
Wylie, Wm., carting contractor, 14 Winchel pl
Wyllie, Sandeman, & Co., Stirling Steam Laundry,
　　52 Abbey rd
Wyllie, Jas., quarryman, 5 St John St

Y

Yates, David, cork merchant, 12 Douglas ter
Yates, John, broker, 12 St John st
Yates, John, dealer, 3 St John st
Yates, Jas., hawker, 14½ St John st
Yeardly, John, engineman, 8 William pl
Yeaman, Mrs Cath., 15 Torbrex
Yellowlees, Robert, leather merchant, 48 Queen
　　st; house—6 Victoria sq
Yorke, Mrs, 3 Glebe cres
Yorkston, Wm., organist, 13 Low. Bridge st
Youlle, Bernard, moulder, 24 Baker st
Youl, J. manager (Lawsons Ltd), 32 Baker st
Young, Alex., carter, 8 Lower craigs

Young, Andrew, 4 Clarendon pl
Young, Arch., joiner, 7½ Weaver row
Young, Arch., quarryman, 20 Bannockburn rd
Young, Joseph, rub. worker, 58 Cowane st
Young, F., shoemkr., 11 Winchel pl & C'wayhead
Young, George, carter, 14 Bow st
Young, James, engineman, 7 Well green
Young, James, pointsman, 7 Nelson pl
Young, John, carter, 41 Main st
Young, Miss E., refreshment rooms, 4 Up craigs
Young, Mrs Helen, 10 Bayne st
Young, Mrs Isabella, 61 Low. Bridge st
Young, Mrs, 25 St Mary's wynd
Young, Mrs M., 3 Glencoe rd
Young, Robert, salt worker, 6 Abbey rd
Young, Robert, dairyman, 6 Well green
Young, Miss, 2 Dumbarton rd
Young, Alex., J.P., Craigview, Causewayhead
Young, Alex., residenter, 71 Barnton st
Young, James, residenter, 71 Barnton st
Young, Joseph, fireman, 20 Forth st
Young, W. H., accountant, Allan pk and 62 Port st
Young, Thos., fruiterer, 56-60 Baker st
Young, Wm., spirit merchant, 5 Drip rd
Younger, Mrs Ann, dressmaker, 45 King st
Younger, Thomas, tailor, 14 Baker st
Yuille, Rev. Geo., 9 Glebe cres
Yule, Mrs Ellen, 42 Up. castlehill
Yule, Wm., policeman, 24 Broad st
Yule, Wm., headmaster, 4 Dean cres

Z

Zeller, Geo., lab., 51 Raploch

OFFICIAL AND OTHER LISTS.

Ancient Free Gardeners.—(British Order.)

Scottish Central District. D.W.M.—John Baird, Grahamston; District Treasurer—John Smith, Lotbrie, Camelon; District Secretary—Wm. Cunnison, Hillside, Causewayhead.

"Flower of the Rock" Lodge, No. 232.—W.M.—David Wallace, 98 Cowane Street, Stirling; Treasurer—George M'Kechnie, Bruce Street, Stirling; Secretary—Andrew Fulton, 9 Well Green, Stirling. Meeting Place—The Hall, 38 Arcade.

"Royal Thistle" Lodge, No. 261. W.M. William Kitchen, 13 Lower Bridge Street, Stirling; Treasurer James Jenkins, 6 Bruce Street, Stirling; Secretary Wm. Rae, Ivy Bank Buildings, St. Ninians; Medical Officer—Dr. Highet. Meeting Place—Baptist Hall, Murray Place.

"Robert de Bruce" Lodge, No. 331.—W.M.—Alex. Penny, The Haugh, Bannockburn; Treasurer—James Johnstone, Ramsay Cottage, Bannockburn; Secretary—James Gillespie, Station Road, Bannockburn. Meeting Place—Masonic Hall, Bannockburn.

Ancient Free Gardeners.—(St. Andrew Order.)

"Stirling Castle" Lodge, No. 77. Secretary—A. D. Campbell, 19 Cowane Street, Stirling. Meeting Place—Derby Hall, Baker Street.

Ancient Order of Foresters.

Denny District. D.C.R., Robert Aitken; D.S.C.R., J. W. Anderson; Treasurer—James Grant; Secretary, Daniel Stewart.

Court "Hope of Snowdon," No. 6087, Stirling. C R., Frank Rae; S.C.R., Andrew Black; Treasurer, George Begbie; Secretary, John Brewster, 36 Queen Street.

Court "Robert de Bruce," St. Ninians.—C.R. James Brooks; S.C.R.—Henry Liddle; S.W. John Wright; J.W. David Cowan; S.B. William White; J.B.—James Carmichael; Treasurer Alexander Laird; Secretary James Bain, Main Street, Bannockburn; Medical Officer Dr. Alexander Chalmers, Williamfield, St. Ninians.

Ancient Shepherds (A.U.)

"Shepherds of the Rock" Lodge, No. 2071, City of Glasgow District.—Secretary—John H. Mains, 23 George Street. Meet in Ambulance Hall, Thistle Street, every alternate Monday night.

Ambulance Corps.

Caledonian Railway.—Captain—Wm. Dow; Treasurer Thos. Arthur; Secretary—Robert Christie, Telegraph Office, Stirling Station.

St. Andrew's (Stirling Branch). Chairman—Provost Thomson; Treasurer—D. Ferguson, National Bank; Secretary—R. Christie, Stirling Station.

Ancient Order of Oddfellows.

Denny District. G.M. William S. Thomson, "Sir John de Graeme" Lodge, Falkirk; D.G.M. William Anderson, "Seth" Lodge, Bo'ness; C.S. John Sinclair, "Rock of Hope" Lodge, Stirling; Treasurer—Robert Muir, "Sir William Wallace" Lodge, Denny.

"Rock of Hope" Lodge, No. 2866, Stirling, M.U.—Noble Grand—Wm. Ramsay; Vice Grand—John H. Oliver; Secretary James MacNicol, County Buildings; Elective Secretary—John Sinclair; Treasurer D. M. Rae; Surgeon—Dr P. F. M'Farlan, 11 Pitt Terrace. Juvenile Lodge Managers—John Sinclair and Wm. Livingstone.

Angling Clubs.

BACK O' THE HILL ANGLING CLUB.—President—James Duncan; Vice-President—Wm. Young; Secretary—John Campbell, 53 Lower Bridge Street.

STIRLING FISHING CLUB.—President—Robert Macluckie; Vice-President—A. D. Steel-Maitland of Sauchie; Treasurer—J. F. Mackie; Secretary—J. M. Macluckie, 22 King Street, Stirling.

Boating and Swimming Club.

President—James Murray, Polmaise Castle; Vice-President—W. Brown; Captain Tom Kinross; Vice-Captain—A. Esslemont; Hon. Secretary—John H. Pride. Headquarters—Club Boathouse, Dean Crescent.

Bowling Clubs.

STIRLING BOWLING CLUB.—President—W. J. Crawford; Vice-President—James Oliphant; Secretary—John Fyfe; Treasurer—W. A. Christie.

SPITTALMYRE BOWLING CLUB, LTD. Club President—Ralph Blackett; Club Vice-President—John E. Thurman; Club Secretary—John Campbell, 53 Lower Bridge Street.

CAUSEWAYHEAD BOWLING CLUB.—Hon. President—J. M. Morries; Hon. Vice-Presidents—Colonel Hare and W. S. M'Dowall; President—R. B. Wood; Secretary—W. Miller; Treasurer—James Strang.

BANNOCKBURN BOWLING CLUB.—President—A. L. Wilson; Secretary—. Nicol.

BORESTONE BOWLING CLUB.—Secretary—J. W. M. M'Innes, Whins of Milton.

CAMBUSBARRON BOWLING CLUB.—Patron—Sir Alan Seton Stuart, Bart. of Touch; Hon. President—James Murray of Polmaise; President—James Jackson; Vice-President—Duncan Wilkie; Secretary—John Lennox; Treasurer—Peter Robertson, jun.

COUNTY BOWLING ASSOCIATION.—President—P. Buchanan, Bridge of Allan; Secretary and Treasurer—T. W. R. Johnston, *Journal* Office, Stirling.

STIRLINGSHIRE CENTRAL BOWLING ASSOCIATION. — Patron—Edmund Pullar, Bridge of Allan; President—T. W. R. Johnston, Stirling; Vice-President—T. L. Reid, Stirling; Secretary and Treasurer—D. Pearson, *Sentinel* Office.

Boys' Brigade.

STIRLINGSHIRE AND CLACKMANNANSHIRE BATTALION.—President—D. G. Young, 1st Bridge of Allan Company; Treasurer—Wm. Cunnison, 4th Stirling Company.

4TH STIRLING COMPANY, BOYS' BRIGADE.—Captain—William Cunnison, Hillside, Causewayhead; Lieutenants—William Kinross, A. M. Paton, Alex. Kinross; Chaplain—Rev. A. S. Andrew.

Building Societies.

STIRLING "MODEL" BUILDING SOCIETY.—Directors—Treasurer Buchanan, 9 Baker Street; A. R. Campbell, 19 Spittal Street; Peter Comrie, 49 King Street; Robert Frater, 73 Port Street; John Lamb, 25 Port Street; Alexander M'Ewan, 35 Cowane Street; William Morrison, 2 Abercromby Place; Peter Scofield, 2 Wallace Street; Eben. Simpson, 16 King Street; James D. Valentine, 1 Port Street. Secretary—James A. Gibson, B.L., 47 Port Street.

STIRLING No. 2 "MODEL" BUILDING SOCIETY.—Directors—Jas. Aitken, St. Ninians ; ex-Bailie Brown, 10 Princes Street ; Treasurer Buchanan, 9 Baker Street ; Peter Comrie, 49 King Street ; William Cunnison, Hillside, Causewayhead ; Robert Frater, 73 Port Street ; John Lamb, 25 Port Street ; Alexander M'Ewan, 35 Cowane Street ; Arch. Oliphant, Armadale, Causewayhead Road. Secretary James A. Gibson, B.L., 47 Port Street.

STIRLINGSHIRE BUILDING AND INVESTMENT SOCIETY.—President, George Kinross, Victoria Square. Directors Asa Clay, 1 Balmoral Place ; Robert K. Common, Pitt Terrace ; Donald Cowan, Princes Street ; Robert Crawford, 49 King Street ; James Currie, Dumbarton Road ; Hugh Ferguson, Port Street ; George Forsyth, 25 King Street ; Alex. Gardner, Allan Park ; H. M. Kirkwood, 6 James Street ; D. L. Morton, 1 Pitt Terrace ; Alex. Moyes, Douglas Terrace ; Alex. Paterson, writer, Port Street ; George Plenderleith, Allan Park ; Adam S. Turnbull, 3 Queen Street ; Ronald Walker, Dumbarton Road ; Secretary Eben. Gentleman, 2 Wolf Craig ; Treasurer—Thomas L. Reid, Royal Bank ; Law Agent—James S. Fleming, Port Street.

Chess Clubs.

STIRLING CHESS CLUB.—Hon. President—John Jenkins ; President John Harvey ; Vice-Presidents—William Brown, John Murray, H. W. Coster ; Librarian—R. M. Pattison ; Secretary and Treasurer—D. Lindsay, *Observer* Office, Stirling.

STIRLING LADIES' CLUB.—President Mrs. J. B. Richardson, Edinburgh ; Vice-President —Mrs. Moorhouse ; Secretary—Mr. D. Lindsay.

CHURCHES.

ESTABLISHED.

§ EAST, St. John Street, ...	Rev. J. P. LANG.
WEST, St. John Street, ...	Rev. MATTHEW MAIR.
§ NORTH, Murray Place, ...	Rev. D. P. M'LEES.
MARYKIRK, St. Mary's Wynd, ...	Rev. THOMAS SKEOCH.

UNITED FREE.

§ NORTH (PETER MEMORIAL), Park Terrace, ...	Rev. J. CHALMERS, M.A.
SOUTH, Murray Place, ...	Rev. JOHN ARNOTT, M.A.
WEST, Cowane Street, ...	Rev. JAMES ANGUS.
CRAIGS, ...	Rev. D. D. ORMOND.
ERSKINE, St. John Street, ...	Rev. THOMAS WRIGHT, M.A.
VIEWFIELD, Viewfield Place, ...	Rev. W. SCOTT, M.A.
§ ALLAN PARK, Dumbarton Road, ...	Rev. JAMES W. PURVES, M.A.
CAMBUSBARRON, ...	Rev. JAS. A. ADAM, M.A.
§ EPISCOPAL—HOLY TRINITY, Albert Place, ...	Rev. R. PERCIVAL BROWN, M.A.
CONGREGATIONAL, Murray Place, ...	Rev. J. C. M'LACHLAN, M.A.
§ BAPTIST, Murray Place, ...	Rev. G. YUILLE.
§ WESLEYAN, Queen Street, ...	Rev. JOHN CARTWRIGHT.
§ ROMAN CATHOLIC—ST. MARY'S, Upper Bridge Street,	Monseigneur SMITH, V.G.

Services at 11 a.m. and 2 p.m. Those marked §, Services at 11 a.m. and 6.30 p.m.

ST. NINIANS.

ESTABLISHED, ...	Rev. J. M. ROBERTSON, D.D.

Service at 11.30 a.m. only.

UNITED FREE (NORTH), ...	Rev. C. MACKENZIE.
Do. (SOUTH), ...	Rev. R. FREW, D.D., Rev. D. SMITH, M.A.

Services at 11 a.m. and 2 p.m.

Session Clerk for Stirling Parish—JAMES BROWN, 10 Barnton Street. Attendance on Fridays, 7 to 8 p.m.

Session Clerk for St. Ninians Parish—T. J. Y. BROWN, 53 Port Street, Stirling.

Session Clerk for Marykirk Parish—W. J. NICOL, 59 Wallace Street, Stirling.

County Council—Central District Committee.

1.—*County Councillors.*—Kippen—Stephen Mitchell of Boquhan; Gargunnock—J. D. G. Dalrymple, Meiklewood, Gargunnock; Logie—Alex. Young, Craigview, Causewayhead; Bannockburn—Arthur H. D. Ramsay Steel-Maitland, Sauchie; Cambusbarron—Sir Alan Seton Steuart, Bart., of Touch; Sauchie—Edwin Bolton, of Carbrook, Larbert; Polmaise and Plean—J. T. M'Laren, Polmaise; Kilsyth—Charles E. Horsbrugh, Blairquhosh, Strathblane; Dunipace and Denny West—James Luke, Duncarron, Denny; Denny East—George R. Ure, Hopepark, Bonnybridge; Bridge of Allan North—R. A. Hill, Garnock, Bridge of Allan; Bridge of Allan South—James Drysdale, Drummond Place, Bridge of Allan; Denny Burgh East—Thomas Shanks, Beechfield, Denny; Denny Burgh West—Wm. W. Hunter, Mount Pleasant, Denny; Kilsyth Burgh East—David Frew, Burngreen, Kilsyth; Kilsyth Burgh West—Daniel Stark, Burnbank, Kilsyth. 2.—*Representatives from Parish Councils.*—St Ninians—John Gillespie, Cultenhove; Denny—James M'Cowan, Blaefaulds, Denny; Dunipace—James Renton, Dunipace, Denny; Kilsyth—John Stevenson, Gateside, Castlecary Station; Gargunnock—Rev. Robert Stevenson, Gargunnock; Kippen—Thomas Welsh—Beechwood, Kippen; Logie—John M'Intyre, Rose House, Blairlogie; Stirling—Alexander Dewar, Cambuskenneth.

Clerks to Central District Committee—Thomas Lupton and J. M. Macluckie.

Road Surveyor—Donald Cox; Assistant—F. Humphreys.

Sanitary Inspector—John Barr; Assistant—Robert Goldie.

County Officials.

Lord Lieutenant—Duke of Montrose, K.T.; Depute-Lieutenant—James Murray of Polmaise; Clerk of Lieutenancy—P. Welsh; Sheriff-Principal—J. M. Lees; Sheriffs-Substitute—A. Mitchell, Stirling; A. Moffat, Falkirk; Interim-Sheriffs-Substitute at Stirling—J. R. Buntine, R. Macluckie, R. Yellowlees, and Provost Thomson; Sheriff-Clerk—John G. Curror; Sheriff-Clerk-Depute at Stirling—Donald Cowan; Sheriff-Clerk-Depute at Falkirk—Alexander Gardner; Convener of County—A. Peddie-Waddell; Vice-Convener—Colonel King; County Clerk—Patrick Welsh; Collector of County Rates—J. W. Campbell (Office: 10 Friars Street); Medical Officer—Dr. J. G. M'Vail; Veterinary Inspector—J. M. Stewart, V.S.; County Analyst—A. Wilson, F.I.C.; Assessor—John Barr, Commercial Bank Buildings; Chief-Constable—John D. Sempill; Keeper of County Buildings—William M'Pherson.

Cricket Clubs.

STIRLING COUNTY CRICKET CLUB.—President—Wm. Forbes of Callendar; Captain—C. W. Forbes; Vice-Captain—W. Wilson; Hon. Secretary—J. A. L. Dunlop, The Brae, Bridge of Allan; Match Secretary—G. S. Orr, Kinnaird, Larbert; Hon. Treasurer—D. Yellowlees, 6 Victoria Square, Stirling. Hon. Secretary, Williamfield XI.—H. D. Sempill, Drummond Place.

STIRLING VICTORIA C.C.

Curling Clubs.

STIRLING CURLING CLUB.—President—C. Harmens; Vice-President—Colonel Bell; Secretary and Treasurer—R. A. Smith; Skips—P. Welsh, T. H. Todd, P. Brodie, R. A. Smith, J. Thomson, Colonel Bell.

STIRLING CASTLE CURLING CLUB.—President—J. M. Page; Vice-President—William M'Kenzie; Treasurer—W. Somerville; Secretary—J. D. Sempill; Representative Members—J. D. Sempill, R. Frater.

AIRTHREY CASTLE CURLING CLUB.—Secretary—Rev. R. Menzies-Fergusson, D.D.

BORESTONE CLUB.—Patron—James Murray; Patronesses—Mrs. James Murray and Mrs. A. D. Steel-Maitland; President—J. T. M'Laren; Vice-President—W. Cunningham; Secretary—W. Forrester; Treasurer—P. Aitken; Representative Members—W. Boswell and R. Oswald; Chaplain—Rev. C. Mackenzie.

STIRLINGSHIRE PROVINCE CLUB.—Patron—Lord Balfour of Burleigh; President—George R. Ure, Bonnybridge; Secretary—Tom B. Jones, Larbert.

FORTH AND ENDRICK PROVINCE.—Secretary—J. Drysdale.

Draughts Clubs.

CAMBUSKENNETH CLUB. Hon. President—County Councillor Young, Causewayhead ; Chairman P. Davie ; Secretary J. Smith ; Treasurer T. Watson.

STIRLING CLUB. President—James Wright ; Vice-President W. Traynor ; Secretary A. Bermingham ; Treasurer H. Welsh.

Educational.

STIRLING SCHOOL BOARD. Rev. Colin Mackenzie (Chairman), Daniel Barker, Arthur Brown, William Brown, Robert Frater, Thomas William Reid Johnston, James Calder Muirhead, Henry Robb, William Simpson. Committees.—High School and Elementary High School Committee Rev. Mr. Mackenzie, Messrs. Arthur Brown, James C. Muirhead, and Henry Robb Rev. Mr. Mackenzie, Convener ; Allan's School Committee Mr. Barker, Mr. Frater, and Mr. Simpson Mr. Barker, Convener ; Craigs School Committee Mr. Arthur Brown, Mr. William Brown, and Mr. T. W. R. Johnston Mr. Arthur Brown, Convener ; Territorial and Abbey School Committee Mr. William Brown, Mr. T. W. R. Johnston, and Mr. Simpson Mr. Johnston, Convener ; St. Ninians School Committee Rev. Mr. Mackenzie, Mr. Frater, and Mr. Muirhead Rev. Mr. Mackenzie, Convener ; Finance Committee Mr. Arthur Brown, Mr. Frater, Mr. Muirhead, and Mr. Simpson Mr. Arthur Brown, Convener ; Continuation Schools Committee Mr. Barker, Mr. William Brown, Mr. Robb, and Mr. Simpson Mr. Simpson, Convener ; Technical School, Cookery, and Saturday Classes Committee Mr. Barker, Mr. Frater, Mr. Johnston, and Mr. Robb Mr. Robb, Convener. Clerk Jas. Brown, 10 Barnton Street. Compulsory Officer R. C. Dickson, Raploch.

ST. NINIANS PARISH SCHOOL BOARD.—J. T. M'Laren (Chairman), Rev. James Allan, Rev. F. Macmanus, James Bain, James Christie, William Wilson, James J. Penny. Clerk and Treasurer James Dobbie, Solicitor, Stirling ; Officer Francis Sanderson.

WILSON TRUST. Clerk J. G. Curror, Solicitor, 2 Wolf Craig, Stirling.

GIRLS' INDUSTRIAL SCHOOL.—Clerk to Managers J. G. Curror.

STIRLING CHILDREN'S HOME. Miss Croall, Whinwell. Branch Home Comely Bank, Largo.

EDUCATIONAL INSTITUTE OF SCOTLAND (STIRLING BRANCH). President George M'Lay, Falkirk ; Secretary and Treasurer Alex. Wilson, Alloa.

STIRLING EDUCATIONAL TRUST. Chairman—Bailie Ferguson ; Clerk—D. B. Morris.

MARSHALL TRUST.—Clerk Wm. J. Alexander, 190 West George Street, Glasgow.

Fine Art Association.

Hon. President His Grace The Duke of Montrose, K.T. ; Hon. Vice-Presidents—The Earl of Mar and Kellie ; Lord Balfour of Burleigh, K.T. ; Sir H. Campbell-Bannerman, G.C.B., M.P. ; Laurence Pullar, The Lea, Bridge of Allan ; Edmund Pullar, Coneyhill, Bridge of Allan ; James Murray of Polmaise ; Captain Stirling of Keir ; A. D. Steel-Maitland, Sauchie ; George Younger of Leckie ; Stephen Mitchell of Boquhan ; Sir James Sivewright, Tulliallan ; Committee of Management—Provost Thomson (chairman), D. Y. Cameron, Henry Morley, J. C. Prowett, James E. Shearer, John Terris, Rev. Dr. Menzies-Fergusson, Rev. D. D. Ormond, Dr. Lowson, Dr. Moorhouse, John Walls, Wm. M. Rodgers, David B. Morris, Hugh S. Robson, Robert Whyte, R. A. Smith, T. W. R. Johnston, Judge Wylie, Bailie Ferguson, Wm. Renwick, M. F. Struthers, H. Kinross, W. Hunter, W. B. Cook, D. T. Ritchie ; Secretary—E. Baker ; Treasurer—D. Ferguson.

Football Clubs.

KING'S PARK FOOTBALL CLUB. President Robert Christie ; Vice-President William Porter ; Match Secretary and Treasurer—Alex. Dun, 37 Murray Place. Secretary of Junior Team—Robert Jenkins, 12 George Street.

HIGH SCHOOL RUGBY CLUB. President A. F. Thomson ; Vice-President—J. M'Gregor Mailer ; Secretary—William Drysdale, County Buildings.

STIRLING AND DISTRICT JUNIOR ASSOCIATION.—President Mr. Stark, Cowie ; Vice-President Mr. Thomson, Alloa ; Secretary and Treasurer John Campbell, Stirling.

STIRLINGSHIRE FOOTBALL ASSOCIATION.— President—J. MacNicol, Stirling ; Secretary D. M. Reid, Camelon.

Golf Clubs.

STIRLING GOLF CLUB. President—His Grace The Duke of Montrose, K.T.; Vice-President—The Right Honourable The Earl of Mar and Kellie; Captain—H. S. Robson; Hon. Treasurer—J. R. Archibald; Hon. Secretary—A. M. Swan, 7 Clarendon Place, Stirling.

STIRLING LADIES' GOLF CLUB.—President—Mrs. Buntine; Captain—Mrs. Robert Whyte; Treasurer—Miss Tasker; Secretary—Miss Ruth MacEwan.

STIRLING VICTORIA GOLF CLUB. Hon. President—William Renwick; Captain—J. A. Crystal; Secretary—James Guthrie; Treasurer—Andrew Scott.

Horticultural Societies.

STIRLING HORTICULTURAL SOCIETY. Hon. President—Sir Henry Campbell-Bannerman, M.P.; President—Captain Stirling of Keir; Vice-Presidents—James W. Drummond, ex-Provost Yellowlees; Secretary and Treasurer—Jas. M'Arthur, 13 Murray Place.

STIRLING CHRYSANTHEMUM ASSOCIATION. Hon. President—Graeme A. Whitelaw, Strathallan Castle; President—Henry Kinross; Vice-President—Wm. Boswell; Secretary and Treasurer—R. C. Dickson, Raploch, Stirling.

ST. NINIANS AMATEUR HORTICULTURAL AND INDUSTRIAL SOCIETY. President—Rev. Dr. Robertson; Vice-Presidents—Rev. W. G. Law and R. Jenner; Secretary and Treasurer—J. F. Macintosh, Bellfield Road.

CAMBUSBARRON HORTICULTURAL SOCIETY.—Hon. President—James Murray of Polmaise; President—Rev. W. G. Law; Secretary—J. Preston.

Insurance Agents.

BRITANNIC.—T. Girvan, Bannockburn.

BRITISH LEGAL.—T. Mowat, 3 Douglas Street.

CITY OF GLASGOW. J. Hamilton, Lawson's Buildings, 32 Spittal Street.

PEARL. W. Gair, 20 Barnton Street.

PRUDENTIAL.—R. Blackett. Office—7 Murray Place.

ROYAL LIVER.—N. M'L. Murphy, 26 Upper Bridge Street.

REFUGE.—J. S. Philps, 5 Well Green.

SCOTTISH LEGAL. W. Leslie, 6 Queen Street.

STIRLINGSHIRE FRIENDLY SOCIETY.—John Ramsay, 14 Bruce Street.

Masonic Lodges.

"STIRLING ANCIENT," No. 30.—R.W.M.—A. S. Greig; Secretary—David Richardson, 80 Port Street; Treasurer—J. Livingstone.

"ROYAL ARCH," No. 76.—R.W.M.—John Hynd, 9 Nelson Place; Secretary—Thomas Hynd, 1 James Street; Treasurer—J. G. Murray.

PROVINCIAL GRAND LODGE OF STIRLINGSHIRE.—P.G.M.—William Black, Falkirk; Secretary—J. G. Murray, 10 Barnton Street, Stirling; Treasurer—A. L. Aitken, Falkirk.

ROYAL ARCH CHAPTER "STIRLING ROCK," No 2.—M.E.P.Z.—T. W. R. Johnston; Secretary—A. S. Turnbull, 45 Murray Place, Stirling; Treasurer—John Steel.

ROYAL ARK MARINERS AND RED CROSS KNIGHTS.—P.W.M.—T. W. R. Johnston; Secretary—A. S. Turnbull.

Military Staffs.

DEPÔT ARGYLL AND SUTHERLAND HIGHLANDERS, STIRLING CASTLE. - Major A. Aytoun, D.S.O., commanding; Captain D. Darroch, Lieutenant G. M'L. Sceales, Lieutenant A. J. H. Maclean, Sergeant-Major J. Lindsay, Quarter-Master-Sergt. J. Sutherland; Lieutenant-Colonel F. Greig, in Medical Charge; Acting Chaplain - Rev. J. P. Lang.

3RD BATTALION ARGYLL AND SUTHERLAND HIGHLANDERS.—Captain and Adjutant H. P. Moulton Barrett, Captain and Quarter-Master A. Beattie, Sergeant-Major W. Hardie, Quarter-Master-Sergeant F. Meston, Sergeant-Drummer A. G. Furr, Sergeant-Piper J. Smith; Sergeant, Orderly-Room-Clerk—T. W. Newns.

MILITARY PRISON—Captain and Superintendent - D. Darroch; Chief Warder—R. D. Holmes; Warder Clerk—J. H. Morison; Staff-Sergeant—C. Jordan: Sergeants —W. H. Jenkins, E. Spittle, S. Catchpole, D. Bisset, J. Binnington; Lance-Corporal—A. H. Phillips.

ORDNANCE STORES, FORTHSIDE.—Major J. A. Stewart, C.O.O.; Captain W. D. Dooner, Lieutenant T. P. O'Connor; Captain, D.C.O. A. Linnell; Lieutenant, A.C.O, W. Dickson; Condrs. - F. S. Smith, W. H. Arscott; Sub-Condr. W. Linsell; Armr.-Sergeant-Major W. J. Cheevers.

Municipal.

STIRLING TOWN COUNCIL.—List of Members, arranged according to Wards, with years of election and retirement :—

I.—King Street Ward.

Elected.		Retires.
1904	Councillor Stewart,	1906
1904	„ Plenderleith,	1907
1905	„ Reyburn,	1908
1905	Judge Ferguson,	1908

II.—Port Street Ward.

1903	Councillor Raffan,	1906
1903	Bailie Steel,	1906
1904	Councillor Macintosh,	1907
1905	Judge Gourlay,	1908
1905	Dean of Guild King,	1908

III.—Baker Street Ward.

Elected.		Retires.
1903	Councillor Brown,	1906
1904	„ Dow,	1907
1904	Bailie Watt,	1907
1905	Councillor Menzies,	1908

IV.—Cowane Street Ward.

1903	Councillor Sandeman,	1906
1903	Provost Thomson,	1906
1904	Bailie Macfarlan,	1907
1904	„ Bayne,	1907
1905	Councillor Judge Wylie,	1908

V.—St. Ninians Ward.

Elected.		Retires.
1905	Councillor Hay,	1906
1904	Treasurer Buchanan,	1907
1905	Councillor Thomson,	1908

The Town Council meets on the Third Monday of each month, at Seven o'clock p.m.
(No Meeting in July.)

Town Clerk—David B. Morris; Depute Town Clerk—David Graham White; Town Chamberlain—James Brown, writer, 10 Barnton Street; Master of Works—A. H. Goudie, Millar Place; Electrical Engineer—A. C. Hanson; Burgh Chief Constable—Thomas Ferguson; Factor, Cowane's Hospital—William Christie, 36 Port Street; Factor, Spittal's Hospital—William M. Brown, 10 Princes Street; Collector of Rates, Registrar of Births, &c.—Eben. Gentleman, 2 Wolf Craig; Medical Officer of Health—Dr. Wilson, 1 Viewfield Place; Veterinary Inspector - J. M. Stewart, V.S., 72 Murray Place; Sanitary Inspector—John Fyfe, 15 Spittal Street; Burgh Assessor—Thomas Currie, 16 King Street; Captain of Fire Brigade—John Duff, Dumbarton Road; Burgh Analyst—Andrew Wilson, F.I.C.; Inspector of Weights and Measures—Peter M'Nab, 38 Craigs; Burgh Officer—Wm. S. Williamson, 23 Baker Street.

STIRLING WATERWORKS COMMISSIONERS.—The Commissioners meet on the first Tuesday of each month, at a quarter-past Seven o'clock p.m.

Town Council Representatives.

Elected.		Retires.
1903	Councillor R. Sandeman,	1906
1904	„ G. Plenderleith,	1906
1904	„ John Raffan,	1907
1905	„ J. F. Macintosh,	1907
1905	Bailie Parlan Macfarlan,	1908
1905	Councillor James Dow,	1908

Ratepayers' Representatives.

Elected.		Retires.
1903	Messrs. John T. Dale,	1906
1903	„ John Duff,	1906
1904	„ Robert Frater,	1907
1904	„ John S. Ralston,	1907
1905	„ Thomas Ferguson,	1908
1905	„ Robert Foster,	1908

Musical Associations.

STIRLING CHORAL SOCIETY.—Hon. President—W. Renwick; President R. Frater; Vice-President—L. Hepting; Secretary—James Macpherson, 26 Port Street, Stirling; Treasurer—Alexander Paterson; Conductor—Dr. Arthur W. Marchant.

STIRLING OPERATIC SOCIETY.— President— Provost Thomson; Secretary—J. R. Archibald, 53 Port Street, Stirling; Treasurer—W. M. Reyburn, Clydesdale Bank; Conductor—W. H. Dobson; Stage Manager—C. Graham.

Parish Councils, &c.

STIRLING PARISH COUNCIL.—David W. Soutar (chairman), Hugh Gavin, John Shearer, Wm. Somerville, Michael J. Hare, Wm. Simpson, Ralph Blackett, Geo. Christie, James Christie, John Corser, John H. Pride, John W. Heron, Robert Smith, Peter M'Neill, John Brown, W. Somerville. Officials—Inspector, Clerk and Collector—John Paterson; Assistant Inspector—Thomas J. Jones; Keeper of Casual Sick House—Frank M'Ginlay. Medical Officers—Stirling District—Dr. Murray; St. Ninians District—Dr. Chalmers.

ST. NINIANS PARISH COUNCIL.—Sir Alan Seton Steuart (chairman), A. D. Steel-Maitland, E. Bolton, J. Grigor, John Gillespie, W. M'Lintock, Major Wilson, G. Wilson, D. Wilkie, J. D. Stevenson, John Edmond, J. Barr, J. Forsyth, and R. Goodall.

STIRLING COMBINATION POORHOUSE.—Clerk—Henry Robb, 2 Dumbarton Road; Governor—D. M'Millan; Matron—Mrs. M'Millan.

Parliamentary.

M.P. for Stirling District of Burghs—Sir Henry Campbell-Bannerman, G.C.B. Constituency—7464. Last Election—Sir H. Campbell-Bannerman, Prime Minister, returned unopposed owing to illness of Unionist candidate.

M.P. for Stirlingshire—D. M. Smeaton. Constituency—18,942. Last Election D. M. Smeaton (L.), 9475; The Marquis of Graham (U.), 5806; Majority—3669; Spoilt papers—94.

Political Associations.

BURGH UNIONIST ASSOCIATION.—Secretary—Henry Robb.

BURGH CONSERVATIVE ASSOCIATION.—Secretary—A. C. Buchanan.

BURGH LIBERAL ASSOCIATION.—President—Jas. B. Smith of Clifford Park; Secretary—Robert Taylor, solicitor, Stirling.

PRIMROSE LEAGUE, "Rock Habitation," No. 1829.—Secretary — T. C. Darling; Treasurer—J. C. Muirhead.

STIRLING UNIONIST CLUB—Rooms, Thistle Street. President—Ex-Provost Yellowlees; Vice-President—A. C. Buchanan; Secretary—J. W. Heron, Episcopal Schoolhouse; Treasurer—Wm. Moir, North of Scotland Bank.

STIRLING WORKING MEN'S LIBERAL AND REFORM ASSOCIATION. — Rooms, Port Street. President—R. Blackett; Vice-Presidents—H. Mathie and D. Mundell; Secretary and Treasurer—C. M. Sneddon, 4 Middle Craigs.

STIRLINGSHIRE CONSERVATIVE ASSOCIATION.—President—The Duke of Montrose, K.T.; Hon. Secretary and Treasurer—Mr. John Monteath, Wright Park, Kippen.

Seven Incorporated Trades.

Deacons.	Trades.	Ex-Deacons.
John M'Gregor,	Hammermen,	James Thomson.
John King,	Weavers	Arch. Forrest.
John Duthie,	Tailors	James Dowell.
J. S. Ralston,	Shoemakers	Peter Schofield.
Judge Daniel Wylie,	Fleshers	William Boswell.
Alex. Denovan, jun.,	Skinners	Walter Stewart.
James Ritchie,	Bakers	John Blyth.

Convener—Judge Wylie; Boxmaster to Convener Court—James Dowell; Boxmaster to Adamson's Mortification—J. S. Ralston; Clerk—David Chrystal, Writer; Officer—John Syme.

Stirling Agricultural Society.

President Edwin Bolton of Carbrook, Larbert. Vice-Presidents A. D. Steel-Maitland of Sauchie; Sir Charles Cayzer of Gartmore; Provost Thomson, Stirling; David Wilson of Carbeth, Killearn; John A. Stirling of Kippendavie, Dunblane; Stephen Mitchell of Boquhan, Kippen. Hon. Directors— Sir Archibald Orr-Ewing of Ballikinrain; James Murray of Touchadam and Polmaise; J. Ernest Kerr of Harvieston, Harvistoun Castle, Dollar; John Risk of Bankier, Carlton, Stirling; Duncan Stewart of Millhills, Crieff; Robert Paterson, Hill of Drip, Stirling. Directors James Binnie of Plean, Bannock-burn (Chairman); William Wood, Townhead, Braco; Henry Gray, Hawkhill, Kincardine-on-Forth; William Dickson, Burnhouse, Denny; Charles M'Farlane, Brackland, Callander; James Orr, Mains, Alexandria; Charles Brown, Kerse Estate Office, Falkirk; Charles Carrick, Baad, Stirling; J. C. Wilson, factor, Tulliallan, Kincardine-on-Forth; Peter M'Intyre, Tignablair, Comrie; J. Scrim-geour, factor, Doune Lodge, Doune; James M'Laren, Alton of Bandeath, Stirling; Andrew M'Farlane, Chalmerston, by Stirling; George Graham, Faraway, Kippen; W. A. Dron, Crieffvechter, Crieff; A. H. Anderson, Kippenross, Dunblane. Secretary Andrew C. Buchanan, 26 Port Street, Stirling. Treasurer Daniel Ferguson.

Stirling District Lunacy Board.

Members for Stirling County—Robert Dobbie (Chairman), Charles Brown, J. D. G. Dalrymple, David Frew, A. Griffiths, George R. Ure; Stirling Burgh—Provost Thomson; Falkirk Burgh—Provost Christie; Dumbarton County—Daniel S. Campbell, William Douglas, William Menzies, Thomas Stirling; Dumbarton Burgh Provost Macfarlan; Linlithgow County—H. M. Cadell, John Marshall, Daniel Robertson; Linlithgow Burgh Ex-Provost Gilmour; Clackmannan County George Cousin, Dr E. E. Dyer; Clerk and Treasurer James Dobbie, Solicitor, Stirling; Auditor W. A. Wood, C.A., Edinburgh.

Stirling Guildry.

Dean of Guild John King; Clerks and Treasurers—Robert MacLuckie and Thomas Lupton; Guildry Officer—Wm. M'Naughton.

Stirling Royal Infirmary.

Chairman of Directors—H. D. Erskine; Vice-Chairman—Provost Thomson; Consulting Physicians and Surgeons Donald M'Fadyen and William Haldane; Visiting Medical Officers J. H. Murray, J. E. Moorhouse, William Eggeling, and J. F. Greig; Consulting Dental Surgeon—L. J. Platt; House Surgeon—Thomas A. Macgibbon; Matron—Miss Peebles; Secretary—Jas. Dobbie, solicitor, Stirling; Treasurer—Robert MacLuckie.

Temperance Societies.

TOTAL ABSTINENCE SOCIETY.—President—Rev. George Yuille; Secretary—Archibald Duncan, 3 Newhouse Villas, Stirling.

ROYAL ARMY TEMPERANCE ASSOCIATION.—

STIRLINGSHIRE NORTHERN DISTRICT LODGE, No. 56, I.O.G.T.—District Chief Templar —Archibald Henderson, New Road, Bannockburn; District Superintendent of Juveniles—Mrs A. G. Duncan, 3 Newhouse Villas, Stirling; District Secretary— Allan C. Harley, 26 Barnton Street, Stirling.

Local Lodges, I.O.G.T.:—"Borestone" Lodge, No. 94, St Ninians; "Sons of the Rock" Lodge, No. 135, Stirling; "Robert de Bruce" Lodge, No. 199, Bannock-burn; "Flower o' Stirling" Lodge, No. 705, Stirling; "Spa" Lodge, No. 905, Bridge of Allan; "Rose of Honour" Lodge, Cambusbarron.

INDEPENDENT ORDER OF RECHABITES. "Liberty" Tent.—Secretary—George Dick, "Bannockburn" Tent.—Chief Ruler—R. B. Proudfoot; Secretary—Malcolm Gillies.

BAND OF HOPE UNION.—Secretary—Charles Johnston, Allan's School.

HOLY TRINITY CHURCH TEMPERANCE SOCIETY.—President—Rev. R. Percival Brown; Secretary—Miss Mackinnon, Maxwell Place.

BRITISH WOMEN'S TEMPERANCE ASSOCIATION (SCOTTISH CHRISTIAN UNION).—President—Mrs Yuille, 9 Glebe Crescent; Treasurer—Mrs Forsyth, 25 King Street; Secretary—Miss Stewart, 10 Melville Terrace.

Volunteers.

HEADQUARTERS STAFF, 4TH V.B., A. & S.H.—Colonel R. Morton, Stirling, Commanding; Major and Hon. Lieutenant-Colonel—E. Simpson; Captain and Adjutant—C. A. H. Maclean; Captain and Quarter-Master—J. Denholm; Sergeant-Major—L. G. Watters, Drill Hall, Princes Street.

"A" COMPANY, 4TH V.B., A. & S.H.—Captain—J. H. Murray; Lieutenant—R. D. Lauder.

"B" COMPANY, 4TH V.B., A. & S.H.—Captain Frew.

13TH COMPANY, 1ST FIFE V.A.—Major—R. C. Highet; Lieutenant—Dr Laidlaw; Instructor—C.S.M. J. G. Taylor; Secretary—C.S.M. John Dun. Headquarters—Old Courthouse, St John Street. Drill Hall—Butter Market.

Colonel A. G. Duff, commanding A. & S. Volunteer Infantry Brigade.

Major H. M'D. Williams, Brigade Major, A. & S. Volunteer Infantry Brigade.

Miscellaneous.

DISCHARGED PRISONERS' AID SOCIETY STIRLING LOCAL COMMITTEE.—Hon. Secy. Thomas J. Y. Brown, 53 Port Street.

No. 11 COMPANY ARMY ORDNANCE CORPS SPORTS CLUB, STIRLING. President Major J. A. Stewart, A.O.D.; Vice-President—Capt. Dooner, A.O.D.; Treas rer O.C. 11th Company, A.O. Corps; Hon. Secretary Sergeant G. H. Jolley, A.O. Corps, 10 Wolf Craig, Dumbarton Road.

ARCADE HALL.—Crawford's Trustees. Agents—Fleming & Buchanan, 26 Port Street.

BURNS CLUB.—President—D. B. Morris; Vice-Presidents—John Craig and Alexander Sauds; Treasurer—Jas. C. Muirhead; Secretary—Ridley Sandeman, 22 Forth Crescent.

COMMERCIAL TRAVELLERS' ASSOCIATION.—President James W. Paterson; Vice-President William Ferguson; Hon. Treasurer—A. Love; Hon. Secretary Jno. A. Paterson, Gowanlea House, Drip Road.

FORTH SALMON FISHERY BOARD.—Superintendent—James Macrae, 18 Union Street; Clerk—Patrick Welsh.

GAS COMPANY.—Chairman—James Johnston; Directors—James Johnston, Robert Johnston, J. S. Fleming, George Forsyth, George Kinross, J. B. Smith, David Chrystal, W. M. Rodgers; Secretary and Treasurer—E. Gentleman, 2 Wolf Craig; Manager—J. D. Smith.

GIRLS' CLUB.—President—Mrs Crum, Auchenbowie; Vice-President—Miss Hunter, Evirallan; Secretary—Miss Cameron, Victoria Square; Treasurer Miss Soutar, Woodcliffe.

GLASGOW STIRLINGSHIRE AND SONS OF THE ROCK SOCIETY.—Preses—Edwin Bolton of Carbrook; Treasurer—J. Wordie; Secretary—Arthur Forbes.

INLAND REVENUE OFFICE.—Collector of Inland Revenue—John Langan; Principal Clerk L. J. Saunders; Clerk—D. Buchanan; Supervisor—J. W. Roberts; Officer—D. Mackie; Surveyor of Taxes—John Barr; Assistant Surveyor—F. G. Mann.

NATIONAL SOCIETY FOR THE PREVENTION OF CRUELTY TO CHILDREN (STIRLING BRANCH).—President—Mrs Murray of Polmaise; Secretary and Treasurer—R. A. Hill, 4 King Street, Stirling; Officer—W. J. Anderson, 7 Murray Place, Stirling. Falkirk Branch.—President—Provost Christie; Secretary—A. Halley, 54 High Street, Falkirk; Officer—W. J. Anderson.

14

OMNIUM GATHERUM.—Deacon—D. M'Donald; Treasurer—A. M'Gregor; Secretary—H. M'Master, 3 Park Lane, Stirling.

PUBLIC HALL COMPANY, LTD.—Directors Colonel Wilson of Bannockburn (Chairman); James Couper, of Craigforth, Stirling; David Morton, Pitt Terrace, Stirling; John M'Ewen, of South Lodge, Stirling; James B. Smith, of Clifford Park, Stirling; ex-Bailie Thomas Menzies, Stirling; Provost James Thomson, Stirling; James W. Drummond, of Westerlands, Stirling. Secretary and Treasurer—R. Taylor, Solicitor, Barnton Street.

RAILWAY STATION.—Superintendent—James Samuel. N.B. Agent—William Graham. Goods Agents—Caledonian—W. Wilson; N.B.—Adam Elder.

REGIONS BEYOND HELPERS' UNION. President—Miss Griffiths Buchanan.

ROYAL NATIONAL LIFEBOAT INSTITUTION.—Secretary of Local Committee—John Jenkins, 80 Port Street, Stirling; Treasurer—Daniel Ferguson.

SALVATION ARMY. Stirling Headquarters—Spittal Street.

SMITH INSTITUTE.—Curator—James Sword; Secretary and Treasurer—J. Jenkins.

SOCIETY FOR THE PREVENTION OF CRUELTY TO ANIMALS.—President J. B. Smith; Vice Presidents Wm. Renwick, D. B. Morris; Secretary—W. L. Thomson, 27 Murray Place; Treasurer Daniel Ferguson; Veterinary Surgeon John M. Stewart, 72 Murray Place; Inspector and Collector—Alexander Mackay, Queen Street.

SOCIETY OF SOLICITORS.—Dean—Robert Whyte; Sub-Dean—T. Lupton; Dean's Council—John Jenkins, James Dobbie, D. Chrystal, T. J. V. Brown, and P. Douglas; Fiscal—D. W. Logie; Board of Examiners—A. C. Buchanan, R. Whyte, and J. C. Muirhead; Secretary—J. C. Muirhead; Librarian—James Brown; Poor's Agents—J. S. Henderson and R. Taylor; Keeper of Library W. M'Pherson.

STIRLING AND DISTRICT PHOTOGRAPHIC CLUB. President—J. J. Munro; Treas.—W. C. Shaw.

STIRLING AND DISTRICT WINE, SPIRIT, AND BEER TRADE ASSOCIATION.—Secretary—D. Richardson, 80 Port Street, Stirling.

STIRLING COUNTY CLUB.—Secretary—Mungo Cochran, Bank of Scotland, Stirling; Club Steward John Sloan.

STIRLING GAELIC SOCIETY. President—Rev. Colin Mackenzie; Secretary—John S. Mackay, Coburg Avenue; Treasurer—J. A. Gordon, 12 Barnton Street.

STIRLING LOCOMOTIVE MUTUAL IMPROVEMENT ASSOCIATION.—President—Mr R. Dobbie.

STIRLING KENNEL CLUB.—President—Hope Paterson; Vice-President—Chief-Constable Sempill; Secretary and Treasurer—W. H. Young, 72 Port Street.

STIRLING MEDICAL SOCIETY.—President—D. M'Fadyen; Vice-President—A. F. Wilson; Secretary and Treasurer—J. Drew, 28 Dumbarton Road.

STIRLING NATURAL HISTORY AND ARCHÆOLOGICAL SOCIETY.—Vice-Presidents—Dr Lowson, Alex. Moyes, and J. E. Shearer; Secretaries—R. Kidston and D. B. Morris; Treasurer—D. Ferguson.

STIRLING NURSING ASSOCIATION.—President—Mrs Johnstone of Alva; Secretary—Miss Graham, 20 Allan Park, Stirling; Treasurer—James W. Campbell, Bank of Scotland.

STIRLING SAVINGS BANK.—President—Ex-Provost Yellowlees; Treasurer—Daniel Ferguson; Actuary—Thomas Muirhead, 4 Port Street, Stirling.

STIRLING UNITED Y.M.C.A. Hon. President—James Gray; President—Thomas Lupton; General Secretary—John Weir, jun.; General Treasurer—D. B. Crockart, Institute, Allan Park; Lecture Committee James Banks, convener. Literary Branch.—Chairman—David B. Morris; Vice-Chairmen—H. G. Mathie and J. T. Davidson; Joint Secretaries and Treasurers—Geo. Forsyth and C. Murdoch.

ST NINIANS YOUNG MEN'S CHRISTIAN ASSOCIATION. President—Rev. C. Mackenzie; Vice-Presidents—Jas. Welsh and D. Y. Taylor; Secretary—R. Weir; Treasurer—Wm. Aitken.

SCOTTISH CENTRAL HORSE BREEDING ASSOCIATION.—Secretary—Jas. Dallas, Forthbank.

STIRLING DISTRICT CLYDESDALE HORSE SOCIETY.— Secretary—R. Paterson, Hill of
Drip.

STIRLING BOYS' AND GIRLS' RELIGIOUS SOCIETY.—Hon. President—Rev. John Arnold ;
President—

STIRLINGSHIRE SOLDIERS' AND SAILORS' FAMILIES' ASSOCIATION (CENTRAL
DIVISION).—President—Mrs Fitzgerald.

HOLY TRINITY HOME.—Sisters of St Margarets, 32 Baker Street.

ST NINIANS EPISCOPAL MISSION ROOM.—25 Bannockburn Road.

TRAMWAY COMPANY.—Secretary—A. M. Wardlaw, Bridge of Allan.

WALLACE MONUMENT CUSTODIERS.—Provost, Magistrates, and Councillors of Stirling ;
First Minister of Stirling, Master of Cowane's Hospital, The Lords Lieutenants
of the Counties of Stirling, Clackmannan, and Perth ; The Sheriff Deputes of
said Counties ; The Dean of the Guildry of Stirling.

WARD COMMITTEES.—Secretaries—King Street Ward—G. Begbie ; Port Street Ward—
Wm. Somers ; Baker Street (vacant) ; Cowane Street Ward—John Merrilees ;
St Ninians Ward—Arch. Duncan.

Justices of the Peace for Stirlingshire.

Aitken, James H., brewer, Falkirk
Abercromby, Lord, 14 Grosvenor St., Grosvenor Sq., London, W.
Alexander, Lieut.-Col. Ed Mayne, Bridge of Allan
Baillie, Robert, Falkirk
Balfour of Burleigh, Lord, Kennet House, Clackmannan
Bamforth, Thomas, Larbert
Barstow, Major, 1st Batt. Seaforth H.
Bauchope, W., Kepdowrie, Buchlyvie
Benton, Alex. Hay, of Polmont Bank, Polmont
Birrell, L.-Col. John, Clober, Milngavie
Blackburn, Lieut.-Col. P., R.A , Killearn House, Killearn
Bolton, Edwin, of Carbrook
Brown, Alex., iron founder, Falkirk
Brown, Charles, factor, Grangemouth
Brown, John A. Harvie, of Quarter, Dunipace House, Larbert
Brown, Thomas, of Dalnair, Drymen
Bruce, Sir W., Bart., of Stenhouse, Stenhouse, by Falkirk
Buchanan, A. W. G., of Parkhill, Polmont
Buchanan, J. H., of Bardowie, C.A., 8 York Place, Edinburgh
Campbell, H. J. F., of Beech Lodge, Wimbledon, Rear Admiral, R.N.
Campbell, J. W., banker, Stirling
Cayzer, Sir Charles, of Gartmore
Christensen, Emil, ship chandler, Grangemouth
Christie, A., cabinetmaker, Falkirk
Clark, Alex., farmer, Bothkennar
Clarkson, R., of Avondale, Polmont
Cochrane, John B., Stenhousemuir
Cockburn, Malcolm, Falkirk
Cowan, David, Clevedon, Cove
Coubrough, A. S., Parklea, Strathblane
Coubrough, John, of Blanefield, Blanefield
Couper, James, of Craigforth, Stirling
Crawford, Euing R., Auchentroig, Drymen
Cribbes, Dr Henry Scott, Airth
Dalrymple, James Dalrymple Gray, of Meiklewood, Gargunnock
Dobbie, Robert, Larbert
Douglas, A. Campbell, of Mains, Milngavie

Drew, Major, Milngavie
Drummond, Colonel C. H. E. Home, of Blair Drummond
Drummond, James W., Stirling
Drysdale, James, Bridge of Allan
Duncan, A. R , Arbroath
Dunmore, Earl of, Dunmore Park
Edmond, David, of Ballochruin, Balfron
Edmonstone, Sir Archibald, Bart , of Duntreath, by Strathblane
Erskine, Henry David, of Cardross
Ewing, Sir A. E. Orr, Bart., of Ballikinrain, B'kinrain Castle, Balfron
Farquharson, J. S., banker, Edinburgh
Ferguson, Daniel, banker, Stirling
Fischer, M., merchant, South Alloa.
Fisher, D., Ballamenoch, Buchlyvie
Fleming, James A., of Balquharrage, 33 Melville Street, Edinburgh
Forbes, William, of Callendar
Forbes, C. W., yr., of Callendar
Fraser, John, of Balfunning, Balfron
Frew, Col. D., Burngreen, Kilsyth
Graham, A. Erskine, of Boquhapple, 19 Inverleith Row, Edinburgh
Graham, J. H. Noble, of Larbert
Graham, Robert J., banker, Kilsyth
Graham, A. G. Barns, of Craigallion, Milngavie
Graham, J. C., Ballewan, Strathblane
Grahame, Robert B. Cunninghame
Griffiths, Azariah, Falkirk
Haldane, Dr., Brdge of Allan
Halket, L.-Col., J. C. C., of Cramond, Edinburgh
Hare, Col. James, of Blairlogie
Henderson, James A., 17 Chester St., Edinburgh
Horsbrugh, C. E., D.S., Blairquhosh, Strathblane
Hunter, Wm. W., Denny
Hunter, Robt., ironfounder, Falkirk
Jameson, R., of Ardunan, Strathblane
Jenkins, A. F., Whins of Milton
Jenkins, R., banker, Bridge of Allan
Johnston, Fred., Woodville, Falkirk
Johnstone, Wm. Barraston, Torrance of Campsie
Jones, James, ironfounder, Larbert
Ker, T. Ripley, of Dougalston, Milngavie
Kincairney, Lord, Edinburgh

King, Col Charles M., Antermony House, Milton of Campsie

King, Sir James, Bart., LL.D., of Levernholme

King, John Westall, yr., of Campsie, Auchenfroe, Cardross

Kinross, Geo., Victoria Sq., Stirling

Lawrie, Sir A. Campbell, The Moss, Killearn

Lees, Sheriff, K.C., Edinburgh

Lennox, The Hon. C.S.B.H. Kincaid, Lennoxtown

Liddell, James, Binniehill House, Slamannan

Livingstone, Jas. F., of Westquarter

Lochhead, Robt. H., banker, Falkirk

Logan, Lieut.-Col. C. A., Glencarron, Denny

Luke, A. M'Naughton, papermaker, Denny

Macadam, John, banker, Balfron

Macdharmid, D., M.B., C.M., Kippen

M'Fadyen, Lieut.-Col. D., Park Ave., Stirling

Macfarlane, Samuel, of Meadowbank, Torrance of Campsie

MacGill, T., shipowner, Grangemouth

M'Grigor, Alex., of Cairnoch, Stirling

Mackay, Andrew Y., Grangemouth

Mackay, Jas., Avonview, Avonbridge

M'Killop, Jas., Polmont Park, Polmont

M'Laren, Duncan, farmer, Cornton, Bridge of Allan

M'Laren, J. T., factor, Polmaise, Stirling

M'Laren, Peter, Falkirk

M'Queen, John F., banker, Denny

Macnab, Charles, Lilyburn, Milton of Campsie

Macqueen, A. Murdoch, of Gateside, Drymen

Maitland, A. H. D. R. Steel, of Sauchieburn, Stirling

Maitland, Keith R., W.S., 5 Thistle Street, Edinburgh

Melrose, William, banker, Drymen

Menzies, Walter, of Culcreuch, Fintry

Mitchell, Stephen, of Boquhan, Kippen

Mitchell, David, of Millfield, Polmont

Mitchell, James, of Auchengray, by Airdrie

Mitchell, Thomas, banker, Slamannan

Moffat, Alex., Sheriff-Sub., Falkirk

Monteath, John, of Wright Park, Kippen

Montrose, The Duke of, K.T. Buchanan Castle, Drymen

Morries, J. M., of Gogar, by Stirling

Morton, Colonel, Stirling

Murdoch, John F. Burn, Colonel, Royal Dragoons

Murray, Adam, Southfield, Lennoxtown

Murray, James, of Polmaise, Stirling

Murray, John C., Pollok Estate Office, Glasgow

Murray, Wm. Watson, Catter House, Drymen

Nimmo, J., of Drumclair, Garfield House, Stirling

Nimmo, James, Edinburgh

Nimmo, John T., 12 Waterloo Street, Glasgow

Paton, James, of Avonhill, 5 Bruntsfield Crescent, Edinburgh

Peareth, John L., Lennox Castle, Lennoxtown

Peile, Horatio R. B., Greenock

Pollock, J. J., of Aucheneden, Strathblane

Pullar, Edmund, Coneyhill House, Bridge of Allan

Rankin, Dr. Walter L., Strathblane

Rankin, Wm. Henry, Pilton Cottage, Laurieston

Rennie, Archibald C., Falkirk

Risk, John, of Bankier, Stirling

Robson, Hugh S., banker, Stirling

Rodger, J., Keir Mains, Dunblane

Salvesen, H. A., Blairbank, Polmont

Shanks, Thomas, Denny

Sheriff, George, of Stenhouse and Kersie, Larbert

Smith, Ronald Kincaid, of Polmont, Colonel, 4th Hussars

Smith, James B., Stirling

Smith, C., 317 St. George's Road, Glasgow

Speirs, P. Alexander, adv., Jedburgh

Stark, Henry, Thornville, Falkirk

Steuart, Sir A. H. Seton, of Touch and Allanton, Bart.

Steuart, R. J. Archibald, of Steuarthall, Stirling

Stevenson, John, of Gateside, Kilsyth

Stewart, Sir Michael H. Shaw, of Carnock, Larbert

Stirling, Andrew, of Muiravonside

Stirling, Sir C. E. F., of Glorat, Bart., Milton of Campsie

Stirling, Commander G. H. Miller, R.N., of Craigbarnet, Campsie Glen

Sutherland, R. M., Wallside, Camelon

Thomson, Alex. F., 19 Galloway St., Falkirk

Thorneycroft, Jas. B., Kilmarnock

Ure, George, of Wheatlands, Bonnybridge

Ure, George R., Bonnybridge

Waddell, A. Peddie, of Balquhatstone, W.S., Edinburgh

Waters, J. C. Dun, of Craigton

Watson, Borthwick, Falkirk

Watson, Robert, Bardowie, Torrance of Campsie

Watt, John, of Drumgray, Airdrie

Waugh, Allan, Avonbridge

White, William, banker, Lennoxtown

Whyte, Robert, banker, Falkirk

Wilkie, P., merchant, Grangemouth

Wilson, Col. Alex., of Bannockburn, Bannockburn

Wilson, Col. A., late 3rd Battalion, A. & S. Highlanders,

Wilson, David, Carbeth, Killearn

Wilson., J, of Finnich Malise, Drymen

Wilson, J., Jinkabout Mills, Polmont

Wilson, W., Viewvale, Bannockburn

Wilson, Wm., quarrymaster, Kilsyth

Wood, William, Burnbrae, Falkirk

Wood, E. A., banker, Grangemouth

Yellowlees, Robert, Stirling

Young, A., Craigview, Causewayhead

Yuill, John W., of Glenmill, Campsie Glen

Zetland, The Earl of, Kerse House, Stirling

The Lord-Lieutenant of the County

The Sheriff-Depute and Sheriff-Substitutes of the County

The Lord Provost, Senior Bailie, and Lord Dean of Guild of Glasgow

The Provost of Stirling

The Provost of Falkirk

The Provost of Grangemouth

The Provost of Bridge of Allan

The Provost of Kilsyth

The Provost of Denny

And the Chairmen *ex officio* of the different Parish Councils for the County

Clerk of the Peace— Andrew C. Buchanan.

Depute-Clerks—At Stirling—George Begbie, James Macpherson ; at Falkirk—Alexander Gardner ; at Kilsyth—R. M. Lennox ; at Lennoxtown — James Macpherson.

VALUATION OF STIRLING.—1906-7.

The abstract prepared by Mr Currie, the assessor, shows the valuation of the burgh to be as follows:—

	1905-1906.	1906-1907.	Increase.
Lands, &c., ...	£102,194 14	£105,102 8 8	£2907 14 8
Railways, Tramways, and Gas Works,...	7,680 0	7,779 0 0	99 0 0
	£109,874 14	£112,881 8 8	£3006 14 8

The following table shows how the valuation has increased during the past twelve years:—

1894-95,	...	...	£83,748 19 4
1895-96,	...	...	86,294 12 1
1896-97,	...	...	87,765 7 4
1897-98,	...	...	89,440 1 9
1898-99,	...	...	92,765 4 1
1899-1900,	...	...	95,351 17 0
1900-1901,	...	...	96 726 14 4
1901-1902,	...	...	98,664 8 5
1902-1903,	...	...	101,903 15 6
1903-1904,	...	...	104,587 7 1
1904-1905,	...	...	107,162 15 3
1905-1906,	...	...	109 874 14 0
1906-1907,	...	...	112,881 8 8

BURGH STATISTICS.—Population at census, 1901—18,403 ; estimated population, 1906, —19,153. Municipal Voters—2989

VALUATION OF STIRLINGSHIRE.—1906-7.

The valuation of Stirlingshire, as made up by the Assessor, Mr John Barr, shows an increase of £10,214. The details are as follows:—

PARISH.	1906-7	INCREASE.	DECREASE.
Dunblane and Lecropt,	£916 14 8	...	...
Buchanan, -	7719 4 4	...	£19 8 0
Drymen, -	15191 15 9	...	15 9 10
Balfron, -	7403 15 9	...	86 11 0
Fintry, - -	4138 0 10	£3 13 6	...
Killearn, -	10917 18 11	48 12 11	...
Kippen E., -	3885 1 2	82 16 0	...
Do. W., -	3511 9 8	...	20 16 1
Gargunnock, -	6636 1 4	...	20 14 6
Baldernock, -	7379 10 4	228 17 11	...
Campsie, -	30308 6 11	575 3 8	...
Strathblane, -	9421 16 10	...	46 8 4
Kilsyth B., -	20000 5 1	783 11 9	...
Do. L., -	30369 13 11	1804 4 4	...
N. Kilpatrick B.,	19832 9 0	1477 11 6	...
Do. L.,	8364 7 5	...	1054 8 8
Stirling, -	516 1 1	...	9 15 3
St. Ninians -	69313 6 3	2441 0 9	...
Logie B., -	26894 9 9	478 10 3	...
Do, L., -	4909 5 6	...	22 14 0
Alva	12950 13 4	242 10 5	...
Do. L., -	3609 17 2	...	595 5 0
Dunipace B.,	2734 5 10	31 1 1	...
Do. L..	6862 4 8	...	488 11 7
Denny B., -	10659 10 1	45 17 5	...
Do. L, -	34050 13 9	1067 17 3	...
Airth, - -	10454 19 10	268 16 4	...
Grangemouth B.,	38024 8 1	971 15 8	...
Do. L.,	32562 16 4	341 8 5	...
Falkirk. -	35134 17 2	1934 7 0	...
Do. Burgh of Grangem'th,	280 12 6	...	1 1 0
Muiravonside,	19494 7 0	...	699 13 1
Slamannan, -	16169 17 4	...	1190 18 4
Larbert, -	13592 11 5	1659 15 4	...

Tota valuation exclusive of railways, -	554276 9 0	...	4273 14 8
Last year -	544062 5 2	...	
Gross Increase, -	-	14487 17 6	
Decrease, - -	-	4273 14 8	

Net Increase, -	-	10214 2 10

POSTAL INFORMATION.

Post Office -Maxwell Place.   Postmaster—Roderick Reid.

HOURS OF ATTENDANCE.

Week Days, 7 a.m. to 9 p.m

Telegraph and Telephone Business, 7 a.m. to 9 p.m.

Money Order and Issue of Licenses, 8 a.m. to 8 p.m.

Savings Bank Business, 8 a.m. to 8 p.m.

Town Deliveries -7 and 11 a.m. ; 2.30 and 6 p.m.

SUNDAYS.

Sale of Stamps, Telegraph and Telephone Business, &c., 8 to 10 a.m.

Delivery of Letters to Callers, 9 to 10 a.m.

Mail Despatch to Edinburgh, Glasgow, and South, 4.20 p.m.

TOWN SUB-OFFICES.

Cowane Street -Miss Jane Hardie; 129 Baker Street W. Gordon ;
Dumbarton Road Mrs. Susan E. Hay.

Hours of Attendance, 8 a.m. to 8 p.m.

Money Orders and Issue of Licenses, 8 a.m. to 8 p.m.

Savings Bank Business, 8 a.m. to 8 p.m.

TOWN SUB-OFFICES AND PILLAR BOXES, WITH HOURS OF COLLECTION (WEEK-DAYS ONLY).

	MONDAYS ONLY—A.M.	MORNING.		AFTERNOON.					NIGHT
Park Place -	- 5.10	8.15	11.45		3.45		7.20		
Abbey Road	- 5.40	10.40		1.30	4.0		7.15	9.35	12.35
Laurelhill, -	- 5.10	8.20	11.15		4.0		7.25	9.10	
Albert Place -	5.0	10.0	11.0	1.40	4.0	5.0	7.15	9.0	12.0
Park Terrace -	5.10	10.0	11.15	1.35	4.0	5.0	7.20	9.10	11.45
Glebe	5.5	10.10	11.20	1.45	1.10	5.10	7.25	9.5	12.0
St Ninians Rd. (Annfield), -	5.20	9.45	11.10	1.30	4.0	5.0	7.40	9.35	11.50
Newhouse(U.F.Manse)		9.35			3.55		7.35	9.30	
Dumbarton Road	5.30	10.10	11.20	1.45	4.0	5.10	7.30	9.40	11.45
King Street -	5.0	10.10	11.25	1.45	4.0	5.0	7.30	9.45	11.45
Railway Station -	5.50	10.15	11.25	1.40	4.10	5.30	7.35	9.45	11.45
Baker St. Sub-Office -	5.0	10.0	10.55	1.20	3.55	4.55	7.15	9.0	12.15
Queen Street -	5.0	10.0	11.0	1.25	4.0	5.0	7.20	9.0	12.20
Cowane St. Sub-Office	5.25	10.25	11.20	1.45	4.0	5.20	7.20	9.25	12.25
Douglas Street -	5.25	10.25	11.20	1.45	4.5	5.20	7.25	9.25	12.25
Craigs -	5.20	10.0	11.15	1.30	4.0	5.0	7.15	9.40	11.45
Corntou Road -	5.15	10.15	11.10	1.35	3.45	5.10	7.30	9.15	

Collection at St. Ninians Road at 8.30 a.m., and at Newhouse at 8.35 on Sundays.

Rural deliveries to Craigmill, Milton Road, South Alloa, Blair Drummond, and Gargunnock, begin at 7 a.m., and Craigend at 6.40 a.m., and deliveries from same, 6 p.m.

ST. NINIANS POST OFFICE.

Sub-Postmaster—John B. Taylor.

Arrivals 6.35 a.m., 2.50 and 6.40 p.m.

Despatches 7.15 and 9.25 a.m. ; 3.45 and 7.20 p.m.

Sunday Arrivals 6.35 a.m.   Sunday Despatches 8.5 a.m.

Letter Post. To and from all parts of the United Kingdom, for prepaid letters Not exceeding 1 oz., 1d ; ½d for every additional 2 oz.

Inland Book Post. The Book Post Rate is ½d for every 2 oz. or fraction of 2 oz.

Parcel Post. Parcels up to 11 lbs. in weight are sent at the following rates :—
1 lb., 3d.; 2 lbs., 4d.; 3 lbs., 5d.; 4-5 lbs., 6d.; 6-7 lbs., 7d.; and 1d. per lb. up to 11 lbs.

Postal Orders.—Issued from 6d. to 2s. 6d.; 4d.; 8s. to 15s., 4d. ; 15s. 6d. to 21s., 1½d.

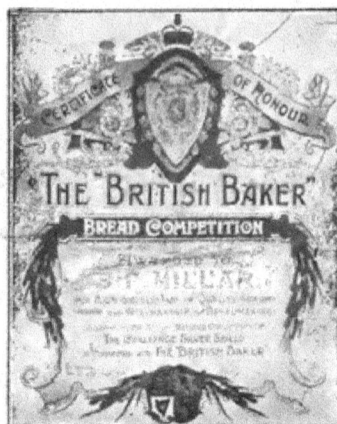

www.ingramcontent.com/pod-product-compliance
Lightning Source LLC
Chambersburg PA
CBHW030734280326
41926CB00086B/1471